MW01067720

 **BRECK**

VAIL RESORTS®

*Includes 17 ski resorts.

SKI
INC.
2020

Alterra counters Vail Resorts;
mega-passes transform the landscape;
the industry responds and flourishes.
For skiing? A North American Renaissance.

PRAISE FOR

Ski Inc. 2020

"Chris Diamond takes the reader to a higher level of understanding on the state of the ski-resort industry than anyone has ever done. Key executives opened up to Chris in a way that is unique to this book; their candor and Chris's astute observations combine to make a compelling read. If you love winter, love mountains, and love to slide on snow, this book is a must-read."

MICHAEL BERRY
Former President, National Ski Areas Association

"*Ski Inc. 2020* accomplished in a matter of hours what I'd failed to do on my own in a decade: make sense of present-day resort headlines in the context of how we got here in the first place. Through countless interviews, hundreds of sources, and deep firsthand experience, Chris Diamond has woven a must-read narrative for anyone hoping to make their career in ski."

GREGG BLANCHARD
Senior Vice President of Strategy, Inntopia
Social media guru @Slopefillers

"*Ski Inc. 2020* provides an almost encyclopedic view of the industry today, from the biggest to the smallest players. It could be a textbook for anyone wanting to understand the landscape of the North American ski business, and how it has changed so dramatically in the past few years."

BLAISE CARRIG
Former President, Vail Resorts Mountain Division

"Essential reading for anyone watching the resort industry carve into this new 'Golden Age.' Chris Diamond (and his colleague, Andy Bigford) deliver invaluable insights into the insular resort industry and its influence on mountain communities. As sweeping changes in resort ownership both challenge and bolster skiing as a business, *Ski Inc. 2020* peeks behind ski country's curtain, revealing the characters, passions, hardships, and money that keep American skiing's oversized impact as vibrant as ever."

JASON BLEVINS
Veteran industry reporter, *Colorado Sun*

"*Ski Inc. 2020* dissects the tectonic shift occurring in the North American ski industry and its significance for resorts, mountain communities, and skiers, providing a detailed and insightful perspective on the transformation of the business of skiing."

BILL JENSEN
CEO and Partner, Telluride Ski and Golf Resort

"If you want to understand the inner workings of today's ski resorts, and what drives their decision-making, *Ski Inc. 2020* is an authoritative, illuminating must-read."

JOHN FRY
Author, editor, and chairman of the International Skiing History Association

"The industry response from the large resorts down to the mom-and-pop ski areas has been strategic and, for some, simply a matter of survival. Chris Diamond's knowledge of the industry and thorough research provide the reader a snapshot into the dynamics of our industry."

JERRY BLANN
Former President, Jackson Hole Mountain Resort

"Chris Diamond does it again. This time he tells the story of how an industry can disrupt itself and reignite growth by creating an exciting consumer proposition. Leaders with vision, passion, and sound business plans can turn around a declining industry. The sequel is a good read for a ski enthusiast or a student of business. He also whets the appetite by introducing the challenges ahead."

STEVE REINEMUND
Former Chairman and CEO, PepsiCo
Former Dean, School of Business, Wake Forest University

"Finely written and deeply researched. This is the compelling story of how changes in strategy and the development of healthy business cultures can improve performance—not just for the two leading companies, but for an entire industry. A winning combination of lower costs, more choice, and an enhanced customer experience has made skiing a sport with a future again."

JOHN ELSTROTT
Emeritus Founder, Tulane University Entrepreneurship Institute
Former Chairman, Whole Foods Market, Inc.

SKI
INC.
2020

Alterra counters Vail Resorts;
mega-passes transform the landscape;
the industry responds and flourishes.
For skiing? A North American Renaissance.

CHRIS DIAMOND

With Andy Bigford

SKI DIAMOND PUBLISHING
Steamboat Springs, Colorado

Published by Ski Diamond Publishing
P.O. Box 774763, Steamboat Springs, CO 80477
Contact the Author at cdiamond1968@gmail.com

Sales and distribution:
West Margin Press
1700 Fourth Street
Berkeley, CA 94710
hello@westmarginpress.com

Book design by Boulder Bookworks, Boulder, Colorado

Proofreading by Kellee Katagi

Cover photo: At 8,171 acres, Whistler Blackcomb is North America's largest resort. Photo courtesy Dave McColm/Vail Resorts.

First Edition

ISBN 978-0-9979784-2-1
Library of Congress Control Number: 2019909294

Printed in Canada

For all those curious about the dramatic, recent changes in the ski business;

about what this means for growth and participation;

about the future;

and about the leaders driving this modern renaissance.

And to all my colleagues;

who gave their time to provide invaluable, honest insights.

I hope this book is worthy of your generous contributions.

CONTENTS

ACKNOWLEDGMENTS

In my Acknowledgments for the original *Ski Inc.*, I thanked Foster Chandler and Preston Smith for taking a chance on me, and for opening the door to a career that has brought so much richness and pleasure. I neglected to thank two wonderful Killington friends, Pat and Joe Heffernan. Their home was a "safe place" for me during those early years when, frankly, I had no clue about where this all would lead. Sadly, Joe passed in 1995. Pat continues her successful career as founder and principal of Marketing Partners, Inc., in Burlington, Vermont.

My wife, Eileen, tolerated my almost daily descent to the "office," where I did the heavy lifting for this book. Combine that absence with my slow recovery from a skiing accident in late spring 2018 (yes, broken femur), and I wasn't much help about the house. Without her patience and support, this book would not have happened.

To my daughter, Elizabeth, who provided her valuable copyediting skills, and son, Keenen, for being so much a part of my skiing life.

To my mother, Mary E. Diamond, who passed away in July 2018 at our family home in Easthampton, Massachusetts. She always wanted to know when I was going to get a "real" job. To her, writing a book made a lot more sense than being a ski-area operator

To my ski industry colleagues and friends who gave generously of their time and provided the content that anchors this book. I had over 100 individual conversations. No one said "no" to an interview.

To my editor, Andy Bigford, who was more of a partner than an editor in this project. Besides his national experience, Andy grew up skiing in the Midwest and knew many of the players. As a result, he was able to open doors and help tell stories that I could never have accessed. Not only is he a great editor, he is known broadly throughout the ski industry and highly respected for his integrity. Where I had trouble gathering information, he would be successful … and as with *Ski Inc.*, we met our deadlines!

CHRIS DIAMOND
Steamboat Springs, Colorado
July 12, 2019

INTRODUCTION

If you're reading this introduction, you're probably familiar with my first book, *Ski Inc.*, published in December 2016. *Ski Inc.* was part-memoir, part-business history of the modern ski resort, with heavy emphasis on my experiences with several of the large conglomerates. I thoroughly enjoyed the writing process and am pleased to note that it was well-received, especially by my peers in the industry. You don't need to have read that book to enjoy what follows, but it does provide great background and history relative to the modern ski industry. So why am I writing another book on skiing?

The short answer: What has happened in the ski business between the time I stopped writing in midsummer 2016 and now (three years later) is simply stunning. The ski world has been turned upside down. As a result, I've had dozens of readers approach me with the idea of a sequel—a follow-up that would help make sense of all that has happened since publication.

Toward the end of *Ski Inc.*, I wrote: "Vail Resorts will also certainly find a way to enter the Northeastern market." I was right. On February 21, 2017, Vail announced a definitive agreement for the purchase of Stowe Mountain Resort. Given its storied history and high-quality facilities, Stowe fit nicely with Vail Resorts' experiential commitment ("Experience of a Lifetime"). Stowe was soon to join the Epic Pass collection, enhancing the appeal of that mega-pass in the Northeastern market. Total pass revenues increased. The Vail business model was cranking on all cylinders.

With the Stowe acquisition in 2016, Vail Resorts owned (or operated under lease) 14 resorts. Most importantly, those resorts provided Vail with a powerful presence in all of the major skiing markets. Although they didn't own a resort in Southern California, they did have Park City/Canyons in Utah and the advantage of frequent, inexpensive flights to Salt Lake City from all major airports in that market. Buying an Epic Pass was a no-brainer for active Southern California skiers. And while Vail didn't own a resort in Washington or Oregon, it did own Whistler Blackcomb, which dominates that Pacific Northwest market. It is, by the way, the largest ski area in North America in terms of skier visits (roughly 2 million) and acreage (8,171).

For Vail Resorts, the competitive landscape at the end of 2016 was something of a yawn. Intrawest, which just a few years earlier had been the largest operator of ski resorts in North America, was a shadow of its former self, having shed a number of properties, including Whistler Blackcomb. Intrawest was owned by Fortress Investment Group (FIG) through a private equity fund and was reportedly being shopped. (FIG had owned Intrawest since 2006, and added Steamboat in March 2007.) How the ski world had changed in just 10 years! Where was the competition?

Fortress had taken part of Intrawest public in December 2014, which provided it with any number of options relative to an exit strategy. Vail Resorts would not be a likely buyer of Intrawest due to antitrust issues, mostly in Colorado, and I did not see a buyer out there who would be interested in acquiring the entire company. I was wrong. In *Ski Inc.*, I speculated that the pieces would be more valuable than the whole and that the resorts would be sold separately, similar to the liquidation of American Skiing Company. At the time, I didn't realize how many players other than Vail were getting active in the acquisition game or how many resort owners were getting ready to sell. In addition to Intrawest, some 15 resorts under the old CNL Lifestyle banner were about to go on the market. KSL, owner of Squaw/Alpine, was looking to grow. Ditto for Aspen Skiing Co. Let's just say that there was more wheeling and dealing going on than I had imagined. The stage was set for a dramatic re-shaping of skiing's competitive landscape.

On April 10, 2017, a partnership formed by KSL Capital (the private equity firm that included Squaw Valley/Alpine Meadows in their holdings) and affiliates of the Crown family (owners of the Aspen Skiing Co.) announced the purchase of Intrawest. Two days later, the partnership announced an agreement to purchase Mammoth Mountain, California (including June Mountain), and its Bear Mountain Resorts (Bear Mountain and Snow Summit in Southern California). Thus began a buying spree by both the new company (soon to be named Alterra) and Vail Resorts that, as of summer 2019, left Alterra owning or operating 15 resorts and Vail 20 resorts (counting the Falls Creek and Hotham resorts in Australia).

In the spring of 2018, the two companies were competing head-to-head in aggressively marketing their Ikon (Alterra) and Epic (Vail Resorts) passes. Between owned and "partner" resorts on those passes, some 60 North America areas were represented, plus dozens more internationally.

And the price was a bargain: Both passes were offered at $899 unrestricted for early purchase; Epic Local was $669, while the similar Ikon Base was $599. Never had skiers enjoyed so many options for so little cost. Somewhere around 1.35 million individuals would purchase those passes. If an accurate count of U.S. skiers and snowboarders is 9.4 million (according to the 2017–18 National Ski Areas Association [NSAA] Demographic study) then 16 percent had purchased a pass from one of these two companies. Because these participants are what we could call "heavy users," the total number of skier visits taken on an Ikon or Epic pass likely approached 16.2 million, or 30 percent of U.S. visits. This assumes an estimated (and somewhat debatable) 12 days of use per passholder. Another way of looking at this transformation: Including non-passholders, the total number of skier visits represented by the resorts that Vail or Alterra own or operate, and those of their pass partners, equals about half of all visits tallied in the United States. Wow.

So why did I decide to write this book? The ski industry as we have known it no longer exists. The airline business consolidated from a dozen to four major carriers (American, United, Delta and Southwest) that now control 80 percent of the business. The result? Expensive fares, added fees on everything from baggage to beverages, and a deteriorating travel experience. In contrast, the ski business saw the consolidation of 35 resorts under two parent companies (with roughly the same number of resorts collected under the next three largest conglomerates). For the consumer, the result so far has been a significant lowering of lift-pass costs and a dramatic expansion of resort options under each mega pass.

Bottom line: The ski resort business has been radically, disruptively and yet positively transformed by the explosive growth of Vail Resorts and the arrival of the Alterra Mountain Company. And this happened with a speed that is simply stunning. From the purchase of Stowe by Vail in the fall of 2016 to the closing on Crystal Mountain, Washington, by Alterra, we're talking two years. The acquisitions have been rolling out at such a frenzied pace that I just assumed more deals would go down from the time that I finished the book in early summer 2019 until its publication that fall. Sure enough, just as I was reviewing the pre-press galleys, Vail Resorts announced on July 22, 2019, its agreement to purchase 100 percent of the outstanding stock of Peak Resorts. We managed to include that groundbreaking transaction, involving 17 mostly medium and small-sized resorts, but apologize in advance for missing any others that occur before publication (recent history indicates Alterra will counter).

Yet this is not just the story of Vail Resorts and Alterra. They figure prominently, for sure. But more broadly, this is a book about the creativity and nimbleness of the other ski areas, and their owners and staffs who have figured out how to thrive amid the new challenges. By doing so, they have positioned skiing for a new period of growth—a renaissance, if you will.

The catalyst for this growth is a combination of the new pricing model, which has been adopted industry-wide, and the breadth of options that many of these passes provide.

The model is simple: Exchange a deep discount for early commitment. The result is a much more stable business platform, with fewer peaks and valleys, which is especially important in the modern context of climate change. What was not immediately appreciated or understood was how wildly popular these passes would be. Rob Katz, Vail Resorts' extraordinary Chairman and CEO, was not the first to recognize the appeal of the value passes. But he was the first to understand the *power* of these passes in the marketplace and to build a company's entire growth strategy around it. By doing so, he has helped reenergize a sport that had languished for years, with flat or shrinking participation, perceived by the nonskiing, general public as a "thing" for the wealthy—too expensive, too dangerous and too much of a hassle for others.

For years, resort business models supported this static approach. Lift ticket and pass pricing was assumed to be somewhat inelastic. Resorts assumed they had pricing power and took advantage. From the resorts' perspective, as long as they kept adding or improving facilities, they could charge a premium and guests would accept it. There just weren't going to be a lot of customers (even with the transformative nature of the value passes, households earning more than $200,000 accounted for 28 percent of skier households in 2017–18, according to the NSAA). For those with the money, it was a pretty good deal. The ski area provided a good experience, generally not too crowded, and, even if it was expensive, it was worth it.

That model got turned on its head when Rob Katz opened the doors to the sport in terms of affordability by selling Epic Passes anywhere, anytime (as long as they were bought before the early December deadline). That drove popularity, commitment—and crowds. Alterra followed the Vail pass model. For the megapasses, like Epic or Ikon, affordability encouraged adventure, enabling guests to explore resorts that in the past had been strictly aspirational. "Let's try Jackson Hole this winter. I've never been there, and the skiing is basically free."

With so many new and exciting options available to these passholders, the experiential side of skiing has come to the forefront, something important to Millennials, a demographic that was forecasted to be "unenthusiastic skiers." How can you possibly get bored, with so many different resorts to check out? The advent of Airbnb- and Vrbo-style lodging products (worldwide, Airbnb has 5 million properties—and counting) also supports this exploration mentality. For Millennials, willing to seek deals at the last minute and less fussy regarding amenities, lodging costs have entered the range of affordability. Passholders are increasing the number of days they ski, exploring new ski areas, and, importantly, often dragging some nonskiing friends along. Without lifting a finger, the ski industry may have found itself a no-brainer in terms of attracting new skiers: Incentivize the millions of passholders to "bring a friend."

My premise in this book is that the Epic revolution, as others have followed Vail Resorts' lead, has initiated a renaissance in skiing. For decades, the media focused on the high cost of skiing, but now the standard refrain is "what a deal" the new passes are. Total skier visits can be expected to grow coast-to-coast, and not just at the mega-resorts. This energy will eventually expand the number of total participants, if that hasn't happened already.

I make these bold predictions knowing that before the game-changing 2018–19 season, when both Ikon and Epic came into play and it snowed, the participation metrics were sobering. While the preliminary Kottke end-of-season study, released in early May 2019, reported 59.1 million skier visits for the breakthrough 2018–19 winter (the fourth best since record-keeping began in 1978–79), the preceding three seasons were much less rosy. They averaged 53.6 million skier visits, a 10- to 12-percent decrease from three-year highs of 56–57 million, recorded a handful of times in the past two decades. Weather and the economy will of course continue to impact future seasons, but we are headed toward an era where the three-year average of 60 million annual skier visits could and should be the norm—and there may be an even more optimistic scenario.

It is my view that these recent changes have rescued skiing from the trend of becoming, in effect, a rich person's sport. What is somewhat ironic is that these consumer-friendly outcomes are the result of a rapid and dramatic consolidation within the ski industry—one that would normally turn heads in terms of providing so much pricing power to a handful of companies. To date, however, the mega-pass competition has been a boon to consumers.

What follows is a lot of detail and history that, I hope, supports my thesis. A special thank you goes out to the dozens of resort industry executives who generously gave their time and insights in often-lengthy interviews, in several cases speaking with me (or my editor, Andy Bigford) not just once but on several occasions. While I sought to personally connect with as many resort leaders as possible, in a book that covers such a broad landscape, I relied on news media accounts and resort websites from across the country when necessary. The email newsletters and archives of *Ski Area Management* magazine (*SAM*) were especially newsworthy, timely, and helpful during these endeavors.

Please note that wherever I use the word "ski," I mean to include snowboarding. It is simply too awkward to keep repeating "ski and snowboard," so I beg the indulgence of my many snowboarding friends. I also apologize for the heavy focus on Colorado and Vermont. These are simply the places where I spent most of my career, and therefore have the clearest insights. Finally, I apologize for the inevitable factual errors that occur in a book as wide-ranging—and on such a quickly evolving, dynamic topic—as this. I can only say they were not intentional.

This is exciting stuff. I hope you enjoy it.

CHAPTER 1

Vail Resorts and Alterra:
Battle Lines Drawn

The North American industry was indeed stunned in the spring of 2017, when a joint venture of KSL Capital Partners and affiliates of the Henry Crown family announced its intent to purchase Intrawest (the deal closed in August). At the time, Vail Resorts' stock was on a distinctly upward trend, with a market capitalization of $12 billion. No one watching the industry anticipated a competitive response to the dominant player. Alterra continued on a buying spree: Two days later, the Mammoth Mountain/Big Bear resorts in California. Then Deer Valley, Utah, in August. All of these assets were merged with KSL's ski assets (Squaw/Alpine in Tahoe), and in January 2018, the new entity got a name: Alterra Mountain Company. These dramatic investments were occurring in the context of global warming and speculation that the ski industry worldwide would be one of its first victims.

Holy Smokes! What happened?

My early view from the sidelines was that the Crown family, longtime owners of the Aspen Skiing Co. (Aspen, Snowmass, Buttermilk, and Aspen Highlands), were observing the inexorable growth of the Vail Resorts' empire and considering the perhaps inevitable marginalization of their properties. It goes without saying that the Aspen and Vail cultures could not have been more different. Aspen and Sun Valley were the early stars in the ski resort world. But Vail Mountain climbed steadily from its modest, Quonset hut beginnings to the pinnacle of U.S. resorts in both volume and image, regularly topping the various resort ranking polls. Remember that Aspen was once owned by 20th Century Fox (along with Pebble Beach). Though currently held by the Chicago-based Crown family (think General Dynamics), many of its longtime investors and wealthy homeowners were connected to the entertainment industry. This West Coast/Hollywood bias contrasted sharply with Vail's East Coast/Manhattan-centric culture.

Aspen and KSL had collaborated in the past. KSL had provided financing to East West Partners for their real-estate development projects at the base of Snowmass. KSL had been alert for many years to any ski resort investment opportunities and was on any seller's short list of potential buyers. It had purchased Squaw in 2010, and then bought neighboring Alpine Meadows in 2011. (As I learned eventually, in November 2016 KSL rolled earlier investors out of the fund that had purchased Squaw and brought in new investors in Squaw as a stand-alone. Aspen made an approximately 10-percent investment at that time.) KSL's leadership team was composed of executives from the former Vail Associates (as it was known back then). Mike Shannon, a former Vail president in the 1980s, had founded KSL and had recently stepped away from day-to-day operations. Its CEO was Eric Resnick, another Vail guy, who had been hired away from Vail to join Shannon's new company in 2001. The KSL team knew the Vail business model as well as anyone, and they knew the industry. The Squaw Alpine CEO was Andy Wirth, a veteran marketing star with experience leading Steamboat's marketing and also Intrawest's, until the great recession forced a significant downsizing. Andy knew the competitive landscape as well as anyone. Arguably, no other investment firm had their combination of financial capacity and industry knowledge. With 20/20 hindsight, they were the logical entity to lead Alterra's formation.

I imagine the conversation between KSL and Aspen went something like this: "Well, are we going to sit back and watch Vail Resorts dominate the market, to our detriment, and limit our opportunities in the ski business, or are we going to respond? And if we do, it better be big and it better happen fast."

First came the acquisition of Intrawest. Initially, industry watchers assumed that the Aspen resorts would be part of the deal. Not so. Aspen would participate in joint marketing, especially as it related to a competitive pass product to challenge Epic, but remain independent.

KSL did not have the corporate structure to operate a large collection of resorts. This was basically a private equity firm that happened to own two ski areas in California. Acquiring Intrawest gave them not only a diverse collection, but it also provided the corporate structure—through Intrawest's Denver offices—to manage that collection.

Two days after the Intrawest announcement came the Mammoth/Big Bear deals. Next came Deer Valley and then the second Edgar Stern/Roger Penske family property in Utah, Solitude Mountain Resort. Fast-rising Alterra now included 14 resorts plus CMH, one of the world's largest heli-ski operators, and a helicopter maintenance company, Aerotec. In December 2018, Alterra would move from the old Intrawest offices in Denver's fashionable LoDo neighborhood to a 34,000-square-foot space at Zeppelin Station in Denver's historic RiNo Art District. The buying would continue, with Crystal Mountain, Washington, joining Altera in 2018.

For some six months after the purchase of Intrawest, the new company searched for a CEO. Eventually, Rusty Gregory, an Alterra board member and the longtime Mammoth Mountain CEO, agreed to assume the leadership role, while David Perry, an Aspen Skiing Co. executive and well-respected industry veteran, would serve as president and COO.

For the 2018–19 season, Alterra launched its own competitive response to the Epic Pass, called the Ikon. In addition to owned resorts, it added a number of others as partners to the pass product. All told, Ikon offered skiing at 15 owned resorts and some 25 partners. By signing up areas owned by Stephen Kircher's Boyne Resorts (most notably Sunday River and Sugarloaf in Maine, Loon Mountain in New Hampshire, plus Montana's Big Sky and Utah's Brighton) and John Cumming's POWDR (led by Killington-Pico in Vermont, plus Copper Mountain in Colorado and Oregon's Mt. Bachelor), Alterra made its Ikon pass product especially appealing in the competitive Northeast market and in Utah and Southern California. *(See the Appendix for a list of resorts participating in the Epic and Ikon passes for the 2019–20 ski season.)*

I don't believe anyone in the Vail organization saw the Crown/KSL juggernaut coming. For Vail Resorts, the self-confidence they felt back in late 2016 must have been shaken. Vail didn't just sit back and watch. Their response in terms of new acquisitions and competitive enhancements to their Epic lineup was stunning, continuing right through to the July 2019 announcement on the purchase of Peak Resorts. While much of the press focused on the evolution of Alterra, little credit has been given to Vail's thoughtful, timely response, both by acquisition and new pass partners.

The rapid industry consolidation we will be describing could not have occurred without the simultaneous availability of both the Intrawest and CNL properties (and then Peak). CNL, a Real Estate Investment Trust (REIT), did own the largest number of U.S. resorts for a time, reaching a total of 16. These were acquired more than 10 years ago and then leased to operators, many of whom were the original sellers. As a REIT, CNL could not be an operator. CNL, as it worked to dissolve its fund, eventually sold most of its ski resort assets to Oz Realty in late 2016, subject to existing leases. In short, if Oz wanted to sell, it would have to complete two transactions: one for the underlying assets and another to buy out the negotiated value of the long-term leases.

(A brief digression for those readers still wondering about the sudden and widespread arrival of REITs on the resort scene. REITs offered resort owners long-term stability by allowing them to basically cash out, but remain engaged with the business as the operator/lessee. A REIT is similar to a mutual fund in that individual investors pool their money together and a manager decides which real estate to buy and which to sell. But unlike a mutual fund, REITs must dissolve at some point. Often, REITs last five to 10 years before they are dissolved and the money is returned to the investors. CNL began its liquidation process at the end of 2015.)

On September 27, 2018, Vail Resorts closed on the purchase of Triple Peaks (Okemo, Vermont; Sunapee, New Hampshire; and Crested Butte, Colorado) in two transactions from Ski Resort Holdings, LLC, an affiliate of Oz Realty, and the Mueller family by acquiring the assets and eliminating the leases. Total transaction value was reported to be $229 million. Vail followed this deal with another purchase from Ski Resort Holdings: Stevens Pass in Washington for $64 million. (This was an anomaly in that the lease was terminable). In early 2019, Vail added two Australian resorts to its lineup.

With the arrival of Alterrra, Vail chose to invite a new, non-owned U.S. "partner," Telluride, to join A-Basin for the 2018–19 season. For the prior year (2017–18), Epic had included only its North American–owned resorts (and Perisher in Australia), plus limited access to some 30 European resorts. Heading into the 2018–19 ski season, Epic also added the six members of the Resorts of the Canadian Rockies (limited to seven days on the full pass), so it now offered access to some 65 resorts in eight countries. Sun Valley and Snowbasin were added for the 2019–20 season, and along with Telluride are also restricted to seven days. According to numerous industry sources, Vail would have added additional resort partners, but was essentially "outbid" by Alterra.

Then, as mentioned earlier, Vail Resorts led the national business news headlines during the record heat of late July 2019. It entered into a definitive merger agreement to acquire 100 percent of the outstanding stock of Peak Resorts, Inc. (SKIS on NASDAQ), at a purchase price of $11 per share, subject to regulatory review and Peak Resorts' shareholder approval. Peak's stock price was $5.10 at the previous business day's close, so the deal represented a 115-percent return for shareholders and an estimated $264 million price tag. The purchase was expected to close in the fall.

The acquisition adds 17 Eastern and Midwestern ski areas to the 2019–20 Epic Pass, including Mount Snow in Vermont, Hunter Mountain in New York, and Attitash and Wildcat in New Hampshire. But the majority are small- and medium-sized areas located near major metropolitan areas, including New York, Boston, Washington, D.C., Baltimore, Philadelphia, Cleveland, Columbus, St. Louis, Kansas City and Louisville.

Vail Resorts, which entered the metro resort business with its earlier acquisition of three Midwestern areas, was now going all in, and also solidifying its pass standing in the Northeast. With this move, Vail is making an even larger bet on urban and small- and medium-sized resorts. Vail's "Experience of a Lifetime" message will clearly have to be modified. It's interesting to note that the announcement included a commitment to spend $15 million on one-time capital expenditures in the next two years to improve the guest experience across those resorts.

Vail Resorts Chairman and CEO Rob Katz called Peak a "powerful network" of resorts. "Peak Resorts' ski areas in the Northeast are a perfect complement to our existing resorts and together will provide a very compelling offering to our guests in New York and Boston. With this acquisition, we are also able to make a much stronger connection to guests in critical cities in the Mid-Atlantic and Midwest and build on the success we have already seen with our strategy in Chicago, Minneapolis and Detroit," Katz said. "The acquisition fully embodies our philosophy of Epic for Everyone, making skiing and riding more accessible to guests across the U.S. and around the world." (See Chapter 8 for the story of how Tim Boyd built the Peak Resorts empire from scratch to a $264 million company in two decades).

So the battle has begun. Vail Resorts and Alterra, through their owned/ leased resorts, account for roughly 37 percent of the skier visits in the country (and that does not include their high-volume Canadian resorts). The remaining two "Mid-Major" companies (now just Boyne and POWDR, since the Peaks acquisition) together weigh in with close to 15 percent. The combined market share of the two passes, Ikon and Epic, which includes non-owned partner resorts, covers areas that represent more than 55 percent of the U.S. lift pass business. I can't think of any comparable market transformation in any American business sector; as mentioned before, the airlines underwent a major consolidation, but in consumer impact, nothing comes close. This is incredible stuff.

Winners to date are the consumers. Never has skiing been so affordable and the options so varied, if one is willing to commit, well in advance of the ski season, to a pass product like Epic or Ikon. As more and more resorts signed up to affiliate with either Ikon or Epic, there seemed to be a new dynamic at work: "fear of being left out." For the few destination resorts that haven't signed up, the future is uncertain. For others, as we'll see, a remarkable, creative response is forming in terms of new regional pass products and business alliances. The landscape of the North American ski industry is incredibly fluid. Prompted initially by a competitive threat from Vail Resorts, the rest of the ski world is re-inventing itself and engendering a renaissance in skiing. Bottom line: The current landscape appears to be a win-win for skiers and ski area operators. That said, there are plenty of obstacles, and we'll take a look at them.

The following chapters explain this dramatic shift in the landscape of North American skiing. What does this mean for the long run? What about the resort communities? Who are the winners? The losers? What about the remaining multiresort operators? What's the future for independents and small ski areas? How will they grow and prosper in this new environment?

CHAPTER 2

Resorts Entering 'Another Golden Age'

I thought the ski business was a "risky business." What has changed? If the number of transactions that have occurred in the past four years (2016–2019) and the premium price for which they were sold are any indication, this is most certainly a seller's market.

Reports surrounding the Deer Valley sale to Alterra had the price at a stunning 14 times EBITDA. Prior to that transaction, the multiple for large, market-dominating resorts was in the 10-times range (and this was a historically high multiple for a ski resort). Granted, these were rather unusual circumstances: It was generally assumed that the Deer Valley owners, the Stern and Penske families, weren't looking to sell. So the price had to be "enticing." And for Alterra, ownership of Deer Valley would position its pass products head-to-head with Epic in the lucrative Southern California destination market. Consequently, that multiple may remain a record for some time. Deer Valley is unique (Sun Valley runs a close second) in North America in terms of its commitment to an absolutely first-class ski experience, encompassing the food, the magnificent grooming, the investment in infrastructure and the quality of its lodging products (Stein Eriksen Lodge, the Montage, St. Regis, and more). Deer Valley caters to the affluent, unabashedly. It still won't allow snowboarders, fearing a backlash from its high-end clientele.

The Deer Valley multiple may remain an outlier, but the reality is that if you own one or more resorts, this is a great time to sell.

Why? Twenty years ago, there were very few individuals or companies outside the industry who really understood the ski business. Since that time, there have been a significant number of ski resort transactions involving private equity firms or institutional investors. These groups are now very familiar with the ski business and know how to value it. The catalyst for this new awareness was clearly Vail Resorts' stunning success story. Instead of just a few knowledgeable buyers, there's now a lot of "new money" looking at the ski business. One major attraction: The resort business is highly unlikely to face new competition. Because of environmental regulations, as well as supply and demand, there hasn't been a new major resort developed since the early 1980s, and that's not likely to change. Investors view the industry as if it had a "moat" around it.

In terms of establishing a successful, high-margin business model, Vail Resorts has been the Harvard Business School case study for the ski industry. A significant number of institutions and private investors own or observe Vail's stock and keep close track of the industry.

As potential purchasers, there are always people just looking to buy because of a personal and emotional commitment to a particular resort. It's a much smaller-scale version of modern NFL or NBA ownership, but let's not discount the importance of ego in many of the ownership decisions. Robert Redford became slightly famous in the ski business for his green stewardship of Sundance Resort, northeast of Provo in Utah; newsman Chet Huntley developed Big Sky; and Bruce Willis once owned Soldier Mountain in Idaho. The latter was sold to a nonprofit in 2012, and then sold again to an Oregon couple for $149,000 plus bank debt. Shay Carl Butler, the YouTube star of the noted Shaytards channel, which has 5 million subscribers, bought Pebble Creek in Idaho. Hedge fund king and conservation philanthropist Louis Bacon purchased Taos from its longtime owners, the Blake family. My old friend and former Heavenly owner Bill Killebrew always used to say, "It's nice to be king." 'Nuff said.

Close observers will remember that the ski business went through a somewhat similar consolidation wave in the mid-1990s, when mega-companies such as Les Otten's highly leveraged American Skiing Company and Intrawest's real-estate-focused outfit gobbled up resorts from coast to coast. This current transformation is different, and less likely to implode—as those did. While those portfolios were put together quickly, they unraveled quickly. *(See the Appendix for a list of the late 1990s conglomerates, and what happened to the individual resorts.)*

We know that both Vail Resorts and Alterra are not done buying, so it's a great time to be a seller. And as we will see, there are more players than just Vail and Alterra looking to expand their ski portfolios.

It's hard to believe that just a few years ago, most investors thought the ski business made money only via real-estate development. Intrawest began as a real-estate developer in Vancouver. It entered the ski business viewing skiing essentially as an amenity to its real-estate holdings. Intrawest was stunningly successful at developing base villages at its initial Canadian ski resort developments (Whistler Blackcomb as well as Tremblant in the province of Quebec). In both cases, entire villages were constructed from the ground up, including a mix of commercial and residential-rental units. These were not small projects. Thousands of condos and hotel rooms were constructed, and these drove enhanced skier visits at the resorts. Strict master plans and architectural guidelines were followed, and the end product proved popular with buyers and vacationers. Tremblant, in particular, maintained the architectural style of the original village in a very pedestrian-friendly environment. Both villages included branded hotels. Parking lots and transit centers were typically oriented to ensure that visitors walked through the villages on their way to the ski lifts, with views of the mountains beckoning. This drove visitation to the commercial units. The formula worked brilliantly at these two resorts, and each occupied the top position regionally in the annual *SKI* magazine popularity poll. Their success was helped by Canadian laws that effectively banned vacant second homes and encouraged warm-bed construction. In Whistler Village, many of the privately owned condos had covenants that restricted owner use to no more than eight weeks a year. The rest of the time, the unit had to be available for rental to tourists. This policy ensured high occupancy and a vibrant village (versus the huge proliferation of vacant second homes and "starter castles" evident at major Western U.S. resorts).

This success was not replicated at other Intrawest resorts. At Copper Mountain and Winter Park in Colorado, the villages often had empty storefronts and never achieved the energy so prevalent in the Whistler and Tremblant villages. With so many beds "cold," the base villages struggled to reach the critical mass that would enable the restaurants and shops to operate profitably. The same lack of success was evident at Stratton, Vermont, and Snowshoe, West Virginia, (both Intrawest resorts) and at Squaw and Mammoth, where Intrawest had partnerships to develop villages.

A big difference, I believe, was the relative absence of nonwinter activities, compared with the Canadian resorts. As a commercial operator (whether lodging, restaurant, or retail), it's challenging to make money outside of the ski season, but rent is due for 12 months, not four. Also, without the vibrant base village, the appeal of owning a condo or private residence diminishes. When the economic crisis of 2008 hit, the resort real-estate business as we had known it basically ceased to exist. Looking back at the Intrawest village formula, it's obvious in hindsight that Whistler and Tremblant were unique—master-planned villages with government assistance from the start. The only other purpose-built U.S. village to match Whistler (it was actually ahead of Whistler) is Vail. Other large-scale base village developments were never as economically viable. There is no doubt the village enhancements improved the resort guest experience and the P&L at those Intrawest properties, and they are still functioning at a relatively high level today, but they never matched the "original models" in Canada.

As the Great Recession took hold, virtually all large, planned base-area developments went on hold. Here in Steamboat, a subsidiary of Fortress Investment Group had acquired the old Ski Time Square commercial center from developers who had purchased the property from the partnership that also owned the Sheraton hotel. Fortress had provided financing for the deal, but as the original developer ran out of cash, Fortress took over. The property is actually two parcels: One is the old Ski Time Square commercial center, and the other the Thunderhead Lodge parcel. They are contiguous and arguably the last large development opportunity in Steamboat. Everything had been torn down except for the venerable and now abandoned Tugboat nightclub. The combined property had been listed for many years, but Fortress was unable or unwilling to complete a transaction until the fall of 2018, when a Washington, D.C.–based LLC, DBT Thunderhead, bought it for $11.58 million. Fortress reportedly had a multiple of that invested in the property, permits, planning, etc.

Conventional wisdom, tempered by the Great Recession, would argue that resort real estate will never be what it was pre-2008. That may be true given the challenges of securing financing for large projects. And considering the "haircut" that many second homeowners experienced post-2008, the demand may not be there (especially for products like a condominium hotel).

That's the popular view. In reality, resort real estate is once again a relatively hot market. Prices are rising, and the inventory is limited (and older) in virtually all major ski resort markets. So it would seem that the right product at the right price would have an opportunity for success. Long-stalled village projects at Killington and Snowmass, which are finally underway; the building boom at Big Sky; and even an attempted resurrection at Tamarack in Idaho will be instructive to watch (and I'll look at them more closely in a later chapter).

At any rate, real-estate profits are not central to the modern ski resort P&L. For many resorts in the West, the real estate priority is to spur development of affordable employee housing (more on that later). During the last decade, most ski resort companies pared back or shuttered their real-estate divisions. Even giants like Vail Resorts now tread carefully in the real-estate space. Back in 2009, when Vail Resorts had a full plate of projects and was working feverishly to close sales against the gathering tide of the recession, it recorded $186.2 million in net revenue from its Real Estate Segment, with $44.1 million in EBITDA. The next year, EBITDA dropped to a negative $4.3 million. Real estate revenues for 2018 were .2 percent of total net revenues! Vail describes its real-estate strategy in its 2018 10-K like this:

"The principal activities of our real estate segment include the sale of land parcels to third-party developers and planning for future real estate development projects… We believe that due to the low carrying costs of our land investments, we are well situated to promote future projects with third-party developers while limiting our financial risk."

Most other ski resorts operators have transitioned to a similar strategy, and generally focus on projects that have strategic value to the resort even if they don't turn a profit. Without the volatility of real estate, well-run ski resorts, both big and small, create significant, predictable cash flow. Healthy EBITDA margins and the relative predictability of results lie at the foundation of current valuations and support the incredible consolidation frenzy that we're witnessing. Ski area operators have worked through multiple recessions, poor snow years, and financial crises over the past 30 years. These companies have figured out how to survive and stay "lean." This—more than any other factor—is likely at the heart of the industry's current financial performance. Below are some other significant changes that have impacted profitability, and help explain the current consolidation frenzy.

Insurance Resolved (Mostly)

Looking back at the late 1970s and '80s, insurance costs were a significant challenge for the industry. Skiing is a risky sport. The potential for serious injury or death is always there. A number of lawsuits turned into plaintiff's victories (the most notable being Sunday v. Stratton in 1978). Insurance companies fled the ski market, and costs rose dramatically. It was unclear how the industry could survive if every accident led to a claim.

At one point it looked as though only one company would remain to insure resorts: AIG, which, fortunately, owned Stowe and understood the business. It didn't hurt that its chairman, Maurice Greenberg, was an active skier and a great lover of the Stowe ski scene.

Since those early days, virtually all ski states have passed legislation that establishes basic responsibilities of both skiers and ski areas. This clarification of "inherent risk" and the evolution of sophisticated risk-management programs across ski country have led to a reduction in claims and lowered insurance costs across the board. (There are exceptions, and California remains a significant outlier.) Although the risk of catastrophic injury is always there, given the variables of weather, snow conditions, and skier behavior, there is no question that skiing is a safer activity in 2020 than it was decades earlier.

Marketing Goes 24/7 Digital

When Killington was growing at double digits annually in the 1960s and '70s, marketing budgets were set at 15 percent of total revenues (based on Vail Resorts' net revenue for fiscal 2018, that would translate to a $301 million marketing budget!). The Killington spend was eventually pared back to 10 percent of lift revenues. Marketing guru Foster Chandler can't remember when the change occurred, but he probably didn't complain about the size of his reduced war chest. (I remember him saying: "I can always spend my way out of trouble.")

Reaching the consumer was an expensive proposition. Branding required a significant magazine spend. There were two prime competitors in terms of ski publications: *SKI* and *Skiing*. Then, *Powder* and *Snow Country*/née *Mountain Living*, plus a number of regional publications. To get out the word on snow conditions, ski areas were forced to buy space in daily newspapers in their region. To communicate near-term deals to the market, intensive radio and newspaper buys were required. Killington actually produced its own ski movie, "North Country Lady," in the '70s. Bob Perry assisted Foster Chandler's team in doing the production, and it won numerous awards. This was a critical sales tool, employed at ski group meetings, ski shows, and more. But it wasn't cheap.

Major resorts (and gear and apparel companies) annually invested tens of millions of dollars on print pages in the national magazines. Two of those (*Snow Country* and *Skiing*) no longer exist, and print ad spending is a tiny fraction, perhaps 20 percent, of what it once was. *SKI* has gone from eight issues annually at its height to four for 2019–20; so has *Powder*. That title and *Transworld Snowboarding*, which in its heyday championed snowboarding's growth, were recently bought by the David Pecker–led American Media Inc., which then owned the *National Enquirer* (it sold the tabloid in April 2019). To the outcry of thousands of snowboarders, *Transworld* announced it would no longer publish print issues. *Freeskier*, the youth-oriented magazine promoting freeskiing (it followed the original, the long-defunct *Freeze*), now has two issues a year and also publishes two issues of its sister mag, *Snowboarding*. So there are just a handful of remaining national publications that focus on the ski market, and they are skin-and-bones compared to their former fat and happy selves.

For the ski business, contrast this former vast publication portfolio in which it invested tens of millions of dollars annually to today's digital marketing and CRM (Customer Relationship Management) efforts, whereby resorts bypass the magazines via targeted emails, as well as Facebook and Instagram posts, tweets, texts, and more. They also spend on digital advertising; in 2018, Facebook and Google scooped up an estimated 60 percent of the total digital spend, which doesn't leave much for the original media outlets.

Meanwhile, snow reports go up on the website, searchable by anyone at any time, and of course into all the social media channels and emails. Web cams provide real-time views regarding weather and conditions, eliminating the old "snow reporting" middlemen (and the cost). And who needs a snow report when you can go straight to video of the resort's snow stake and see for yourself? Even more critical today with 11th hour vacation planning are snow forecasts, which the popular OpenSnow dangles enticingly. (Resort leaders from Pres Smith to Les Otten used to curse the TV meteorologists, particularly those in non-ski country, who sounded the alarm to avoid the roads and hunker down inside whenever a snowstorm threatened. Today's skiers know better than to listen to such advice.)

The most sophisticated resorts have detailed information regarding their customers, segmented into at least a half-dozen demographic categories, and they communicate regularly (via email or text) with targeted special offers

Companies like Vail Resorts have invested enormous amounts in digital marketing, and in their own internal marketing and CRM. Vail even bought its own ski-news website in 2010, *On the Snow*, and published its own 300,000 circulation custom magazine, initially called *PEAKS* and then *Epic Life*, until ceasing publication after the 2016–17 season (my editor, Andy, served as its editor and publisher for eight seasons).

The large resort conglomerates have larger customer databases (email lists, Facebook fans, Instagram followers, and such) than the magazines. They create their own custom content and push it out daily. Although this lacks the independent "stamp of approval" that once set the magazines apart, and the custom content is at times less than believable, it does not seem to matter. Resorts now work directly with their customer base to develop their brands, and in most cases they are doing an admirable job.

Vail Resorts' Epic Mix, which tracks vertical-feet-skied and awards badges for an assortment of accomplishments, launched in 2010. Epic Photo, its image companion (with on-mountain photographers taking photos of guests and immediately uploading them to your app), debuted for the next season. This all put marketing clout in Vail's customers' hands. Even in the uncertainty of the Great Recession, Rob Katz had the confidence to invest millions of dollars to install gantries at the entries to all of the company's lifts, thereby allowing Epic Mix to track lift rides. It remains hugely popular … the investment paid off.

It's hard to put a price tag on the domino effect of guests sharing on social media their smiling, "best-day ever" powder shots, or their stats from bagging 100,000 vertical feet on a ski vacation. Multiply that by hundreds of thousands of visitors, and you get tens of millions of mostly positive impressions. Many resorts (Aspen is a standout) have made savvy use of social media to organically support and promote their brands, but Vail remains the leader. Its latest innovation is Emma (Epic Mountain Assistant), billed as the world's first A.I. resort-guest helper.

Bottom line: Total marketing costs, when you consider investments in IT, internal content creation, and the digital ad spend may not have dropped significantly. But resorts are now able to reach substantially more customers more often and through more channels—ultimately driving revenue at a much lower and effective CPM (cost per thousand customers). Even the smaller guys are good: When a potential season-pass buyer is looking at options on the website for the Les Sommets resort in Quebec but hasn't pulled the trigger, it generates an email from the resort asking, "Need help deciding?" The responses were so substantial, according to *SAM* magazine, the marketing team had to get help from the customer service team. On average each email generated $30 in revenue!

Will the demise of large, independent media chronicling and supporting the sport hurt it in the long run? It's hard to argue the importance of the role *SKI* and *Skiing* played in the early years of the sport, when they were the only place to find nationwide, quality information on resorts, gear, and instruction. Their sales staffs were also the gateway to the New York City–based corporate world, helping resorts forge alliances with brands, from liquor to automotive, and sponsorships of a range of important on-mountain events. *Transworld* was the bible of snowboarding when it exploded on the snow scene, with issues running 300-plus pages. *Powder* employed numerous iconic editors, writers and personalities over the years, and played a role as predictable contrarians, which in their view kept focus on the core values of the ski experience.

My editor Andy, as a former *SKI* magazine editor-in-chief and then publisher, waxes nostalgic about the loss of these once heavyweight brands, the long cast of characters behind them, and their role supporting the sport over eight decades. He feels the loss has weakened the sport's foundation. But the world has changed, and the negative impacts from their disappearance are difficult to pinpoint. The magazines still do solid digital work, and there are numerous independent ski-news websites churning out good daily content. The ski world has moved on.

Snowmaking/Grooming Improves

In *Ski Inc.*, I mentioned the impact of snowmaking technology on the health of the business. Snowmaking costs have been lowered by a significant reduction in annual energy consumption (KWH) that, depending on the resort, probably ranges from 50 to 75 percent of historic norms. Areas with the greatest savings have fully automated systems. Again, these savings flow to the bottom line. But, more importantly, modern snowmaking has allowed smaller ski areas in warmer climes to succeed. The critical component is water. Where the area has significant water resources, the snowmaking system can quickly rebound from adverse weather, inevitable in many regions. Erratic weather patterns can still impact profitability, but it is no longer a life-or-death situation for many ski areas. I would argue that modern snowmaking has allowed the industry to prosper and, to date at least, mitigate the impacts of climate change.

Anyone who looks back 40 or 50 years into the early days of skiing and talks about the "good old days" doesn't have a very good memory. The social side and the physical exhilaration were wonderful, but remember cold, wet socks? Permanent blue stains on your lower body from those wet jeans? Limited and erratic grooming (no power tillers)? Slow lifts? Day tickets stapled to your Army surplus jacket? Unreliable "releasable" bindings? Those plank-like 210-centimeter straight skis that were nearly impossible to press into an arc? Nope. Don't want to go back. The ski resort industry has been successful because the overall experience has been transformed from those early days. There are still frustrating hassles (mostly getting there and back), but the modern ski day is generally predictable, fun, safe, social, and energizing. The adrenaline rush is still there for those so inclined. As I noted in *Ski Inc.*, "No one wears a GoPro while golfing." But they are ubiquitous on the slopes.

Vertical Integration Now Standard

One major, beneficial change in the industry that has facilitated both increased profitability and a better experience is "vertical integration." In the early days, most ski areas saw themselves as uphill-transportation companies. Their principal job was to operate the lifts, safely and efficiently. Food had to be provided, usually via bland cafeterias, as did goggles, gloves, and anything else that might have been left behind. Many services were leased out. Nowadays, virtually all elements of the experience are owned and operated by the ski area: rental/demo/retail shops, varied food offerings, lodging, retail, ski school, reservations, and new summer venues.

For many resorts, the rental/demo department has emerged as a strong bottom-line contributor, particularly with destination-resort visitors who don't want to pay increased baggage fees to haul gear on a flight and want the flexibility to rent the best skis for the current snow conditions. High-end demo operations, which can get 30, 40 or even more rental days out of a pair of skis, and then sell them at season's end (and recoup the original investment), are a relatively new and important profit center. Many resorts boast a 70 to 75 percent net income profit margin from rentals/demos.

For many years now, NSAA has provided member areas with "best practices" relative to rental-shop operations, knowing from experience and customer feedback that the rental-shop experience was often a weak link in attracting new skiers to the sport. Most rental shops have been significantly enhanced as a result, and gear companies have helped with simplified ski-boot-binding rental systems that don't even require a screwdriver for adjustments. This has led to dramatically increased efficiency and profitability. Assisting this trend is the arrival of new, in-room ski delivery companies, like Black Tie Ski Rentals.

In terms of profitability, the next most important revenue center is ski school. While deals abound for learn-to-ski or -ride programs, the most significant contributor to profitability is the private lesson. At major destination resorts, the cost of an all-day family private is almost the same as an unrestricted mega-pass. Yes, skiing has become more affordable, but there are still many who will shell out the big bucks for the convenience (and lift-cutting privileges) of a private lesson.

Food and beverage operations are also being run with more attention to quality, variety and service. Smart resort F&B operators today offer options that are healthier, greener, and a huge step up from the burgers and chili-cheese fries of yesteryear. Cafeteria lines are being replaced with high-end food courts. Resorts are bringing the food product up on the mountain where the guests are and where they want to dine. There are even remote food-service operations, such as Steamboat's Taco Beast, essentially a food van mounted on the back of a snowcat. The Taco Beast can show up virtually anywhere on the mountain, complete with music system, lounge chairs, and, of course, cold beer. Bottom line: A healthier bottom line and a dramatically improved dining experience.

In the case of Vail's Colorado operations, vertical integration extends to Colorado Mountain Express, a regional shuttle operator (now rebranded as Epic Mountain Express). They can't be missed on I-70, headed to or from the airport, given their large and colorful "Epic" signage. This vertical integration allows the resort to cross-market its products and leverage the profitability of each operation. The rub comes when the resort competes head-to-head with older community operators and enjoys what some might see as an unfair competitive advantage.

Ski Towns Matter

One of the more significant changes in the modern ski industry is the role that the larger ski resort community now plays. Back in the 1980s and '90s, conventional wisdom held that for continued success a ski area needed to keep getting bigger, offering more and more variety for its guests. Customers understand that the resort business has matured, and that you don't have to (and realistically cannot) have a new lift or expanded terrain every year. Much more important is what's happening in town.

Prior to the advent of high-speed lifts, most skiers spent a full-day on the slopes. In today's world, three- to four-hours of skiing is about all most guests can handle. (The next lift ticket pricing tool might establish specific hours of use and price appropriately. This might be a boon to smaller resorts which need to turn over their parking lots to park as many cars as they can in a day.)

When guests at a modern resort start early, the afternoon is largely free. Vice versa, if they get off to a late start, there's plenty of time for a walk and breakfast downtown prior to hitting the slopes. And the communities have evolved to provide a much higher-quality experience and greater variety than in the past.

Using Steamboat as just one example, it is almost impossible to experience all of the community's offerings in a week. Consider the options: hot-air ballooning, the famous hot springs in Strawberry Park, snowcat skiing on Buffalo Pass, Tread of Pioneers Museum, the Steamboat Art Museum, more than a dozen art galleries, historic Howelsen Hill (the oldest continuously operating ski area in the U.S.), Strings Music festival, and the list goes on. In reality, most guests probably spend more time off the mountain than on. What a change. It's the total vacation experience that matters, not just what happens "on the mountain." The ski experience is still reason No. 1 for the visit. But in terms of a decision to return, it will be the total vacation experience that determines whether one comes back. *The guest's view of the relative appeal of ski areas has become defined by the community in which they operate, not just by the ski area.*

This reality has led to a new level of cooperation and coordination between resort communities and their ski areas. Joint-marketing initiatives have long been in play, especially in the summer, and most Western destinations have community-supported airline subsidies.

The town matters. It follows, then, that the relationship between the ski company and its host community must be positive, synergistic, and carefully maintained. The popular view of Vail Resorts is that its area COOs are not allowed much independence. With the company's focus on promotion from within, there is a constant churning of leadership, as executives progress from roles at smaller to larger resort properties. This can lead to a shorter tenure than some communities might prefer.

Alterra, on the other hand, has publicly committed to local management and maintaining the independence of each brand. The company promotes this as a significant point of difference with Vail. The company's website proclaims: "We honor each destination's unique character and celebrate the legendary adventures and enduring memories they bring to everyone." This is understandable as a marketing/positioning strategy, but the reality is that the ski towns have their own distinct personalities, regardless of ownership. Steamboat has seen three *very* different ownership groups over the last 20 years. The town has survived each. *The towns matter.*

Summer Operations Flourish

For decades, resorts have searched for an answer to the financial challenge of high seasonality: golf courses, mountain biking trails, alpine slides, water parks, and so on. Despite some significant investments over the years, few areas were able to meaningfully impact their seasonality.

Vail Mountain, for example, could get 20,000-plus skiers on its lifts on a busy winter day, but summer was a different animal. Visitors to Western destination resorts in summer have historically been a different breed, with tighter budgets and interests that don't align with the actual ski resort property: hiking and fishing on U.S. Forest Service land, sightseeing, shopping, and maybe staying at an RV camp.

More recently, ski towns have become summer destinations in their own right, and sales tax collections have skyrocketed over the past decade at dozens of Western destinations. The weather is delightful, with cool nights and warm, but not too warm, days. Lodging and services are much less expensive than during the ski season, and occupancy rates have risen steadily. The recreational and cultural offerings are incredibly varied.

Big initiatives, like Vail Resorts' Epic Discovery and its many iterations at other resorts, are further altering the summer dynamic. Although the situation is quite different region to region, for the most part a whole new menu of summer attractions has changed the landscape: zip lines, mountain coasters, high-end miniature golf, summer tubing, and more. Vail Resorts was one of the first to make a significant investment in its Lionshead area back in the 1990s, where a number of new activities have been available in summer. It then went all in with its $25 million Epic Discovery. The all-day, unlimited pass, which includes everything from the gondola access ride to adventure courses, tubing, mountain coaster, climbing wall, and zip line is priced around $100.

Coasters and zip lines have potential for use during the winter season as well as summer, providing a stronger economic argument. Because the summer season is so short, investments need to be very high margin, leverage existing infrastructure, and, ideally, provide revenue in winter as well as summer (which Vail does).

For destination resorts in the West, these new facilities took advantage of existing high occupancy rates in the mountain towns (daily rates are still about 50 percent lower than winter). In other words, the new attractions were activities that guests already in town might enjoy. In the case of more regional resorts or ski areas near major urban centers, the investments tend to focus on the drive market and are likely the main reason for a visit. Snowbird's annual Oktoberfest, which is more about brats and beer and riding the tram than physical activity, has evolved into a bigger draw than those famous powder days at this Wasatch resort.

Summer activities are now so important that they have their own annual trade show, where new ideas are presented to industry representatives. The trade publication *SAM* has taken the lead in organizing and promoting these Summer Ops Camps. The *SAM* team also produces a trade publication targeting this new market for summer activities. *Adventure Park Insider* has reach well beyond ski resorts, appealing to all summer adventure facilities. According to *SAM*, summer operations now contribute an average of 15 percent of a ski resort's total revenue. This is an increase of 20 percent from just five years ago. Summer is beginning to count.

New Lodging Options Abound

In light of the popularity of resort towns with seniors, it is not surprising to note that one of the significant economic changes in recent years has been that of the multigenerational family. Those graying seniors, the Baby Boomers, are providing free room and board to the kids and grandkids. This is most notice-able over the traditional school-vacation periods and summer recess. Those generous grandparents are providing an extra economic boost to ski resorts and their communities.

It was not unusual for skiers to drop out of the sport for a few years when faced with the time pressures and expenses of raising children. Most would re-turn after this hiatus, but when the grandparents have remained active in the sport (and have that lovely, large vacation home that their kids can use), that "break" doesn't have to occur. Millennials have also left their mark, as resorts now cater to this generation with everything from food truck-like venues to craft beer festivals and special events that target group participation rather than individuals. And yes, plenty of live free concerts.

The arrival of Vrbo, Airbnb, and the like has dramatically increased the warm bed base at hundreds of resorts, giving visitors another excellent option for lodging. The platforms are so pervasive that traditional lodging reservation outfits lean on them heavily for their own bookings.

Airbnb and Vrbo are perfectly timed for bargain-hunting Millennials. They are inveterate shoppers and can find deals at ski resorts that were simply not available in the past. This helps with their commitment to the sport, not to mention the new business for area operators. I had my wake-up call to this new trend when my daughter and her husband converted a downstairs bed-room/family room in their Steamboat townhouse into an Airbnb unit.

Tax Law Changes Fuel Capital Investments

Recent tax-law changes have also benefited the ski industry. It's a capital-inten-sive business, and the ability to write off up to 100 percent of major capital ex-penditures is a material change. In the fall of 2018, the *Denver Post* carried an article on the surge in lift construction, not just in Colorado, but nationwide. Leitner-Poma lift company, headquartered in Grand Junction, Colorado, was constructing five lifts just in Colorado. According to Jon Mauch, sales manager: "Our business right now couldn't be better. We are having the biggest year we have ever had in the U.S." The article noted that the tax-code changes impacted the manufacturer's decision-making, as well as that of the resorts. The company had accelerated its investments in new manufacturing equipment for the Grand Junction facility. It's a good time to be a ski-lift manufacturer.

Mega-Passes, Value Passes Explode

My last thought in terms of what has changed in the economic model of the ski industry is the most critical today: historically cheap, multiresort passes, with Epic and Ikon at the top of that heap.

Winter Park was the first to introduce a bargain-priced, single-resort pass in the Colorado market (after Mike Shirley pioneered a $199 pass for Bogus Basin, Idaho). It was called the Buddy Pass. My old friend Jerry Groswold, the longtime Winter Park president whom we lost in 2015, used to remind us that it wasn't brilliant marketing behind the new product, just survival. The resort faced a financial crisis, and feared it would not make payroll in the summer of 2000. So for the 2000–01 season, four people could sign up in person (it was designed to target only Colorado residents, but some ambitious destination skiers flew in to make the buy). The cost for the Buddy Pass was $199 per person, an unheard of bargain at the time.

The market responded. On the first Labor Day weekend after Winter Park unveiled its Buddy Pass, Colorado resorts once again pitched their exhibitor tents outside Gart's Sportcastle in Denver for the annual Sniagrab sale ("Bargains" spelled backward), to sell products like the four-ticket packs. According to Chris Jarnot, now the executive vice president of Vail Resorts Mountain Division but then serving as the marketing director for Vail and Beaver Creek, when Winter Park began selling its Buddy Pass on the Friday of the holiday weekend, the line of eager buyers stretched all the way down Broadway and snaked around the block. Its competitors were lonely. The next day, Copper would match it with a similar offer, and its line equaled Winter Park's. By Sunday, Vail Resorts was on board with an even bigger offer, and its inexpensive Keystone/Breckenridge/A-Basin pass had the longest queue of all.

For many years, the season pass had been considered "inelastic." In other words, conventional wisdom held that a drop in price could not be offset by an increase in volume. That had remained true for remote destination resorts, where purchasers were largely local residents and second-home owners, but for those areas close to major ski markets like Denver, big discounts drove big increases in units sold.

For most regions of the country, this was viewed as a largely "Colorado thing." And even in Colorado, there was an effort to "fence" the sale of deeply discounted passes so that your typical destination guest could not easily take advantage of the deal. For example, Intrawest's multiresort passes were sold for years only through Christy Sports locations in the Front Range. In the example of Steamboat, the value-oriented "Rocky Mountain Super Pass Plus," which included Steamboat along with Winter Park, Copper, and Eldora, allowed only six days at Steamboat. This effectively isolated the product from those who wanted a traditional, unlimited pass for Steamboat (which cost several hundred dollars more). Requiring a fall purchase at a Front Range location also blocked the product from destination guests who were planning to come for a week, and for whom the six-day pass was an attractive and cheaper option.

While the competition was going through the mental gymnastics of "fencing" and protecting lift-ticket yield, Vail Resorts developed a simpler strategy. It offered an unrestricted Epic Pass—alongside the Epic Local, with its reduced access and blackouts—to *everyone*. And it promoted these deals everywhere. *"Voilà!"* Sales went through the roof. For the 2018–19 season, Vail Resorts sold almost 1 million passes. A staggering number. It had detailed information on each purchaser and could target additional product sales through its vigorous CRM systems. Here, the benefits of vertical integration and customer intelligence would really pay off.

While some heavy users of an Epic Pass can count 100 days, there are many others who over-estimate their expected ski days and bring down the average, increasing the yield for Vail. For 2018–19, the average days skied began to move upward in response to great snow and the increasing awareness of the value of the mega-passes and their new pass partners. Skiers took advantage of these new opportunities by skiing more resorts and skiing more often.

For those who didn't make the pass commitment: Welcome to ticket-window shock, otherwise known as "dynamic pricing." Vail Resorts (and other operators with similar passes) were now managing the ticket pricing based on time of year and quality of snow conditions. The single-day price has edged above $200 at Vail and Beaver Creek for peak demand periods ($219 for the 2018–19 Christmas holiday). The lesson to anyone forking over that much dough at the window: Plan ahead, and buy an Epic Pass next year. At a minimum, go to Vail's website and find the best deal available.

For years, high-window pricing had been a negative for the industry in terms of the "pricey" image of the sport. This, despite the availability of all sorts of deals on-line or via multi-day packages. The public and press would only remember the expensive "window" price. Now, any complaint about the high window price leads to a discussion about the deeply discounted passes. As a result, one could argue that the public perception of the cost of skiing is nowhere near as negative as it has been in the past. This doesn't eliminate ticket window shock. But it does mean that fewer and fewer transactions occur "at the window." Consumers are figuring it out. And Vail Resorts has addressed ticket-window shock for the 2019–20 season—but we'll get to that later.

Although full-priced, unrestricted Epic gets most of the press coverage, there are other popular pass products targeting different income and usage demographics. There's the Epic Local, as well as super-value products, like the Keystone/A-Basin pass (which ended after the 2018–19 season, when A-Basin pulled out of Epic). There's also the military pass, and frequency products, like the four- and seven-day passes. (For the 2018–19 season, Alterra chose to keep its product mix simpler, offering only Ikon and Ikon Base.)

The other significant business advantage of the Epic is that Vail Resorts gets commitment early via a down (or full) payment each spring. The balance is due before the lifts begin operating. From a business point of view, this has effectively eliminated the need for working capital and materially softens the impact of a poor snow year. It should be noted that while this does have down-side protection, it also limits the "upside" when Mother Nature is unusually generous (as in the winter of 2018–19). The best pricing comes with the earliest deadline, and then the prices start to jump in increments steep enough to drive early commitment. Eventually, the value passes are not available.

The new competitor to Epic is Ikon. Because of some differences with partner-resort ticketing systems and a short time period for the launch, Alterra could not develop the software in time to offer a deposit-type program. If you wanted an Ikon pass for the 2018–19 season, you had to make a full payment by April 9. After that date, the price increased by $100, until October, when the price increased by another $50. There was some trepidation within Alterra that full payment would negatively impact their sales in the first year, but that doesn't seem to have been the case. Perceived value is so high that there was little resistance and the market responded enthusiastically. (For the 2019–20 season, Alterra did offer a payment plan.)

While I've focused here on Vail Resorts and Alterra, the trend toward deeply discounted passes has swept the industry. Peak Resorts offered its Peak Pass, essentially an Eastern regional version of Epic. There are a number of other regional passes that include multiple resorts. Even for individual, stand-alone ski areas, the clear trend has been to trade a deep discount for early commitment. It is difficult to get data on pass penetration as a percentage of all skier visits, but it must have been close to 50 percent for the 2018–19 season. In spring 2019, yet another multiresort pass emerged, this one organized by an independent marketing group. The "Indy Pass" is a product for small- to medium-sized, independently owned resorts, as an alternative to the mega-passes. "Our resorts represent the scrappy soul of skiing, and the Indy Pass is the antithesis of Epic and Ikon," says Doug Fish of Fish Marketing in Bend, which launched the effort. "So far we have 30 resorts committed with a few more in the pipeline," he said in mid-June 2019. No doubt there will be more partners, and more pass offerings, shortly after this book rolls off the presses.

What It All Means...

So for all the reasons noted in this chapter, the U.S. ski industry is on a stronger financial footing than ever before. EBITDA margins, on average, have moved from the low 20s to 26–27 percent. Some of the largest resorts operate with margins over 40 percent.

More than a handful of CEOs are dubbing it the "Golden Age"—it may have been Michael Berry who first used the term. I'm not sure I'd go that far. The real Golden Age was arguably when hundreds of resorts were being built in the 1950s through 1970s. But as you will see, it's not just the big guys who are finding success. It's a broad, deep transformation of an old business model that has many prospering. "Renaissance" might be a better word.

CHAPTER 3

Vail Resorts:

Analyzing Its Success

On August 15, 2016, shortly after the purchase of Whistler Blackcomb in British Columbia, Vail's stock closed at $153.53. That was a stunning, fourfold increase since CEO Rob Katz took over in 2006. The stock reached a 2018 high of $302.76 in September. Vail Resorts has been a darling on Wall Street, and deservedly so. That said, investors are struggling with the impact of Alterra on Vail's long-term growth prospects. The stock price was beaten down in early 2019 to $210, 30 percent off the high-water mark. By the end of June 2019, it was at $225. The day after the Peak Resorts acquisition, its stock jumped 4.25 percent to $235.

Where is it headed? I'm not going to speculate, but for those who do, it's important to recognize the company's strengths before trying to calculate how the changed competitive landscape might impact their future performance. There are many reasons for the company's success, but in my view four come to mind: first, the ability to deliver strong results when facing adverse weather conditions; second, the quality of its resort facilities; third, its coordinated acquisition and Epic Pass strategies; and fourth, the leadership of Chairman and CEO Rob Katz.

1. Financial Results

In the West, the two winters preceding the 2018–19 season were less than ideal from a snowfall perspective. Much of Colorado was experiencing moderate to severe drought conditions. Telluride, in southwestern Colorado, experienced arguably the most negative effects. It had fewer than 200 acres of skiing open for the busy 2017–18 Christmas holiday period.

Over that same holiday period, Vail Mountain was unable to open its legendary Back Bowls. Although conditions eventually improved in Colorado, the season was less than stellar from a snowfall perspective. In California, the drought was even worse. Late-season storms brought a modicum of relief, but for the most part, the damage had been done to the state's ski industry. Raging wildfires during the summer of 2018 are testimony to the lack of moisture. The East Coast was a mixed bag in terms of weather. Yet given these challenging conditions (it is unusual to have so many regions of ski country experience adverse weather in the same year), Vail performed well. Financial results for the 2018 fiscal year were exceptional. The Vail business model is based on two fairly simple premises. First, that the large collection of resorts is worth more than the individual assets. And second, that the Epic Pass strategy drives commitment and loyalty to the company. In executing that strategy, Vail has acquired highly visible resorts in all of the major U.S. markets while continuing to build an international portfolio. This scale has enhanced the appeal of its trademark Epic Pass and provided significant economies of scale from a financial performance perspective.

Yet even with the success of Vail Resorts' pass-sales strategy, the key to annual financial success remains managing the business day-to-day in a manner that maximizes results. Vail's local management teams are exceptional at this. Multiyear snowmaking investments certainly paid off, especially at Heavenly and Northstar. Keystone in Colorado covers virtually all popular terrain and is a longtime snowmaking leader. (It needs to be, because the resort is disadvantaged in terms of annual, natural snowfall, based on unique geographical conditions.) The Vail organization shares best practices across its divisions, relative to mountain operations. This translates to competitive snow surfaces provided by well-trained and well-equipped snow groomers.

The Vail Resorts culture insists on commitment to centralized purchasing. This can be particularly challenging for new acquisitions, where there may be a long-standing tradition of favored suppliers. Snowcats are a good example, where the local team may have a clear preference in terms of supplier, but Vail Resorts' corporate will dictate the decision, based on the technical specs the resort provides. Vail Resorts simply does not tolerate any "independence" in terms of purchasing, at least for big-ticket items. Although this creates a certain amount of resentment at the local business level, especially with new acquisitions, the impact on the bottom line is hugely positive. The local impact may be overstated since each resort provides central purchasing with its detailed performance specifications. A sophisticated purchasing team then employs those specs, along with other historic metrics of down-time, etc., to make a final decision. The analytics apply to just about everything it buys, and the price is driven down by its multiresort leverage, like buying 25 snowcats instead of two or three. When capital budgets go farther, the individual resort managers see the benefits.

Other resort holding companies are known for their focus on purchasing to save costs, but in terms of scale, Vail Resorts is the leader. Their offices in Broomfield are filled with analysts looking for any possible cost savings and then driving their purchasing plan through the company. Shared best practices (and insistence on conformity with those) and razor-sharp purchasing support the argument that the collection is more valuable than the sum of its parts.

Bottom line: Despite the weather vagaries of 2018, the company recorded 12.345 million skier visits. Mountain EBITDA rose 4.5 percent over the prior year, to $591.6 million. Mountain revenue rose 6.9 percent. The company was sitting on $171.1 million in cash or cash equivalents at year-end (July 31, 2018). Vail Resorts delivered in 2018.

2. High-Quality Facilities

One of the issues that troubles investors when looking at the ski industry is its capital-intensive nature. There's a lot of hardware out there, and it's expensive to replace or update. Many large resorts operate grooming fleets with as many as 16 cats, at an average cost of, say, $375,000 each. These need to be retired on a schedule, usually based on hours. A typical metric is "four years and gone." So do the math: A 16-cat fleet with a four-year rotation means roughly $1.5 million per year (there is some trade-in value from the older cats). That's before fuel costs, track repairs, and other miscellaneous maintenance.

A modern, detachable six-seat chairlift runs about $10 million. Older, fixed-grip lifts can be safely maintained for many years, but at some point this equipment needs to be replaced. And current expectations from skiers are that the new lift represents an upgrade in terms of comfort and capacity. That often means replacing an older, fully depreciated, fixed-grip lift with a new detachable. Big bucks are required.

To the extent that a ski company has high operating margins, these replacement costs are a manageable challenge and just a reality of the business. But most of the industry does not achieve margins comparable to Vail's. In recent annual reports, Vail has committed to spending approximately $150 million annually in CapEx. When you look at how this breaks out in terms of spending per resort, the reality is that few non-Vail resorts will be able to match that level of internal investment. In my view, this is one of the biggest challenges Alterra will face as it moves to position itself as a serious competitor to Vail Resorts. More on this later.

Any knowledgeable observer of the ski business would have to agree with the statement that, in broad terms, Vail's ski resorts have more modern, up-to-date facilities than the competition. This, in fact, has been the company's "promise" to its guests for many years. There are certainly many ski resorts that can meet those standards, but looking across the industry, it's just a fact that the ongoing Vail investments have differentiated their resorts from a qualitative perspective. In terms of future financial challenges, Vail does not face the same "CapEx hangover" as the rest of the industry. According to the 2018 10-K: "We systematically upgrade our lifts and put in new lifts to increase uphill capacity and streamline skier traffic to maximize the guest experience."

Not having to play catch-up creates the opportunity to further distance themselves from the competition. In talking to some of the still "independent" operators, this is their greatest concern looking forward. Many simply do not have the cash flow to compete from a capital-spending point of view. In summary, the quality of Vail Resort's facilities provides an existential competitive advantage in today's marketplace and limits the need to commit future CapEx to those existing facilities, a luxury most of the competition doesn't have.

3. The Epic Strategy and Acquisitions

This brings me to the third reason for Vail's popularity among investors: the seamless marriage of an aggressive acquisition strategy with its proven Epic model.

Epic Pass sales provide a significant early financial cushion, with 47 percent of annual lift revenues coming from pass sales (per the 2018 10-K). This compares with 43 and 40 percent respectively for 2017 and 2016. The ability to secure $413 million in pass sales (estimated for 2018), most of this in the bank prior to the beginning of the ski season, dramatically stabilizes annual revenues and EBITDA.

For a decade, the Epic Local has been priced just below the full-price Epic. The Local targets the regional markets (Tahoe, Summit County, and others), whose skiers are willing to trade some blackout days and restrictions for a discounted price. Both Epic and Epic Local have "buy by" dates, after which the price goes up or the passes are no longer available. The company also offered two products for those who didn't want the full season: the Epic 7-day and the Epic 4-day. They provided access to the same resorts for those respective days total (with some blackouts). These also were not available after certain dates. Those who didn't purchase any of the above products were consigned to "checking the web" for the best price or heading to the dreaded ticket window for the day's surprise price. Targeted marketing of thoughtfully developed pass products, covering virtually all pricing segments and demographics, anchors Vail Resorts' success. Add in dynamic pricing and its higher yields, and the result is industry-leading profitability.

As 2016 ended, Vail Resorts had made a much predicted move into the Northeast with its acquisition of Stowe. The Epic Pass strategy operates to drive commitment and loyalty. Regionally, the result is higher volume at its owned resorts, which Stowe is most assuredly seeing. From a destination-resort perspective, it also drives higher volume, because passholders, with their pass paid for, are highly likely to visit a Vail-owned resort when travelling west. Simple. From an EBITDA perspective, the destination component is the most important because it brings a higher total spend from ancillary services the company operates.

To provide a range of pricing options for customers, Vail Resorts introduced the Epic Local, which as stated captures buyers who can accept some limitations (such as blackout dates) in exchange for a price discount. (Alterra has rolled out a similar product called Ikon Base). For anyone even remotely considering a trip out West to one of Vail Resorts' properties, an Epic Pass purchase, with Stowe now included, would be very attractive. One can only assume that the addition of Stowe enhanced Epic Pass sales in the Northeast.

Then came Alterra, and the world changed.

For the 2018–19 season, the Epic and Ikon passes drew more attention and focus from skiers than the individual resort brands. How quickly this happened was stunning. Marketing dollars that once might have promoted individual resort brands were redirected to the pass products. This transition had already occurred at Vail Resorts' mountains, where even legacy brands like Vail Mountain have been subjugated to the Epic mission. But with the advent of Ikon, the "pass is the brand" movement truly exploded. Confirmation of this transition came with the October 2018 edition of *SKI* magazine. For some 30 years, this issue had presented its annual rankings of ski resorts, including regional rankings. This was a much watched and anticipated event. For years Vail took top slot; Deer Valley enjoyed a long run; and Whistler Blackcomb also had its time at the top. In the 2018 issue, the top three resorts in North America were . . . drum roll, please . . . well, kind of hard to figure out.

For 2018, the whole ranking system was discarded in favor of a listing of resorts by pass affiliation and a highlighting of their key attributes. If you look carefully at the text, there is a "Best of the West" category, and the winner was Aspen Snowmass. Other regional "bests" and categories were awarded, but they were difficult to discern, and there were no regional rankings. The pass was now the brand.

Looking at the Northeast, Alterra dramatically eliminated Vail's "Stowe advantage." Not only were the Intrawest resorts (Stratton; Tremblant, Quebec; Snowshoe; and Blue Mountain, Ontario) part of Ikon, but Alterra had signed up the Boyne Resorts (Loon in New Hampshire, and Sunday River and Sugarloaf in Maine) and POWDR's Killington and Pico for seven days at each resort.

Vail responded with the purchase of the Triple Peaks resorts from the Mueller family and Oz Real Estate. This brought Okemo, Sunapee, and Crested Butte into the fold. For protecting market share in the Northeast, it was a brilliant move.

Its next move was in the Pacific Northwest, where it had a strong advantage given its ownership of Whistler Blackcomb. It strengthened that by acquiring Stevens Pass from Oz Realty. This move anticipated Alterra's pass partnerships in that market and, possibly, its eventual purchase of Crystal Mountain. Without Stevens in the Epic portfolio, Vail would have seen its market share advantage in this lucrative market virtually disappear.

Back in July 2015, Vail Resorts closed on the purchase of Perisher Ski Resort in Australia. This was Vail's first international resort acquisition. Immediately, Perisher pass holders became eligible for Epic benefits. Perisher is the largest snow resort operation in the Southern Hemisphere, with the highest terrain, the most lifts and the most skiable terrain. Australia has been a strong market for the major Rocky Mountain resorts. Vail Mountain, in particular, had been promoting itself there for many years with considerable success. So all those new Perisher Epic passholders considering a ski vacation in the states would naturally gravitate to Vail itself or one of its sister resorts. Australians typically take extended vacations during their summer, often combining a week's ski vacation in the Rockies with a second week in Hawaii. So this acquisition met Vail's qualitative standard; it came with regional dominance and positively enhanced the company's international visitations.

In February 2019, Vail Resorts announced that it had entered into an agreement to acquire Falls Creek and Hotham resorts in Victoria, Australia. Rumors of this transaction began circulating in December 2018. The purchase price was in the range of $174 million (AU).

"We are thrilled to welcome the guests and employees of both Falls Creek and Hotham into the Vail Resorts family and further strengthen our position in Australia, which is one of our most important international markets. The acquisition of the leading mountain resorts in Victoria is part of our continued strategy to drive season pass sales and build loyalty with guests from around the world," said Katz.

Upon closing, the two resorts will join the 2019 Epic Australia Pass and the 2019–20 Epic Pass. In promotional materials, Vail Resorts highlights the fact that the Epic Australia Pass pays for itself in just four days of skiing. Alterra has no owned resorts in Australia, so with this most recent transaction, Vail dominates that market, owning the three largest ski resorts. Australia already provides a significant number of destination visits to U.S. ski resorts. Epic Passes will be very attractive to those travelling Aussie skiers.

By way of personal anecdote, I was riding the Steamboat gondola in late February 2019 and struck up a conversation with two Aussies. They were planning to travel to Vail following their week at Steamboat and had visited one of Vail's Japanese Epic partners earlier in the winter. They owned both Epic and Ikon passes! As we unloaded the gondola, one of them said, "We can basically ski the world and ski year-round for just a bit more than we used to pay for our local passes." How the ski world has changed.

Vail Resorts had been looking for international opportunities for many years. John Garnsey, a longtime ski resort executive and former president of Beaver Creek, was closely involved with the international racing community because of the Beaver Creek World Cup events. This led to contacts with resort operators around the world, but especially in Europe. John spent the tail end of his career chasing those opportunities, but none materialized at the time. The complex, historical pattern of ownership makes acquisition by an outsider very difficult. However, the relationships that were established as a result were no doubt a catalyst for the dramatic expansion of Vail's international partners in the 2018–19 Epic Pass. The offerings in Europe are simply stunning: 30 resorts across France, Switzerland, Italy, and Austria. Les 3 Vallées in France is, I believe, the largest ski complex in the world. I've had the pleasure of skiing there many times. It contains more ski lifts than the entire state of Colorado. It is an absolute bucket-list destination for any serious skier.

Vail Resorts leads in this international space in terms of the competitive appeal of its Epic Pass. Alterra has countered with partner offerings in Japan, Chile, New Zealand, and Australia, but these pale by comparison with the Epic menu. The Alterra international offerings are largely a "value add" for passholders. They are not driving pass sales in the way that Vail is through acquisitions, like those in Australia.

Given the relatively few opportunities for growth in the U.S. (via large resort purchases), Vail is likely to continue its international focus. This could mean additional acquisitions, new pass partners, or even new businesses to facilitate ease of travel for U.S. Epic passholders who want to venture out internationally. Very few North American skiers have actually visited a European resort. From my perspective, doing so is part of the complete skiing experience. Vail is facilitating that and by doing so, driving commitment and loyalty to its pass products. It will be interesting to watch how the Epic skier visits to Europe grow over the next few years.

On December 7, 2018, Vail reported its first-quarter results. The impact of new acquisitions caused the Q1 EBITDA loss to widen year over year from $54.1 million to $72.5 million. Epic Pass sales were projected to hit 925,000 versus 725,000 the prior year. However, 100,000 of those were deeply discounted military and family passes, at $99 each. So while units grew substantially, revenues increased only 10 percent, a smaller YOY increase than either of the prior two years. On the earnings call, Rob Katz was questioned on the impact of Ikon. He noted weakness in the Utah and Northern California markets, but overall he reported that the arrival of Ikon was raising awareness of value passes and confirming VR's Epic strategy. Katz confirmed overall guidance for the fiscal year. He also highlighted VR's capital-investment strategy for the coming year and detailed major projects by resort. Total spending: $175 to $180 million. This would bring the total investment to $1.2 billion over the decade. Look for VR to continue to trumpet its capital spending, because few competitors will be able to keep pace.

The stock fell about 18 percent that day, the largest single-day drop since going public in 1997. It had corrected by 5 percent by the end of that week.

The Wall Street Journal carried an article in December that was over-ambitiously titled: "Vail Expansion Plan Goes Aggressive and Wipes Out." The piece didn't provide any evidence to back up the disaster headline. It referenced analysts who thought Vail might have paid a premium for recent acquisitions and acknowledged the arrival of the new competitor, Alterra. The meat of the story covered geographic distribution and how that strategy might mitigate variable weather conditions. It missed the fact that the ski world has shifted in its buying preferences. Epic was transformational. Ikon and others are simply copying the proven model. Yes, Vail has more competition, but that doesn't alter their ability to continue to deliver stellar financial results. What is different: the low-hanging fruit in terms of potential North American acquisitions been plucked from the ski tree.

For calendar year 2018, the Vail stock was virtually unchanged, at approximately $212 per share. Its high for the year was just over $300. One could argue that at $300 the stock was pricey, but taking the longer view and recognizing the company's fiscal discipline, it will likely resume an upward march. Epic Pass sales for 2018–19, as noted, were 925,000. Stunning. As we'll see, advance sales for 2019–20 show continued growth ... despite Alterra. Those numbers will only increase with the addition of the resorts formerly under the Peak umbrella, with previous passholders having the option of upgrading to Epic.

4. Chairman and CEO Rob Katz

Would the Vail Resorts' story be the same without the leadership of Rob Katz? Unlikely. He joined the Board of Directors in 1991, representing the interests of longtime employer Apollo Global Management, LLC. He loved the company, the people, and his work on the board, and he took every opportunity to ski at Vail. He was a lifelong, passionate skier, explaining that he started "at age 11 in jeans at Hunter Mountain."

In mid-March 2019, Katz gave an insightful, candid, and somewhat surprising talk in Park City, reflecting on those early days. His presentation on leadership was part of the town's 25th Annual Community Leadership Lecture, organized by legendary land planner Myles Rademan.

In the presentation, he described his successful early career in finance with Apollo in New York City, during which Katz thrived in complex analysis, dissecting companies, and giving concise investment advice. Then he and his wife, Elana Amsterdam, the founder of Elana's Pantry, decided on a lifestyle change. On the heels of 9/11, they moved with their two children to Boulder. What hardly anybody knew before that evening's revelation was that he was considering a rather incredible career change to become ... a psychotherapist.

Here was Wall Street wizard Rob Katz, hanging out in his leafy Mapleton Hill neighborhood, unshaven, wearing cargo shorts daily, meditating, practicing yoga, and spending perhaps 20 percent of his time consulting with large-valuation companies. He was pondering the oft-futile group leadership efforts and retreats he'd witnessed on Wall Street, and wondering what he could bring to the subject as a friendly, experienced adviser, essentially a leadership coach. In the take-no-prisoners world of high finance, he related, they say that if you want a friend, buy a dog. With further training, Katz imagined he could be the high-stakes counselor who would help develop better leaders. He had actually completed prerequisite courses for admission to Boulder's Naropa University master's program in psychology. So leadership was—and is—a big thing for Katz.

Then Adam Aron, at the time Vail Resorts' CEO, departed. The board named Katz to head the search committee for a replacement. The search smartly circled back to the guy running it, Katz, and in the resort world the rest is history. In 2006 he took over the reins as CEO and, in March 2009, the chairmanship as well.

In his early years, Katz says he was developing his own leadership skills and was often tested—and he made mistakes. He had a common habit of being so enthusiastic about an issue that he would "talk over" his management team, he says. He has worked hard to address that, even warning his team in advance that he was likely do so on a topic.

There's a view, however, that high-level executives like Bill Jensen and

Roger McCarthy might not have left the company in Katz' early years if their relationship with the CEO had been more positive.

There's an old saw that "leaders who don't listen end up with followers who have nothing to say," and Katz has worked hard to avoid that trap. While he has strong opinions, I've had former executives confirm that he does take input and feedback from his team, and he has now adopted a schedule of visiting individual resort managers, speaking to their employees, and doing community talks for an impressive total of 60 appearances a year. He classifies himself as an introvert, and says he had to repeatedly practice to become an accomplished public speaker. There's no doubt he's good at it now; he is a commanding presence before groups, but with self-awareness and humor—and still amazingly youthful in his appearance.

When he started as CEO, Katz learned quickly that Vail Resorts' employees were passionate about their work and talented, and they loved the mountain culture, but they did not like the company. He set out to change that and has made leadership—which can be practiced by a lift op as well as a department head, he stresses—a priority and cornerstone at Vail Resorts. Google his Park City talk; it's well worth watching for his walk through of what he's learned about leadership in the field.

In 2016, *Fast Company* named Vail Resorts one of the World's 50 Most Innovative Companies, and in 2018 *Forbes* designated it as one of America's Best Employers for the fourth straight year. Impressive.

When you examine Katz's career, it's evident that no other individual has had a comparable influence on the ski business, ever. His driven style remains—this is, after all, the leader who on his first day announced the move of Vail Resorts' headquarters from the ski town of Avon to Broomfield, which back then caught a lot of people off guard. The local take was that Vail would lose many tenured, committed employees and its "mountain soul." In retrospect, the move was a slam dunk given what Katz had planned for the company.

He came into the business not shy at all about ridding Vail Resorts of what he considered to be the old and ineffective habits of the ski industry. One that really bothered him (and was noted in his Park City speech) was how some resorts fought the emergence of snowboarding, banning it from their lifts, when it was ultimately their savior. Katz embraces change as part of his leadership role and shows no outward regret about making tough decisions, such as severing ties with a longtime executive or pulling out of Colorado Ski Country.

The results speak for themselves. True leaders distinguish themselves not in the good but in the tough times, and Katz deserves extra credit for the difficult, at times painful, decisions he made to steer the company through the financial crisis of 2007–09, while also taking a $1 salary himself. Vail Resorts gives back $12 million annually in the communities where it operates, and Katz personally has set an incredibly high bar in philanthropy. Along with his wife, Elana, he created a $58 million, self-advised nonprofit that supports charitable social services in the mountain communities where Vail Resorts operates.

As noted earlier, Katz is responsible for validating the current business model for conglomerates and establishing value passes as foundational to the modern ski experience. I visited with Rob in February 2019 at the Vail Resorts corporate offices in Broomfield, Colorado, midway between Denver and Boulder and, importantly, a short drive to Denver International Airport. There remains a kind of community love/hate relationship surrounding the company, and Katz hasn't entirely extinguished that with his initiatives, partly because it has grown *so much bigger* since he took over.

Katz pretty much sees this as part of the landscape and doesn't allow such animosities to distract him. More than 2,000 employees now work in the company's headquarters, seven floors of busy-ness in a modern, if humdrum, office park. Dining options are more than a walk away, so the company provides a staff cafeteria. Except for the large, back-lit Epic sign over the entry, you would have no idea, walking from the parking lot to the front door, that this facility housed the largest ski company in the world.

Just a few miles away is the city of Boulder, home to the University of Colorado, where Rob lives. For as long as I can remember, Boulder has been a very desirable place to live, with home prices reflecting that popularity. Many of the Vail execs call Boulder home.

Unlike most ski industry leaders, Katz, as mentioned earlier, came to skiing via a stellar financial career with Apollo. Although he started as an outsider, he is now a 13-plus year veteran (not including his Vail Resorts' board of directors involvement, which goes back to 1991), and is, inarguably, the most knowledgeable, successful ski resort executive in the industry's modern history.

Right now, while he shares my view that skiing is in a very good place, he is quick to point out issues and clouds on the horizon. Looking back, he noted that some 30 years ago, the arrival of snowboarding and shaped skis rescued the industry. These days, instead of new technology, a combination of affordability (via value passes) and an improved guest experience is driving participation.

Katz's biggest concern is the lack of diversity in skiing. As we walked to his office, he said, "Look, we're part of the problem. Do you see a lot of diversity here?"

He quickly corrected himself in noting success in terms of engaging women with the company. His current Mountain Division president is Pat Campbell, who started her career as a ski instructor and worked up through the ranks to a leadership role at Keystone, then her current president role. Kirsten Lynch, who came to VR in 2011 after serving as top marketer for PepsiCo and Kraft, is mentioned as having the intellectual stamina to be a potential successor to Rob. But in terms of people of color, Rob is spot on. "Even if we succeed in attracting minorities to our resorts, how do you think they feel when they arrive? Staff members are largely white, which is intimidating by itself if you're not. And the systems we've devised to serve skiers really have been developed by skiers, white male skiers, who may not understand the issues that minorities face."

And, at his Park City leadership talk, Katz also voluntarily acknowledged that Vail Resorts, seeing the abundance of affordable-housing stock during the Great Recession, got way behind in prioritizing this critical need (as did the towns). Vail Resorts has refocused and stepped up its efforts to make up for the shortfall. Likewise, the company did not respond quickly enough with wage increases to meet the rising cost of living and is addressing this as well.

We spoke at length about the arrival of Alterra and its impact. In the big picture, beyond the short-term hit to the stock price, Katz feels that Alterra has validated the VR business model. He also argues that increased promotion of and awareness about value passes, even from the competition, is better for all. The emergence of value passes has shifted the image of skiing from that of an expensive, niche sport to one that is much more accessible and affordable. This is not just a significant change. This is transformational. Ikon's arrival has magnified the Epic value message. Seldom does one read about the "high cost of skiing." Instead, the media's focus is on the high-value pass products. This is driving participation, as played out in the 2018-19 ski season, the fourth best on record. Yes, weather played a huge role, arguably more than the mega-passes, but these results would not have been achieved without the new pricing model.

Does Vail Resorts have a bright future? Absolutely. Does Rob Katz have a few ideas to grow his company and compete? You can be sure of that. The Alterra competition will drive new, creative responses. Katz and his company have a lot of levers to pull, given their depth of resources and head start relative to Alterra. The recent Peak acquisition is just one example. The bigger question for Vail employees and stockholders: Who will replace him?

So this is the company that Alterra was formed to challenge. The next chapter will take a closer look at Alterra and where this new competition might be headed.

CHAPTER 4

Alterra's Ascent
In One Word: *Speed*

The weekend before the KSL/Crown announcement that would lead to Alterra's formation, I happened to be in Aspen for a friend's wedding. I shared a beer with Aspen Skiing Co. CEO Mike Kaplan, and asked him about the rumors circulating regarding Aspen's purchase of Steamboat. (Aspen executives had been spotted in Steamboat, probably on their due diligence mission for the joint venture). According to our local real estate offices, a deal was "definite." Of course, I was skeptical, given the way rumors had a way of moving through our real estate community. Mike was appropriately noncommittal. But my takeaway was that something was happening. I thought it was just Steamboat being purchased by Ski Co., which was partially true at an earlier stage, as I would later learn. But the negotiations eventually advanced to buying all of Intrawest—and through a new entity.

According to reporting by Jason Blevins, who scoured the SEC filings, more than 170 potential bidders had lined up to buy all or part of Intrawest's stable of resorts. This included 16 "strategic partners in the global ski industry," 63 financial firms, and 51 high-net-worth individuals. (Blevins, the nation's leading ski industry reporter, wrote the story for his longtime paper, the *Denver Post*, in May 2017; he has since moved on to the independent *Colorado Sun*.)

One of the stranger twists in Alterra's evolution was the participation (or not) of the Crown ski assets in the new company. Announcements from the start were vague on this issue. At the time, there were those in the industry who concluded that once the Mammoth deal was done, the Crowns insisted on a higher valuation for their Aspen Skiing Co. mountains, and the numbers simply didn't work for the new company. So, for whatever reason, the Crowns went forward as investors, but the Aspen resorts remained independent (but joined in the new pass products). I had the opportunity to meet with Alterra President and COO David Perry in January 2019, and I asked him why it took so long to get clarity on Aspen's decision from an equity perspective.

"How do you value Aspen?" David answered. I can imagine what the internal discussions must have been like on that subject. Given Aspen's iconic position in American skiing, the work-in-progress rebirth of Snowmass, and the unusual nature of Crown ownership (where maximizing annual EBITDA might not have been a driving force).

Mike Kaplan stayed on as Aspen CEO, and David Perry was announced as the new company's president and chief operating officer on July 31, 2017. He would report to Bryan Traficanti, a KSL executive, who had assumed the role of interim CEO. A public CEO search was underway. It was now clear that the Aspen resorts would not be part of the new company. And the new entity still didn't have a name.

There was a quiet period until January 11, 2018, when the joint venture announced its name: Alterra Mountain Company. Shortly after, on February 7, Alterra board member and Mammoth CEO Rusty Gregory was announced as the new CEO.

When we look back on Alterra's formation, the collection of owned resorts and pass partners heading into the 2018–19 season, one thing stands out: *speed.*

It wasn't until I had a chance to talk in-depth with David, Rusty Gregory, and Eric Resnick as background for this book (early in 2019) that I finally understood how they were able to move forward so quickly. Each has his own perspective.

The idea of a competitor to Vail Resorts goes back five years. Two dynamics were involved. First, unbeknownst to many in the ski business, Aspen itself had been on the acquisition trail, and second, it was the Mountain Collective Pass that provided the roadmap for Alterra to quickly assemble its acquisition targets and, on a parallel track, bring so many major pass partners to the table for Ikon.

David Perry is a lifelong ski guy. The Canadian native got the bug working as a heli-ski guide with Canadian Mountain Holidays (CMH), the world's largest heli-ski operation. After ascending through the marketing ranks at Whistler Blackcomb, he was hired away by Colorado Ski Country USA as its executive director. In 2002, he headed to Aspen Skiing Co., starting in marketing and then piling on mountain-operations responsibilities. In 2014 he was named COO. Being deeply involved with the Alterra Mountain Company's formation, he took over as its president and COO in 2017.

For those who have been students of the Colorado ski industry, it's no secret that Aspen, prior to the arrival of Mike Kaplan and David Perry on the senior leadership team, was an important player, but not a competitive one. Snowmass had struggled to maintain market share. To say its village core was "tired" would be kind. The Aspen demographic skewed to the extreme high-end and was aging; nightly rental properties were being converted to second homes; and, very importantly, Aspen had lost much of its earlier "vibe" with the younger demographic. The current management team addressed these deficiencies. The loud horn blast that announced things would be different was the signing of the X Games in 2002. Downtown Aspen now has a new, trendy Limelight hotel that replaced the old one. Snowmass is in the throes of a major redevelopment, and so on. Although Aspen still has challenges, especially in the lack of affordable nightly rentals and employee housing, there's no question that the resort is in a better place thanks to Kaplan, Perry, and their team.

According to the folks I interviewed, Jim Crown noticed these changes. He was pleased with the financial results and the fact that all this had been accomplished within a culture that was very supportive of staff and committed to taking an industry-leading role in combating climate change, values the owners cherished. Ownership gave the green light to pursue acquisitions and grow the company beyond the existing resorts. This was obviously a team that could do more and was encouraged by the Crowns to do so.

The original Aspen vision was a collection of premium resorts that would be regionally dominant destinations. Both Kaplan and Perry had extensive relationships among the resorts and began feeling out potential partners. They were also testing the water in terms of a pass product that might appeal to the remaining independents concerned about competition from Epic or the Intrawest passes (mostly marketed in Colorado). Thus was formed the Mountain Collective Pass (MCP). In its first year, it included the Aspen areas, Whistler

Blackcomb (this was the year before Vail completed its acquisition), Jackson Hole, Snowbird, Alta, and Squaw Valley/Alpine Meadows. The following year, Whistler dropped out given its new owner, Vail, but others were added, including Sun Valley, Taos, Revelstoke, and Big Sky. As described elsewhere in this book, the pass (good for two days at each resort with discounts for subsequent days) worked well to encourage trial while "fencing" season-pass prices at the partner areas. Mammoth was approached but initially declined, expressing concerns about diluting their regional market share. They joined the following year. As of 2018–19, the MCP had 17 partners, all talking to one another (remember, the agreement to join the collective for 2018–19 occurred before the finalization of Ikon).

In mid-December 2018, I spoke with Ralph Scurfield, who owns and operates Banff's Sunshine Village in Alberta, Canada, which had just joined Ikon. "We had a relationship through the Mountain Collective, so it just seemed the right thing to do. Ikon is an amazing destination product," he said. He had already seen a measurable impact on skier visits from U.S. Ikon passholders, and it was prior to the Christmas holidays when we talked.

In terms of today's resort landscape, the legacy of the Mountain Collective lies in the relationships that were established. This group of independent operators enjoyed working together, traded ideas beyond mega-passes, and found they had many shared values. All strived to maintain the strength of their own brands (precisely what Alterra seeks to do with its collection of resorts) while exploring cooperative efforts through the new pass products.

The seeds of the Intrawest acquisition go back to the MCP discussions between Aspen and Squaw/Alpine, owned by KSL. There were more than just industry relationships at work here. Aspen Skiing Co., as mentioned earlier, had become a minority investor in 2016 in Squaw/Alpine. That put them on the advisory board and helped forge their partnership with KSL. Another important element of their relationship was that KSL had provided funding for the ongoing Snowmass redevelopment. So KSL and Aspen folks were talking on multiple levels. I always assumed, and heard from many knowledgeable industry pundits, that it was ultimately an agreement between Jim Crown and Eric Resnick that led to the Intrawest purchase and additional investments. Both shared the view that Vail Resorts was dominating the industry and that their resorts would be marginalized if they didn't respond—and do so in a big way.

Resnick was generous with his time in early February 2019, offering his view on how everything had come together. I had heard from many colleagues and spent enough time with him to know how passionate he is about skiing. He started at age 4 at Camelback in Pennsylvania; his parents taught both Eric and his sister to ski, and they became a classic East Coast skiing family. They enjoyed their local mid-Atlantic hills, and for one week a year they would head off to Vermont and then, eventually, Colorado. Their first trip west was to Steamboat when Eric was in the fifth grade. "I thought I had died and gone to heaven," he says, recalling winning a medal on the NASTAR course. Skiing in general and skiing out West, specifically, became aspirational from a very early age.

His talent with spreadsheets must also have revealed itself early on. After that first vacation, his parents gave him the task of deciding the next trip, as long as the budget remained below the $2,000 cap for the family. From then on, Resnick planned the annual event.

After college at Cornell, he joined McKinsey & Company's Washington, D.C., office as a business analyst. He wound up being mentored by Terry Williams, one of the company's senior execs. (In another ironic coincidence, Williams led the McKinsey team that looked at a potential merger between SIA and NSAA, and the establishment of an industry-wide demand-building strategy, "Ski It to Believe It." I was on the NSAA team that met multiple times in the Amelia Earhart Room at Chicago's O'Hare Airport as Terry helped us put together the ill-fated USIA. Small world!)

Williams suggested that Resnick try to "find a way to marry your vocation with your avocation" and introduced Resnick to Ralph Walton, owner and chairman of Crested Butte. Walton's suggestion was that he write to some key industry execs outlining his passion for skiing, that he should prepare himself for a pay cut, and that he would need to travel on his own nickel for an interview. Resnick's persistence was rewarded when he interviewed with Harry Mosgrove (Copper), John Rutter (Keystone), and Andy Daly and Betsy Cole (Vail). Rutter said he was interested but had just hired an analyst. After many twists and turns, Resnick wound up at Vail in May 1996, not knowing that Apollo owned Vail and was about to close a deal for Keystone and Breckenridge. So he started with a bang, working closely with the Apollo folks on the deal and Rob Katz in particular. He tells the story of showing up at a meeting of Keystone executives just after the deal closed and seeing Rutter again. John said, "Haven't we met?"

By January 2001, Resnick was Vail Resorts' treasurer and vice president of strategic planning and operational finance, and was sitting on its executive committee. Mike Shannon, who had engineered Vail's rise from the ashes of bankruptcy, had left to form KSL years earlier. Resnick joined him later in 2001 as CFO. He kept a home in Vail and maintained all those key relationships from his tenure there. And he skied whenever he could.

Resnick learned many things during his time with Vail, none more powerful than the recognition that a multiple-area pass product, offering value and choice but requiring early commitment, was the model for success. The Colorado Pass (good at the four Vail resorts) was born 20 years ago and morphed into the Epic some 10 years ago.

In his early years with KSL, he focused on the golf and resort portfolio. KSL would attend ski area auctions, but until Squaw became available, they did not successfully close a deal. They probably had a larger "book" on ski industry metrics than any other potential buyer.

Squaw was attractive because it was a great mountain with lots of issues, problems that Resnick felt could be solved. So in 2010, they made a bid attractive enough to keep ownership from moving forward with a public sales process. Resnick says that, at the time, they were optimistic about the ski business but regionally focused. They were intrigued by other opportunities and had bid on Intrawest ('06), and then Steamboat ('07), losing out to Fortress. When the financial crisis struck, Fortress was forced to sell off a number of assets, including Whistler Blackcomb, which was taken public on the Toronto Stock Exchange on November 9, 2010. Intrawest retained a minority stock interest and eventually sold that ownership position to KSL, who then took seats on the board of directors. Resnick and his team wanted to acquire control of Whistler and merge it with Squaw/Alpine, creating a strong regional player. They spoke with the Aspen team about forming a partnership to accomplish this, but unfortunately, Vail was also interested. "It was very complicated because of Whistler being publicly held," Resnick said. He was sad to see it go to Vail, but acknowledged that "it got the juices flowing."

Then in January 2017, both Intrawest and Mammoth came on the market. Peter McDermott, the KSL CIO who played a key role in the Squaw/Alpine acquisition, told Resnick, "We're missing things."

In other words, if they could figure out a way to do both Intrawest and Mammoth, and merge those assets with Squaw/Alpine, they had a powerful business model. It would work. Meanwhile, the Aspen Skiing Co. initially wanted only Winter Park, Steamboat and CMH, and had offered as much as $1.129 billion for the three properties, according to the SEC documents cited in Blevins' story. It also offered as much as $878 million in cash for just Winter Park and Steamboat. But Intrawest wanted to sell the whole company, so Aspen came on board on two levels. First, through their investment in Squaw/Alpine, which was rolled into the new deal, and second, through direct investments by the Crown family.

Between January and April of 2017, the hard work was done. Resnick acknowledged that the Aspen areas would not be part of the new company, but that they would be pass partners and serve as the aspirational destinations for the new company's pass products.

On a parallel track, final purchase and sale agreements were being drafted while the pass strategy was being finalized. I don't have all the details, but Mammoth was reportedly shifting back and forth from buyer to seller during negotiations. The Aspen and KSL teams hired McKinsey to do the research that identified partners for the Ikon pass as well as potential acquisition targets. KSL looked at where people were skiing in North America and where they aspired to ski.

"We looked at all sorts of resort combinations and conducted thousands of interviews with skiers," Resnick said. "We essentially 'curated' our pass." During those three months, they actually visited each of the potential portfolio ski areas (six Intrawest resorts, plus CMH, Mammoth, and the Big Bear Resorts).

When Aspen and KSL came together, they bid $23.50 a share for Intrawest, according to Blevins' account. Intrawest countered with $23.75 a share, and the $1.7 billion deal was forged.

The plan had been to announce both the Intrawest and Mammoth deals on the same day, but there were delays that put off the Mammoth announcement by two days. Resnick acknowledged losing some sleep during those 48 hours, anxious that Vail Resorts might try to insert itself in the Mammoth deal. Obviously, that didn't happen. Ultimately, KSL and its investors took the majority position, with the Crown money assuming a minority position, in the Alterra joint venture. Aspen's four mountains joined Ikon, providing five or seven days of skiing, depending on the product.

The day Mammoth was announced, Resnick called Lessing Stern (owner/partner of Deer Valley) to inform him of the transactions. (This is a common courtesy. Calls are assigned to senior executives to make sure key industry leaders and partners get a personal heads-up call.) Stern said, "Hey, we should talk." They did, and the new company closed on Deer Valley on October 10. Solitude, which the Deer Valley group owned, followed in June 2018. An agreement to purchase Crystal Mountain in Washington followed in September.

It's worth looking back for a moment at Intrawest and how that company, once the largest ski conglomerate in North American, wound up being sold as step No. 1 in Alterra's formation.

In 2006, Fortress Investment Group, through a private equity fund, bought Intrawest. The total value of the transaction, including Intrawest's existing debt, was approximately $2.8 billion. This was a tidy premium of 20 percent over Intrawest's closing price on February 27, 2006, the last trading day before the company announced its intentions to pursue "strategic options." In March 2007, Fortress added Steamboat to the collection for an additional $265 million.

Alex Wasilov, then president and CEO of Intrawest, said in a company press release: "The acquisition of Steamboat represents another milestone in our long-term strategy to develop, market, operate, and provide our customers with access to the world's premier network of experiential destination resorts." At this, Intrawest was unquestionably the largest ski resort operator in North America. *(See Appendix for a chart comparing Intrawest with Vail Resorts in April 2007.)*

There was a period of considerable uncertainty following the Intrawest and Steamboat transactions, while Fortress took a deeper dive into the organization. The biggest issue was leadership. CEO Wasilov was a former board member but otherwise had limited experience in the ski business. On January 8, 2008, we got clarity. Fortress had recruited Bill Jensen from VR and he would replace Wasilov on June 1, 2008. Wasilov had been CEO for 15 months at the time and would return to his position on the board in June. Jensen was a seasoned ski resort professional, having most recently served as co-president of Vail Resorts' Mountain Division. I was viewing all this from the perspective of my role at the time as president of Steamboat, having to attend seemingly endless meetings in Vancouver, regarding the new company's organization and business practices. There was an awkward transition period between the January announcement and June 1, when Jensen finally took over (the delay was related to Jensen's non-compete agreement with Vail Resorts). Beginning that June, with Jensen's leadership, meetings had more structure and direction. The company seemed to be moving forward.

From my perspective, Jensen's biggest challenge lay in refocusing the company on core ski operations (where operating margins were significantly lower than Vail's) and "rightsizing" the real estate division. He never had that opportunity. The Lehman collapse in the fall of 2008 brought a hard stop to resort real-estate development and, as the recession deepened, the company's survival came into question.

Intrawest began to shed resorts: Panorama, B.C.; Mountain Creek, N.J.; and Copper Mountain in Colorado. Most painful for longtime Intrawest folks was seeing Whistler leave the fold through a public offering in Canada (Intrawest held a minority interest for a while but eventually sold its remaining shares to KSL).

With these dispositions, Intrawest survived as a much smaller holding company, with five resorts and a 50 percent interest in Blue Mountain, Ontario. Still in the fold was CMH Heli, a handful of hotels, the time-share division, and a few other interests. The offices had been relocated from Vancouver to Denver.

In 2014, Fortress took most of Intrawest public again, this time on the New York Stock Exchange at $12 per share. Inside the company, there was much speculation over whether this was just a necessary step for Fortress (as it began to plan its exit strategy from the ski business) or whether there really was a plan to grow the core business again. That question was quickly answered when Jensen departed in November 2014. Bill later explained to me that months earlier he had negotiated his separation from Fortress, but agreed to stay on until a replacement was named. Apparently, the only other person in Intrawest aware of this was the corporate attorney, Josh Goldstein. For everyone else, it was a "deer in the headlights" moment. The new CEO was Tom Marano, a career Wall Street executive, with senior-level experience at Bear Stearns and with Ally Financial's Residential Capital mortgage unit. Clearly, it was his job to sell the company. In *Ski Inc.*, I intimated that the pieces would be more valuable than the whole, because I didn't see a buyer out there with the capacity to absorb the "new" Intrawest. I was wrong. The KSL/Crown partnership knew Intrawest was being shopped and put a deal together.

Starting in the spring of 2017 with a small core of Intrawest staff members in its Denver headquarters, David Perry, working with the KSL executives and, eventually, CEO Rusty Gregory, built a whole new organization in just over one year. Alterra relocated from the Intrawest offices to a new, larger space in Denver's RiNo Art District in December 2018. Some 200 staff members— including some from Squaw, Mammoth, Aspen and Intrawest, but most new to the company and in some cases the ski business—were now managing Alterra's affairs from the new headquarters.

Incredibly, Alterra in a handful of months, had managed to put together a viable competitor to Vail, something that would have been inconceivable just a year earlier. And in broad strokes, the empires were comparable. By fall 2018, Vail Resorts owned or operated under lease 20 resorts. Alterra owned 15 resorts. In terms of skier visits, Alterra was just 20 percent smaller. Collectively, these two holding companies accounted for some 32 percent of all North American skier visits.

It might have played out differently. At the time KSL and the Crowns were looking at Intrawest, Rusty Gregory was talking to both buyers and sellers. There were people beyond the KSL/Crown group interested in Mammoth. He had to do best by his partners, so the conversation with KSL, although it had begun years earlier, went back and forth up to the last minute, explaining the two-day delay.

Rusty Gregory is another ski industry character: unique, driven, competent, a well-respected leader with a deep love for the sport. He has an independent streak, partly innate, given his athletic background, but more importantly a reflection of years working directly for Mammoth founder Dave McCoy, who was always inclined to "go it alone." McCoy and Killington founder Pres Smith were two sides of the same stubborn yet successful coin. Anyone familiar with the Mammoth culture would not have been surprised when they "passed" on joining the Mountain Collective in its first year.

Gregory came to skiing late, growing up in Southern California, spending most of his time playing team sports and surfing. His friends all went to Mammoth on weekends. He was unable to tag along.

Football took him to the University of Washington, where he saw his first snow. Rusty still carries a linebacker's build (industry myth had it that he played pro ball; he says, "I spent time on practice squads!"). In his senior year, completing a degree in business and finance, he had his first ski experiences: four trips to Snoqualmie Pass and two to Crystal Mountain. "I fell in love with skiing. I was hooked," he said.

So, he took a year off and went, finally, to Mammoth, working as a lift operator. (Bill Jensen's successful career had followed exactly the same path.) Given his college training, he was able to provide financial guidance (while honing his business skills) to partners in setting up what became Mammoth

Heli-Skiing. He secured the appropriate permits and established the business platform. He continued to work at Mammoth, developing a close relationship with McCoy, and by the late '80s, he was chief administrative officer. He remained with Mammoth until taking the CEO position with Alterra in 2017. What is somewhat unique for a ski resort executive: He sold the same company three times during this tenure.

The first time was in 1995. The combination of California droughts and no snowmaking made it a challenge to meet payroll, and Mammoth was broke in 1991. Gregory then led a four-year restructuring effort that brought in Intrawest as a base-area developer and ski resort equity partner in 1995. A 33 percent investment by Intrawest allowed him to resolve the liquidity issue, refinance the company, and buy some time. Rusty also bought a 15 percent stake. The original company now had $27 million in equity, allowing Gregory to buy out five of McCoy's six children. Helping engineer all this was Mammoth's banker, Jim Donohue (Eric Resnick's future father-in-law), who went on to become a major ski industry player, eventually as CFO with Vail Resorts. Intrawest increased its investment to 58 percent in 1998.

During those early years, Gregory learned the "power of the pass." In 1999, facing another round of financial challenges, Mammoth dropped the price of its season pass from $1,200 to $379. It was an early adapter of the value path that Mike Shirley had pioneered at Bogus Basin and which Winter Park also would follow. Sales skyrocketed from 2,000 to 36,000, providing roughly $13.6 million in upfront revenue. Mammoth was figuring out a way to deal with its year-to-year volatility (a.k.a. draught). Added snowmaking further smoothed out the financial performance.

The second sale, at a much improved value, was to Starwood Capital and partners (including Gregory) for $400 million in 2005 (KSL was the backup bidder). Intrawest remained a 15 percent owner, eventually selling its stake. In 2014, the company acquired Snow Summit and Big Bear for $38 million, a sum that industry pundits viewed as a very good deal for Mammoth. While those SoCal properties experienced considerable volatility in terms of annual skier visits, in a good year, they could add 700,000 visits. It was a big deal. Along with the announcement of the acquisition, Mammoth unveiled a new Cali4nia Pass, unlimited access to its now four mountains for $689. These passholders, a built-in, loyal audience, provided the foundation for Ikon sales in Southern California for the 2018-19 season.

On April 12, 2017, the Mammoth purchase was announced. Gregory again became an investor in the new company. During his tenure, he had seen Mammoth's skier visits move from a low of 450,000 to a high of 1.6 million, a tally that in some years is close to tops in U.S. skier visits.

When I spoke to Gregory in March 2019, my first question was, "Why didn't you retire?" Through a rambling discussion on the state of the ski industry, I learned that essentially he felt this was an unbelievable time of opportunity. "The landscape has changed," he said. Like many, he had shared the fear that Millennials would not backfill the skier population as Boomers exited the sport. Like Bill Jensen, his view was that lots of resorts would drop by the wayside.

Then there was the power of the pass. He and fellow investors began with a view that assembling unique destinations and making them affordable would be the foundation of their business model—not unlike Vail Resorts, but with emphasis on the "mountain" experience. Now there's a second element: preparing for generic growth in the ski sport that few had foreseen. Gregory shares my view that the ski business is getting a second wind. This will require a level of capital reinvestment in his Alterra resorts that probably wasn't contemplated in the original business plan. How things change.

He believes the mountains have always drawn people in a very compelling way. "Like the beach, it's where we find the best version of ourselves. Millennials just do it in a different way from Boomers, wanting no obstacles to their experiences. They want life and work to be fused in a continuum, and they favor experiences over material goods," he explained. Technology has facilitated this, allowing Millennials to relocate to mountain towns as they work remotely. This is putting new pressures on small resort communities which, he feels, need to begin investing along with the resorts to maintain their quality of life.

Gregory has brought Alterra a very long way in a very short time. Just like Rob Katz, he's not done. He talks about Asia and the fact that China's president has established a goal of 300 million winter-sports enthusiasts by the next winter Olympics. Many of these will be skiers. Hundreds of new ski areas are yet to be built. Ikon China? In Japan, where dramatic demographic shifts managed to shrink an overbuilt ski industry from 100 million annual visits to 30 million, there are also opportunities. That's still a lot of skiers! Ikon Japan?

Yup. It's not over yet—it's just getting started.

CHAPTER 5

Ikon Meets Epic:
A Regional Perspective

Just looking at their owned resorts, Alterra and Vail Resorts control about 20 million skier visits in the U.S. alone, about 37 percent of the nationwide total. (This does not include the Canadian powerhouses of Alterra's Tremblant and Blue Mountain and Vail's Whistler Blackcomb, which add roughly 3.25 million more skier visits). When you put in the pass partners, the Epic-Ikon reach extends to about 30 million in the U.S., more than half the business.

Vail Resorts is larger by ownership. But in terms of "reach" via pass partners, Alterra has the bigger hand: Their partners collectively account for an estimated 10 million skier visits in North America. The Epic Pass had 10 of *SKI* magazine's Top 30 Resorts for 2018 (back when the magazine still published those rankings), while the Ikon had 16.

Vail Resorts has been a big player for two decades. How did Alterra put together such a large portfolio of pass partners in such a short time? And why didn't Vail Resorts try to thwart some of these partnerships?

Remember that Copper Mountain and Eldora had been Intrawest pass partners for many years (Intrawest once owned Copper). They were now owned by POWDR, which also owned Killington in Vermont. POWDR agreed to join the Ikon pass, with unlimited access to Copper and Eldora (as in the past) and limited access at Killington. John Cumming's father, Ian, had purchased a majority interest in Snowbird in 2014 but did not put it in the

POWDR ski portfolio. Ian passed away in February 2018, at age 77. John made the decision to bring Snowbird into the Ikon pass for 2018–19. Because Snowbird and Alta were already joined at the hip (you could buy a pass allowing access to both resorts), it was inevitable that Alta would come along as well. With the long-term POWDR/Intrawest relationship and Snowbird's participation in the MCP, it was predictable that its portfolio would join Ikon.

Looking at how this played out regionally, it's hard to overstate Ikon's impact on the Southern California ski market. Ever since the Epic pass was introduced into this market, with unlimited access to Park City and the Canyons, Vail had enjoyed significant growth in pass sales and visitation to Park City. In terms of raw size, Park City/Canyons was the largest ski resort in North America. With cheap, multiple daily flights to Salt Lake City from virtually all the major airports, Epic was a no-brainer for California skiers and probably accounted for a significant portion of Vail Resorts' overall pass-sales growth in recent years. Then came Ikon for 2018–19. Deer Valley had not been for sale. To complete a deal, Alterra reportedly paid an unheard-of multiple of 14-times EBITDA. This multiple looks excessive until one considers the way Ikon has transformed the Southern California market and the incremental revenues it now provides to Alterra. Suddenly, unless one had a strong affiliation to or preference for Park City/Canyons, Ikon was the better choice for Utah and Southern California skiers: access to Deer Valley, Solitude, Brighton, and Snowbird/Alta, as well as Mammoth and the nearby Big Bear resorts. Vail's deal with Sun Valley for 2019–20 also brought up-and-coming Snowbasin into the Epic fold, somewhat strengthening Vail's situation relative to Utah and Southern California skiers.

Even more important than Alterra's POWDR relationship was that with Boyne. Stephen Kircher, president of Boyne Resorts, had long-standing relationships with many of the Alterra executives, notably David Perry. Big Sky was an MCP partner. Boyne had been managing Loon Mountain in New Hampshire; Sugarloaf and Sunday River in Maine; Brighton, Utah; Cypress, B.C.; and the Summit at Snoqualmie, Washington, under long-term leases from the CNL REIT, then its successor, Oz Real Estate. On May 8, 2018, Boyne announced the closing of a transaction to acquire those six resorts and the Gatlinburg scenic chair-lift attraction from Ski Resort Holdings, LLC, an affiliate of Oz Real Estate. Kircher now owned the resorts he had been managing under leases.

Adding the Boyne Resorts strengthened Ikon's appeal immensely, especially in Utah, where it added Brighton. Ikon now provided access to a Park City–area resort (Deer Valley), as well as both Little Cottonwood (Snowbird/Alta) and Big Cottonwood (Brighton/Solitude) canyons—quite the value proposition for Utah residents, not to mention the Southern California market. (Note that Deer Valley provided only limited Ikon access as it wanted to protect its high-end clientele and continue to market its $2,400 season pass.)

How do the pass battles play out regionally? In the Northeast, for a Boston-based skier, I'd give the nod to Ikon based on historical visitation patterns, even with Vail adding New Hampshire's Attitash and Wildcat via Peak (Boston tends to favor New Hampshire and Maine). For the New York market, it's more of a toss-up with a tilt toward Vail because of its Peak acquisitions of Mount Snow and Hunter. Connecticut Gold Coast families have favored Okemo, while New York Metro patrons exhibited more loyalty to Stratton. In terms of favored Western resorts, NYC has long been fertile ground for Vail and Beaver Creek. So the pass sales probably wind up being split in that market. In Eastern Canada, Vail signed up Stoneham and Mont-Sainte-Anne (seven days each), providing a competitive alternative to Tremblant and Blue. Either pass is very attractive if you're a Northeast skier. It will be interesting to see how actual sales sort out. But one thing is very clear: More skiers are deciding first which pass to buy and not necessarily which resort they plan to visit during the upcoming winter.

You have to give both Altera and Vail Resorts credit for the way in which they recruited pass partners. From a regional perspective, Epic and Ikon provide great value for consumers, encourage trial, and enhance overall visitation in the Northeast. From a destination perspective, had Vail not responded with the Triple Peaks deal, they likely would have seen fewer destination visits from that market (mostly to their Colorado and Utah properties).

The Pacific Northwest is one of the stronger skier markets in the U.S. in terms of active skiers per capita. Just about all major resorts market aggressively in a region that is, arguably, the most underserved in terms of ski facilities. There are really three major players in Washington: The Summit at Snoqualmie (including Alpental), Stevens Pass, and Crystal Mountain. Subsequent to its Triple Peaks deal, Vail continued discussions with Oz Real Estate (remember that Oz owned the Triple Peaks Resorts, subject to long-term leases that had to be bought out). Stevens was not subject to a lease. Karl Kapuscinski, a seasoned, well-respected ski resort operator, had held the leases for both Mountain High in Southern California and Stevens Pass, but he defaulted on those cross-collateralized leases during the drought years. He managed to maintain Mountain High by bringing in a group of investors (Mountain High Reunited) to purchase the ski area from Oz on October 6, 2017. ("Reunited" reflects the fact that these were the same investors who had owned Mountain High prior to selling it to CNL.)

Vail quickly put a deal together for Stevens Pass and closed on August 18, 2018. Vail was already a major player in the Washington market, given its ownership of Whistler Blackcomb. So sales to skiers planning multiple destination trips to Whistler primarily drove Epic sales. With Stevens Pass, there was now a regional option, and one could expect Epic sales to increase dramatically. Certainly, any Stevens Pass skier who was contemplating a Whistler trip would be onboard with Epic.

Alterra quickly responded with the purchase of Crystal Mountain. Crystal had been a part of Boyne for 20 years, but on March 31, 2017, it was split off and sold to Stephen's brother John, who had tired of the large-company's operations and wanted to focus on a single resort. However, just a year later John sold to Alterra. He commented on the transaction: "If you own a large to midsize area that is not on a collective pass, that's a problem." So Crystal joined Ikon, and "*voilà*," the expected Epic advantage in the Pacific Northwest virtually evaporated. Alterra now had two regional powers: Crystal through acquisition and Snoqualmie via the Boyne pass partnership. From a quality perspective, Crystal and Stevens were viewed as regional leaders. From a volume perspective, Boyne-owned Snoqualmie was top dog.

Ikon also offers limited access to Cypress (which is on the road from Vancouver to Whistler) and Revelstoke, plus Banff Sunshine, Lake Louise, and Mt. Norquay (SkiBig3). These resorts are significant players in their marketplace. Revelstoke is an up-and-comer, with almost 6,000 feet of vertical. Ever alert, Vail Resorts added the Resorts of the Canadian Rockies.

How will this competition sort out? I'll give the nod to Ikon, marginally, but had Vail not made its move with Stevens Pass (which meets the Vail "experiential" promise), it could have seen a material erosion in Epic sales from that market. My guess: With the Epic/Ikon competition, total pass sales and skier visits in the Pacific Northwest will increase, maybe dramatically (given average snowfall).

While looking at the pass competition from a regional perspective, it's appropriate to focus now on the situation in Colorado, which has the highest percentage of pass ownership in the country. Vail Resorts has the big four: Vail, Breckenridge, Keystone, and Beaver Creek. Together they account for some 40 percent of Colorado's skier visits. The Front Range of Colorado (running from Fort Collins in the north through Denver and its suburbs, to Colorado Springs in the south) is fertile ground for pass sales. The economy is strong and the population keeps increasing, with many drawn to Colorado specifically for the mountain activities. Epic has been around for a long time and is the dominant player. That said, for many years Intrawest provided an attractive alternative, priced virtually the same for unlimited access to Winter Park, Eldora, and Copper Mountain, and limited access to Steamboat. Prior to Vail's purchase of Crested Butte, it also participated in the Intrawest pass, with limited access.

Market share between the two passes had remained about the same for several years. Loyalties are pretty well set, and not that many Colorado skiers have historically ventured out of state (this is changing). For those who do, both passes provide attractive options.

But things change. Pass partners can change affiliation. On February 18, 2019, Arapahoe Basin announced that it would not continue its Epic partnership with Vail Resorts for the next season. This partnership had been in place since before the founding of the Epic Pass (when Vail's attempt to purchase A-Basin was denied on antitrust grounds, but they were allowed to establish a "pass" relationship). Most Epic holders who took advantage of the A-Basin option did so early and late season. A-Basin received an agreed-upon "per scan" fee from VR, but that payment was reportedly modest. Since early and late season are historic A-Basin strengths, the goal would have been to increase revenues during these key time periods. A-Basin had made significant recent enhancements to the operation (more than $40 million in the last 15 years). Clearly, the resort was in a position to generate more revenue going it alone or by negotiating a better deal with new partners—Ikon perhaps? On his blog, COO Alan Henceroth commented: "These actions are designed to preserve that special culture and vibe people expect when they chose to spend a day at the Basin." Henceroth soon unveiled a $399 early-buy 2019–20 pass price, and he told Basin loyalists that while the ski area was still considering pass affiliations for 2019–20, the Basin pass would offer the only unrestricted access. Throughout the 2018–19 season, it had offered a three-day pass, unrestricted, for $189, perfect for those who arrive in Epic-dominated Summit County without having made an Epic deal. (It will presumably offer a similar product for 2019–20, though by late June 2019 it was not listed on the resort's website.)

Immediately, Vail Resorts responded with a new Keystone Plus Pass, as a replacement for the Keystone/A-Basin pass, which had historically been a very popular choice for Summit County skiers and locals, being a very reasonably priced product, at less than $400. Vail Resorts, which for years had been circumspect in establishing its closing dates, had already announced an extended 2018–19 season for Breckenridge and was touting Keystone's snowmaking expansion. The Vail Resorts' team clearly saw the A-Basin change coming and, presumably, had not been able to negotiate a new deal. So they had begun to position their resorts for a new future, preparing to capture early and late season skiers.

The new pass will provide unlimited access (with holiday restrictions) to Keystone Resort and unlimited spring skiing at Breckenridge (after April 1) plus five days at Crested Butte (with holiday restrictions). Cost for the 2019–20 season: $369 for adults, $259 for kids.

According to Kirsten Lynch, Vail Resorts' chief marketing officer, "We are excited to offer a new pass that provides skiing and riding from mid-October through Memorial Day at Keystone and Breckenridge, at an incredible value." Breckenridge could not secure approval to operate its Peak 7–8 access gondola, the BreckConnect, from May 1 to Memorial Day, so it is busing skiers to Peak 7, which served as the base hub (the resort closed Peak 8 guest services).

Vail Resorts dropped another big new offer into the spring pass-sales frenzy: With early purchase, all the company's unlimited season-pass products will include 10 buddy tickets, an increase from the six previously offered. This timely, thoughtful response is just another example of how focused Vail Resorts remains in the newly competitive ski world.

So in Colorado, Vail Resorts gains Crested Butte, but loses A-Basin (which in early August joined Ikon as a restricted partner, seven days on the full pass and five on the Base). Keystone and Breckenridge will adjust their operating plans to compete early and late season. In terms of market share going forward, let's call it a draw.

Back to Alterra: *Speed*. That has been the defining characteristic of the Alterra story, from my point of view. During the summer of 2018, Alterra enhanced the broad appeal of its pass product by adding Taos, the iconic New Mexico resort just now beginning to reinvent itself. I mentioned Boyne Resorts earlier as pass partners but didn't single out Montana's Big Sky, the crown jewel of the Boyne family. This is an up-and-comer with plans for stunning future investments designed to create a resort community that will compete with the best of the Rockies. Big Sky has been "bucket listed!" Its addition, along with Jackson Hole (both limited access), will certainly help Alterra sell more Ikon passes. In turn, the resorts will gain from exposure to and trial by skiers who might not have ventured there otherwise.

As noted earlier, Vail Resorts has put together a very attractive collection of international partners, notably in Europe and Australia. Alterra has countered with pass partnerships in Australia (Thredbo), New Zealand (Coronet Peak, The Remarkables, and Mt. Hutt), and Japan (Niseko United). To me, the Japanese resorts are the most intriguing, given their reputation for extraordinary snowfall.

Looking back on the Alterra/Vail Resorts pass battle, the one thing that stands out is the quick decision-making and competitive responses by both companies. Clearly, they intend to compete head-to-head in all major markets.

So, now we've taken a look at how Vail Resorts and Alterra have altered the ski industry landscape over the past three years. It's tempting at this point to start prognosticating on where this all might be headed and "who's on first?" There will be plenty of time for speculation at the end of this book. But before doing that, we need to remember that there are hundreds of other ski areas out there. Vail and Alterra—Epic and Ikon—grab all the press. They are the big dogs. But what is truly amazing, and what I hope the following chapters will demonstrate, is how resilient the industry is—and how other resorts are realigning, reengineering, and reinventing themselves to compete. It's a fascinating study in how swiftly and effectively competitors can move forward in a transformed competitive landscape.

We now turn to the "Mid-Majors," the conglomerates that occupy an important second segment of the ski industry, one of which, Peak Resorts, has just been purchased by Vail Resorts. We examine how they hew to their own strategies and cultures, and are managing not just to survive, but thrive.

CHAPTER 6

The Mid-Majors:
First Up, Boyne Resorts

Boyne Resorts is the first of the Mids, both in its history and size. Boyne doesn't get much attention or respect, and that's a shame. Of all the major players, Boyne can claim the longest-running (and arguably most colorful) history, going on 72 years, plus an impressive record of innovative "firsts" in the ski industry. It is next in line behind Vail and Alterra in skier visits, with an estimated 3.8 million annually (it does not scan at every resort, remains privately owned and, therefore, does not divulge company-wide visits). Boyne positions itself as the country's second-largest privately held ski resort company (behind Alterra), with 10,500 employees at its resort and golf operations.

Despite its scale and geographic diversity, Boyne continues to be pigeon-holed by skiers (and even the industry) as a Midwest regional player. This, despite Boyne's four decade-long ownership of Big Sky Resort in Montana and ownership of a trio of New England heavyweights: Sugarloaf and Sunday River in Maine and Loon in New Hampshire. (Boyne had managed the three New England areas for CNL since 2007, and subsequently acquired them in 2018).

The company's story began back in 1947, when patriarch Everett Kircher, an independent, visionary, and often irascible businessman, bought a 40-acre former apple orchard in the northwest Lower Peninsula of Michigan for the grand sum of $1. Thus began a five-decade-plus run of innovation in the ski industry. "Everett was the only other guy besides Dave McCoy, who built

Mammoth Mountain, to really think outside the box," opined filmmaker War-ren Miller, who traveled extensively with his camera to ski resorts from the 1950s and through the '90s and closely studied their operations. (A personal observation: Warren should have referenced Killington's Pres Smith, who was not just "outside the box," he was sometimes out of this world in his thinking!)

Born in St. Louis, Kircher moved with his family to Detroit, when his dad got a job for $5 a week at the Ford Motor Company. Kircher attended the University of Michigan for a year, but left to fill in for his mother in the family garage business when she had to step down due to a serious injury. Later, he would start his own mobile-home business, with a $3,000 loan from his father, and enter the auto business.

During World War II, when both the trailer and car dealerships stalled, Kircher made nose cones for Navy rockets, and afterward he opened a Stude-baker dealership (becoming the youngest owner in the Studebaker system). He was an avid outdoorsman, a world-class fly-fisherman, and a dedicated skier, this at a time when the U.S. had only a handful of resorts. His first visit to Sun Valley was in 1938 on a $150 all-inclusive ski-week package (including the Union Pacific train fare). He would return over a dozen times, mixing it up with Sun Valley celebrities like Bing Crosby, and noting how the resort's amenities elevated the winter vacation experience. Those experiences made a lasting impression.

On his Michigan hill with just 500 feet of vertical, Kircher would sculpt Boyne Mountain into an all-inclusive destination resort. He bought Sun Val-ley's Dollar Mountain single chair (the first chairlift constructed in the U.S.) for $2,000, and then paid $3,000 to have it transported to Michigan. The lift is still operating on site, albeit with lots of upgrades. By the early 1960s, Boyne had enough beds and amenities to serve 425 skiers. "This is a ski resort, not a ski area," Kircher told *Sports Illustrated* in 1963, for a feature story titled "Mountain Out of a Molehill."

"We want people to feel the togetherness. We don't want them to have to look elsewhere for anything," Kircher explained in the article. Boyne's tar-get market was families and singles, and Kircher wasn't shy about promoting the social side of skiing. "Sex, sex, sex," Kircher exclaimed. "Sex brings the girls north looking for guys. And vice versa. You can call it anything you like, but it's just plain sex. I've often wondered just how much the improve-ments we make affect this boy-meets-girl urge. But skiing must have something to do with it. Otherwise," he chuckled, "they would keep coming after the snow melts."

Kircher and his longtime GM Chuck Moll were already making a study of demographics, and for Kircher the "sex" thing was critical in developing long-term loyalty. He knew that when those single skiers got married, they would drop out of skiing for a few years. But once the kids were 5 or 6 years old, and dad was climbing the ladder at Ford or GM, they were fair game again. Boyne's goal was to make the return as seamless as possible.

Kircher was breaking new ground in the ski industry and reinvesting the profits back in the resort. What allowed him to continually re-invest was another outside-the-box move: building the Gatlinburg Sky Lift in Tennessee near the Great Smoky Mountains National Park in 1954. A local hotel owner, reading about the new chairlift at Boyne, had contacted him with the idea for a sightseeing attraction. Kircher bought a used chairlift from Sugar Bowl in California and ran it up the 1,800-foot peak of Crockett Mountain after securing appropriate long-term leases for the land. The lift operated 364 days a year, regularly attracting more than 500,000 annual riders. It is located amid a number of sightseeing attractions and in the tourist magnet of Gatlinburg. The Sky Lift was an absolutely critical cash-flow provider for Kircher, particularly from the 1950s to '70s, when he was expanding his ski resort footprint and needed outside capital, and through the Great Recession. In May 2019, Boyne added another attraction, a 680-foot-long Sky Bridge at the lift's summit, the longest pedestrian-only suspension bridge in North America, bringing a unique mountain experience to the south.

Boyne was an early adopter of extensive, full-resort snowmaking and an innovator in efficiency with the fan gun. Its circa-1950s Duck Bill Snowmaker was followed in the 1970s by the Boyne Snowmaker (aka Highlands Snowgun), which was patented, licensed, and eventually used at hundreds of resorts around the world. An inveterate tinkerer, Kircher was obsessed with making snow. He had evolved the systems first employed at Grossinger's in New York, at Wilmot in Wisconsin, and at other resorts in the early 1950s. Even at Boyne's northern elevation, winters could be fickle, and Kircher would need to cover 100 percent of his terrain.

Boyne also installed the first triple chairlift (a bubble at Boyne Highlands in 1963), the first four-person chair (Boyne Mountain in 1964), and America's first six-seat detachable in 1992. In the 1960s, Kircher was one of the early resort leaders to adopt and promote the "Ski Week," attracting families from Detroit's affluent, automotive-industry-fueled suburbs, 250 miles south, and even from Chicago. An up-and-coming congressman—the future President Gerald Ford—and his young family were regulars at Boyne and supporters of Kircher. Guests came for up to seven days, taking learn-to-ski lessons. They would begin not on the ubiquitous and dreaded bunny-hill rope tow, but on a chairlift that Kircher insisted on installing. "The toughest thing in skiing is learning to ride those damned ropes," Kircher told *Sports Illustrated.*

His pro staff was led for a short time by Olympic gold medalist Stein Eriksen, always bareheaded and wearing a brightly colored sweater. Kircher had sold Eriksen a Studebaker when he was headed home after the Aspen FIS Alpine World Ski Championships in 1950, and asked if he might be interested in directing the Boyne ski school. Eriksen said he'd consider it after the following season. Kircher eventually telegrammed a $5,000 offer. Eriksen asked him to double it; Kircher did, and brought him to the U.S. to start his post-race career. Next in line to run the ski school was the blonde, blue-eyed Austrian Othmar Schneider. Also an Olympic gold medalist, Schneider would spend 14 winters there.

Visitors discovered the magic of après ski in the purpose-built village, with its token clock tower, and soaked in the heated outdoor pool— the first built east of the Mississippi. The whole experience was a Midwestern version of Sun Valley: Stein doing flips on skis, the heated outdoor pool, ice skating, and sleigh rides.

Kircher was among the first resort operators to push into four-season operations. Desiring to keep some of his staff employed in the summer, he built a nine-hole golf course at the base of Boyne Mountain, along with an airstrip. After acquiring Boyne Highlands in nearby Harbor Springs in 1963 and developing its ski facilities, Kircher hired Robert Trent Jones Sr. to design the 18-hole Heather course that opened in 1966, debuting as one of the "Top 100 Courses You Can Play" in the country. Boyne Resorts currently owns 13 championship courses (the vast majority are in Michigan, but the collection includes Boyne South in Naples, Florida). The Heather was just named the 2019 Golf Course of the Year by the National Golf Course Owners Association.

Boyne is now led by Everett's son, Stephen Kircher, who has been a top executive with the company for more than 25 years. Stephen looks a decade younger than his mid-50s age; he is thoughtful and studious, measured yet passionate about the business and the outdoors. He played on the Division I golf teams at both Northwestern and Michigan State University as an undergraduate, and then went to Boston College to earn his MBA, partly because he foresaw Boyne's eventual entrance into the New England market. He shares a kinship and mutual respect with fellow industry titan John Cumming, who founded POWDR, a friendship born from the similarity of their childhoods: looking up at hard-charging and at-times-difficult fathers, and growing into their ski industry roles as the relative little guys amid giants like Vail Resorts. Both also want to see their companies continue as family-owned for generations to come.

Boyne Resorts was a family business from the beginning, with Everett's three other children (John, Amy, and Kathryn) all involved at various times. Stephen says it was a given that he'd dedicate his life and career to Boyne. He recalls a "family board meeting," back when he was all of 10 years old, called to decide the fate of a proposed resort acquisition. Everett was interested in buying Telluride, which Joe Zoline had opened in 1972, and the entire family went on a fact-finding site visit. "He was reviewing our thinking and the pros and cons," Stephen recalled in a 2013 interview with *Traverse* magazine. "Then we voted on it, and we voted it down. I remember feeling fully empowered and involved, and that was a first spark. He made us think that at least we made the decision with him." The family also passed on Jackson Hole, but gave an overwhelming thumbs up when they drove into a remote Montana valley and looked up starry-eyed at 11,167-foot Lone Peak. "It was love at first sight for all of us," says Stephen, who recalls sitting in the back seat of the station wagon (middle seat!) when he got his first glimpse. The family did buy Big Sky in 1976, just three years after Chet Huntley had opened it.

Kircher had an early appreciation of the benefits of geographic diversification (e.g., the Gatlinburg project) and made that central to Boyne's future growth plans. As a pilot who eventually had a fleet of planes and pilots, it would be easy for him to oversee resort operations in far-flung locales.

In 1986, Boyne acquired Brighton, in Big Cottonwood Canyon near Salt Lake City. It bought Washington's Crystal Mountain in 1997, and in 2001, it purchased Cypress Mountain outside of Vancouver. Cypress would host the freestyle and snowboard events for the 2010 Olympics.

Although Everett Kircher was a visionary, he was an old-school manager and infamous for his non-PC ways, a hardheaded businessman who would acquire the nearby ski competitor only to eventually shut them down. He preferred not to share budgets with managers, which in his mind were a green light to spend money. He wanted his managers to bring any spending requests to him for approval, and he expected them to passionately own and argue their case. This was fine when Boyne was a small operation, but unworkable as it expanded.

A classic example of tight-fisted quirkiness: Boyne's maintenance vehicles were outfitted only with a driver's bucket seat, with no room for a passenger. "He did that to focus on efficiency; he didn't want anybody talking instead of working," Stephen Kircher says. A biography of Stephen's father, *Everett Kircher: Michigan's Resort Pioneer* (Pocket Books), is a must for any ski resort history buff, and can be bought used on Amazon.

Stephen Kircher's office is still located where it all began, at Boyne Mountain. The far-flung Boyne properties vary greatly in terms of size and their local markets. Only Big Sky is a true destination resort. Because of their uniqueness, Stephen insists on a strong on-the-ground management presence. The company's leadership team is composed of department heads, such as finance, HR, marketing. They operate as a traditional corporate staff, but Stephen allows them to work remotely, and then visit the individual resorts on a regular basis. Rick Kelley, the 40-year veteran who has led Loon Mountain for decades, is the COO for all Eastern resorts plus Michigan. John McGregor, who began his career at Boyne Highlands, oversees all the Western resorts, with Taylor Middleton continuing to directly oversee the crown jewel, Big Sky, as its president and GM. Barb Rooney, who began her career at Big Sky in 1991, is the senior vice president of lodging, spa, and ownership services.

Department heads typically hold weekly conference calls; the arrangement requires discipline to stay in touch but seems to work smoothly. Vertical integration is so ingrained in the Boyne culture that Stephen doesn't think of it as anything but standard operating procedure. In his case, it extends to the company's retail arm, Boyne Country Sports, which has five metro locations in Michigan as well as a presence at all its resorts. (Boyne purchased a majority stake in the respected, 50-year-old, multi-location Bavarian Village retail group in 1999, and then rebranded the stores, which immediately began selling lift tickets and packages to its resort properties.)

Boyne is still known for a kind of stubborn independence. I recall their frequent purchases of used lifts and their relocation to various resorts. Some of these moves may have raised eyebrows, but bottom line: Boyne was able to stretch their capital dollars. Being lean and mean is part of the corporate character.

The Kirchers have endured their share of bumps along the road. The signature Boyne Mountain actually lost money for an astounding 23 straight years, from 1980 to 2003. Boyne was an experts' mountain and as the years passed, its amenities were no longer competitive. Skiers preferred the easier terrain and lodging at its sister Boyne Highlands, which was flourishing 27 miles to the north in Harbor Springs. The popular Ski Weeks also eroded when affordable, frequent air travel became prevalent in the 1970s, and it was just as easy to fly west as to drive the 250 miles north.

The choice was to shut down the flagship or dramatically reinvent it, with more beginner terrain and beds. Building a first-class resort hotel was a major step, and Everett, then in his mid-80s, wanted it opened before he died. Stephen, who found the company extended with the construction of the Bay Harbor Resort and a $56 million hotel at Big Sky, nonetheless charged ahead. Despite two poor Midwest winters and handshake bank financing, Everett reached into his own pocket to put up $5 million and work began. Just as the steel frame was rising out of the ground, Boyne's financing stalled—and then came 9/11. Rather than a testament to the Mountain's renaissance, the unfinished project served as a glaring reminder of Boyne's ongoing struggles, and Everett would die in 2002 with the project stalled.

Stephen persevered. Construction began again in 2003, and the 220-room hotel project was completed in 2006. With the addition of two major condo projects, Boyne had increased its bed base from 700 in 1998 to more than 2,500 by 2005. Today, the Mountain Grand Lodge and Spa is a focal point of the resort, as is the connected and popular Avalanche Bay Indoor Waterpark, the perfect hedge against uncooperative weather and a facility that is busier than the mountain on poor weather days.

Boyne Resorts entered into a sale and leaseback agreement with CNL Resort Properties for Gatlinburg and Cypress in 2005, and then Brighton in 2006, with 40-year leases. With new cash resources thanks to that transaction, Boyne attempted to buy Steamboat Resort but, according to Stephen, Fortress outbid them by $5 million. I was president of Steamboat at the time and always wondered how things might have evolved had Fortress not made the purchase.

Later in 2007, Boyne went after the American Skiing Company assets in Maine, buying Sunday River and Sugarloaf in Maine, and then entered into the same sale and leaseback arrangement with CNL. It also negotiated the takeover of the Booth Creek assets from CNL (Loon, and Snoqualmie). As the Great Recession loomed, Boyne also finalized another loan with CNL, using Big Sky as collateral, with the Midwest's Fifth Third Bank to take out Bank One—just before Lehman's bankruptcy. With all those maneuvers, Stephen's foresight had paid off, and Boyne was geographically diversified and a player in most major ski markets

In 2018, Stephen Kircher succeeded in acquiring ownership of the CNL resorts he had been operating under long-term leases (the actual transaction was with an affiliate of Oz Realty, which had acquired the CNL ski properties). This was accomplished through a B2-rated, $400 million bond offering. "Today is exceptionally gratifying," he said when the announcement was made on May 10, 2018. He was now fully in control of the company's future.

Boyne continues to look outside the box for business. For summer 2018, that included adding a new wrinkle to off-season amenities. On a 200-acre adjacent farm parcel that the company had been eying for some 60 years and finally bought, Boyne built fields for soccer and lacrosse, one of the nation's fastest growing sports. It also organized an array of revenue-producing camps and tournaments to fill hotel rooms and village shops during the off-season. It is believed to be the first such diversification by a ski resort, though of course many resort towns have such facilities

Stephen and his older brother, John, had worked alongside each other as co-presidents at Boyne for years. Over the past decade, because of a desire to focus on a simpler lifestyle, John relinquished much of the load, except for operating Cypress and Crystal in the Pacific Northwest. Stephen was hardwired to run a large, sprawling company and had the stomach for endless spreadsheets, while John seemed more content hiking and skiing in the mountains. In 2017, John decided to set out on his own, buying Crystal Mountain out of the family portfolio and running it as a rare independent outfit. His wife, Kim, was a longtime Crystal patroller who had become the resort's patrol director.

Then everything changed overnight. Vail Resorts bought Crystal's competitor, Stevens Pass, and it joined the Epic Pass. Given the new competitive climate, John and his family decided to sell to Alterra in a deal that closed in the fall of 2018. Washington now has Vail Resorts and Alterra going head-to-head in a hot market that has arguably the largest percentage of skiers among its population. It is also the most underserved in the number of ski areas.

Meanwhile, for Stephen Kircher, the corporate philosophy hasn't changed, with the goal of maintaining all of the resorts' independent character, and doing what makes sense locally. The company mantra is: "We love creating unique playgrounds to enjoy lifestyle sports."

The massive "sidecountry" terrain expansion at Sugarloaf that launched in 2011 is a perfect example, with the resort eventually opening access to 653 hike-to acres on adjacent Burnt Mountain, all without a lift or any brick-and-mortar (and adding snowcat access for 2018).

"We respect the DNA of a resort," Kircher told Michigan's *My North* magazine in a 2013 interview. "We understand that every resort is different. Each has its own culture, its own set of qualities, and every community is different, too. We want to showcase that DNA, the things that make it different. That is in great contrast to others who have tried a cookie-cutter approach, tried to make them all the same. Sharing best practices is important, but to do so to the extent that the individual brand is diminished ... that can be very detrimental. Sunday River and Sugarloaf in Maine are perfect examples. Those are iconic brands in the East, and with unique DNA." A previous owner had tried to manage both under one leadership team, and each brand seemed to dim as a result. I had a very personal experience with this exact-same model in the 1990s when we tried to operate Killington and Mount Snow under one umbrella. It was not successful.

To initially compete against the stunning ascent of the Epic Pass, Kircher partnered with Cumming's POWDR and with Bill Jensen, the CEO of Intrawest, to create a collective pass. For the 2015–16 winter, they created the M.A.X. Pass, which Kircher dubbed the "Epic Vaccination Pass." It originally offered five days of skiing at 22 resorts in a dozen states and Canada (Jensen had left Intrawest by then but was instrumental in the early planning). Working together on these collective-pass efforts fostered closer relationships between the resort partners, eventually leading Boyne to join with Alterra.

Boyne's current CMO is Ian Arthur, who was marketing director of Vail/Beaver Creek in the early 2000s and would return to the ski business to work for several years again with Bill Jensen at Intrawest before departing in July 2014. He certainly understands the competitive landscape created by the mega-passes, and he has been hard at work on Boyne's software infrastructure to more seamlessly connect all Boyne's properties and its patrons. The art and science of communicating, segmenting, marketing, and selling to all those customers across a portfolio of properties can take the company to the next level in customer relations marketing. This sort of effort is going on industry-wide, says Arthur, and will help skiing catch up with other travel sectors, representing a fertile frontier.

Kircher is bullish on the future, noting the benefits of the collective season-pass bonanza, and in particular the leveling of the field with the rise of Alterra and its strategy to partner with smaller conglomerates and independents. By becoming pass partners with Alterra for the 2018–19 season, Kircher gave Alterra a huge boost by elevating the competitive appeal of Ikon in new markets.

"You don't have to beat Vail Resorts," Kircher says. "We can all win while competing. It's not a win-lose, it's a win-win."

Kircher says the industry has emerged from decades of chronic instability and unsustainability (often tracking with weather and economic conditions) to a new era of sustainable vitality. "We are in another Golden Age of the ski industry," he declares.

Beyond the major boost from mega-passes, Kircher cites the benefits of summer operations and an uptick in overall professional management. But he also pins progress on across-the-board "dynamic pricing" (with everything from hotel rooms to tee times), plus the accelerated appreciation in the recent Trump Administration tax-law changes, which mirror what happened in Europe over the past couple decades. Those immediate write-off benefits have led Boyne to plan $1 billion in capital improvements at its resorts over the next dozen years, kicking off for the 2018–19 season with an eight-place high-speed lift at the crown jewel Big Sky, along with an impressive array of other resort and private-developer projects.

Kircher views the recent tax law changes as paramount and draws a comparison to Europe, which until a couple of decades ago was a disheveled world of T-bars and antiquated facilities, compared with the cutting-edge U.S. ski industry. Since those early days, European governments have begun subsidizing the ski industries in Austria, Germany, France, and elsewhere. Put bluntly, the EU left America in the dust in terms of the quality of new infrastructure. "Compared to Europe, we were like a Third World country, but now we are catching up, and the tax changes are a big assist," Kircher says. Europe is still relatively dominant in terms of capital investments; the average lift age is seven years, compared to 27 in the U.S. In Alpine-crazed Austria, where the homegrown ski racers are superstars like our LeBron James and Tom Brady, the tiny nation—about the size of Vermont, New Hampshire, and Maine combined—records roughly the same number of skier visits as the entire U.S., as does France.

An astounding one-third of Boyne's revenue comes from Big Sky, which is located 45 minutes from Bozeman and has, arguably, one of the brightest upsides of any resort in the country. Anchored by Lone Peak, the resort's 5,800 ski acres, third most in the U.S., drew more than 500,000 skier visits for the first time in 2017—18, blew well past that mark for the 2018–19 season, and has its sights set on passing 700,000 in the near future. Although the 2017–18 total is just a third of Vail Mountain's business and puts Big Sky in the medium tier of resorts for volume, it is in the midst of a building boom both at its base and on the mountain. It also features intriguing village-to-village connections (Moonlight Basin, the private Yellowstone Club and Spanish Peaks). Big Sky provides the closest thing in North America to a European ski experience.

For the 2018–19 winter, Boyne claimed another first by installing North America's first eight-person chairlift, a high-speed Doppelmayr with heated, ergonomic seats (the new lift replaces the old Ramcharger quad). Kircher didn't reveal the price tag for the new Ramcharger 8, but he noted that each chair costs "as much as a Porsche." With the new capital investment incentives, Big Sky also replaced the Shedhorn lift with a high-speed quad and is forging ahead with its 2016 master plan pledge, called Big Sky 2025, in which the mountain company plans to invest roughly $150 million on the mountain as part of a larger, community-wide $1 billion in spending. Besides more lift upgrades, including roughly eight new lifts and another four to be relocated, Big Sky plans to add transformative European-style on-mountain food and beverage facilities; develop a new, 160-acre, high-end, ski-in-ski-out community; overhaul its current resort village facilities; and renovate the Summit and landmark Huntley hotels.

That's a mouthful—and there's more. The private development underway is simply stunning. Big Sky never had a real downtown, but built a Town Center from scratch. A new Marriott Residence Inn, named for Woodrow Wilson, who signed the act creating the National Park Service, opened in summer 2019. Two luxury hotels are planned, one at Spanish Peaks and another at Moonlight. The median single-family home price has nearly doubled from 2012 to 2017, when it reached $1.24 million, and that doesn't include sales at the Yellowstone Club, where condos start at $3 million and many homes are in the $25 million range. Local scuttlebutt has it that dozens of Vail homeowners, the ".1 percenters," upset at the Epic crowds, are selling their homes and moving to the Yellowstone Club or Big Sky area.

Boyne Resorts has stayed the course for seven decades. The company is built on its early foundations: lean staffing; significant investments in snow-making; innovations in lifts; early transition to four-season destinations; geo-graphical diversity with Gatlinburg's summer cash flow; and always a willingness to think out of the box. Everett's visionary estate planning allows Boyne to claim that it is the longest-running ski company in the world (the founder moved the company to his kids' ownership way back in 1976). Stephen is now the majority owner. Everett would be proud.

For 2019 Q1, revenues were up 12 percent over what was a record 2018 Q1 for both revenue and EBITDA. Ikon was a great next step after M.A.X., with added growth and no adverse impact on paid skier days or individual sea-son-pass sales. The Big Sky locals complained loudly about Ikon Pass visitors, but like the story at many other resorts, the local passholders were out in force for a huge powder winter and way outnumbered the interlopers.

So Stephen is excited about the future, for Boyne and the industry. While sections of the country (Midwest, New England) will have to swim upstream because of demographics and other issues, the West in general—and markets like Denver, Salt Lake, Seattle, Vancouver, and even little Bozeman, gateway to Big Sky—will be assisted by a strong downstream current. An increase na-tionwide to a three-year average of 60 million skier visits a year, roughly a 12 percent increase, is viable in five years, he thinks. In a decade, he says, maybe a new benchmark of 65 million—if disrupters like climate change and partic-ipation challenges are solved. He is more than ever focused on the big picture. In terms of governance, he's recently added three outside directors and trimmed his direct reports from 21 to 13.

With Boyne Resorts and the industry on the upswing, it's no surprise that Kircher has no interest in selling to an Alterra or Vail Resorts or anyone. He would like to keep Boyne in the family for a third generation and beyond. "What would I do with half a billion dollars?" he laughs. "And what would *I* do? What would the motivation be?" Kircher shares the independent, stubborn streak of his father, is passionate about the resort business, and loves what he does. He's more likely to be buying than selling.

CHAPTER 7

POWDR Promotes Adventure Lifestyle

Park City–based POWDR owns nine ski resorts, including Copper Mountain, Killington, and Mt. Bachelor, with roughly 3.5 million total skier visits. Throw in Snowbird, which shares the same Cumming-family ownership, and the number rises above 4 million. POWDR also owns and operates a half-dozen Woodward camp facilities, the popular ski and adventure-sports incubator for kids. POWDR's history begins in a most unlikely place, a tent near the summit of Mount McKinley in 1992.

John Cumming had graduated from the University of Colorado in 1991 with a degree in French studies, but was enjoying a rebellious respite, working as a senior mountain guide for venerable Rainier Mountaineering Inc., a guide service created in 1969 by Lou Whittaker and Jerry Lynch. John had already led more than 50 climbs up Rainier when his father, Ian, called with an unusual request: He wanted to climb Denali, an arduous task for any mountaineer. Foul weather delayed the ascent near the summit, and father and son hunkered down in a tent for the night.

Ian told John how proud he was to see him following his passion. And John revealed how much he enjoyed the guide mindset, the routine, the lessons it taught about patience and responsibility. He also admitted that he was tired of always being broke and that he'd really like to merge his love of the outdoors with a viable business career. That decision led to his current role with POWDR.

Two decades earlier, when Ian turned 40 and John was just 3, the two learned to ski together at Alta. It was the year before Dick Bass opened Snowbird down the road in Little Cottonwood Canyon. Ian became an investor in Snowbird, where the family bought a slopeside condo, and over the years it was where John and his younger brother, David, spent time with their busy father, who would fly back from New York City on weekends. The experience stoked John's growing love of the mountains. "I became me in the mountains," Cumming concisely says. When the Cummings finally had the opportunity to acquire the majority interest in Snowbird in 2014, they referred to it as an "heirloom" rather than an "asset." Snowbird is not officially part of the POWDR portfolio, but it has the same shareholders and is managed by POWDR. Snowbird insiders say that while the Bass family is the "founder" of the resort, the Cummings will be the "finishers," and they have recently embarked upon several major capital projects.

Back in the mountaintop tent, John Cumming was ready for a change, but he didn't want to wear a suit and tie and commute back to the concrete canyons of New York City or some other metropolis, as his dad did every week. Ian, who was born in Vancouver and had earned an MBA degree from Harvard in 1970, was a self-made billionaire. Along with a Harvard classmate, he built Leucadia National Corp. into a turnaround machine, investing in companies in diverse fields from mining to manufacturing, vineyards to real estate, and even casinos and debt collecting, according to the business journal *Crain's*. By the time Cumming retired in 2013, Leucadia was valued at $6.8 billion, according to *The Salt Lake Tribune*.

Together in the tent with his father, recalls John, "We cooked up a career." John's first move was on the gear and apparel side. He managed to arrange credentials to attend the Outdoor Retailer industry trade show, still held in Reno back then, on behalf of his guide outfit, Rainier Mountaineering. He met with Jack Gilbert and Paul Kramer, industry veterans who had worked for The North Face and then helped found Sierra Designs. After an unsuccessful attempt to acquire Sierra Designs, the family settled on the idea of a new company and Mountain Hardwear was born. Gilbert and Kramer led the effort. "Those guys made Mountain Hardwear," John says of co-founders Gilbert and Kramer, but it was the Cummings who provided the capital, and John played an important role by insisting the company make products that guides would embrace and use.

Around that same time, in the early '90s, Nick Badami was pondering the future of his Park City and Alpine Meadows ski resorts. His original day job was as the head of the manufacturing and retailing giant BVD. Badami subsequently channeled his capital into his personal passion, buying Park City in 1975. Badami was a huge supporter of the U.S. Ski Team, the chairman of its board, and along with his son Craig had transformed World Cup ski racing by creating "America's Opening" races at Park City in late November, which emphasized live music and a party atmosphere alongside the competition. The plan was to have Craig eventually take over the helm. But Craig, the resort's director of marketing, died tragically in a helicopter crash in November 1989, while he and resort crews were cleaning up after hosting the World Cup races.

The Cummings met with Badami and struck an agreement whereby John would learn the business from the ground up, serving as an "assistant to the chairman" and getting an on-site MBA from the veteran Badami. John diligently went about his duties, making snow, grooming terrain, working race crew, and taking reservations. He even had a desk next to Badami. After a trial period, Badami concluded, "I think I can teach him the business." Cumming still mentions Badami as a critical mentor and often cites one of Nick's favorite sayings: "Luck is the residue of design."

Ian Cumming provided the capital for the eventual acquisition of Park City and Alpine Meadows, a loan at 8 percent, and John was off and running. This loan, and a smaller one to start Mountain Hardwear, would hang over John for decades. There's a general industry view that he was handed the keys to the castle by his billionaire dad, but John says that's not the case. "He was the financier, but POWDR and Mountain Hardwear were my deals." He continued to work under Badami for several years before ascending to the CEO position.

He also paid his father back, with interest, in full, and on time. He's been fighting the dual stigma of the mistaken impression that he was just spending his dad's money all along, plus the obvious psychological trials of "having my dad be my banker." (Not just a dad, but one who happened to be among the foremost businessmen in the country. *Forbes* once wrote that "few can match wits with corporate bottom feeder Ian Cumming when it comes to wringing money out of white elephants.") Deep down, John believes he and the teams he's assembled built and made POWDR, and he knows that in some situations he learned to do the exact opposite of what Ian preached. He is now at peace with all that.

From the beginning, John Cumming had a vision, but, by his own admission, not a clear plan for execution. He wanted to become the largest privately held ski resort operator in the country—and the most profitable one (so the apple didn't fall far from the tree). But he sought "enduring profitability," quite the opposite from the fix-and-sell, turnaround mantra of his father. As it grew, POWDR would not depend on developing real estate. In a resort business that was already topsy-turvy from season to season, he didn't need to further exacerbate the peaks and valleys by rolling the dice in the speculative world of real-estate development and sales.

Cumming is continually guided by a mountaineer's mentality, and he peppers his conversation with climbing terms and sayings. Chief among them is this piece of wisdom that climbers use when approaching a difficult summit in adverse conditions and considering what to do next: "Up is optional; down is mandatory." Or this one: "There are a lot of old climbers, and a lot of bold climbers, but not a lot of old, bold climbers."

He favors the craft-beer approach to resort operations, with an emphasis on working with the community where it operates, not trying to bend them to a corporate dictate. POWDR would be the Sam Adams of resort companies, not the Anheuser-Busch.

So Cumming applied a circumspect discipline to an industry that was already rife with wreckage, and that in the late 1990s would see the launch of resort conglomerates that would be relatively short-lived, such as American Skiing Company and then Booth Creek and even Intrawest. POWDR would concentrate on delivering mountain adventure and the attendant lifestyle, not $25 hamburgers or luxury condos. He also inherited a "high-pain tolerance," which would be a core requirement for surviving the bumpy years ahead.

Back in the turbulent '90s, ski resorts could sometimes be bought for five or six times cash flow, though interest rates were high and capital scarce. The Cummings had capital, and in 1995 they bought the small resorts of Boreal, installing Jody Churich as president and GM, and Soda Springs in California. In 2001, POWDR acquired Mt. Bachelor in Oregon, a Pacific Northwest gem, but had to overcome a hostile battle with some shareholders to eventually close. In 2003, POWDR added Lee Canyon outside of Las Vegas.

POWDR next stepped into the hypercompetitive Northeast market, and sparks flew. In 2007, POWDR bought Killington, the "Beast of the East," and nearby Pico for $85.2 million from the remnants of the American Skiing Company (To make this happen, he had to sell Alpine Meadows; it was an extremely difficult personal decision for Cumming, who loved the Tahoe day-skier area).

Killington, in Cumming's view, was a ski industry "franchise," like an NBA or NFL team, one that needed to be nurtured for multiple generations to realize its ultimate value. But to get there, he would have to "take it down to the studs."

An Eastern institution, Pres Smith's baby, and the place where I started my ski career, Killington was ground zero for many of the resort industry's most important innovations and best management practices. At one time it recorded close to 1 million annual skier visits. Cumming knew all that and held its history in the highest regard. It was also plagued by prior owner ASC's uneven oversight, with an over-emphasis on selling Grand Summit Hotel units as quickly as possible to hold off the banks, capital expenditures that didn't pay off, and a load of deferred maintenance headaches, particularly a snowmaking pipe system that was rotten to the core. While recognizing these ASC failings, he gives a nod to Les Otten. Cumming says ASC "was so close to pulling it off."

Cumming is fond of noting that "you can't pay payroll with skier visits." The POWDR team concluded that Killington needed to focus on the yield per customer, on vertical integration, and on controlling fixed costs. In that regard, this rigorous, expense-focused strategy in many ways mirrored Ian Cumming's Leucadia.

The transformation would take a lot of tough love, time, and investment. Shortcomings needed to be addressed. But POWDR, by Cumming's own telling, stumbled badly out of the gate. The rocky start included a decision to revoke lifetime season-pass privileges from some 800 Killington holders, a benefit that had originated when investors plunked down $1,000 to fuel the resort's growth in the 1960s and '70s. The move made good business but not good political sense, embroiling the company in a public-relations nightmare and triggering a class-action lawsuit (which POWDR would eventually win). POWDR also ended the Pres Smith tradition of Killington being the first resort in the East to open and the last to close, a policy that was key to its identity in skiers' minds but could also be inefficient and costly to execute. (The resort has since reverted back to its "first and last" commitment.)

Cumming said he tried to warn the community that the forthcoming changes "might hurt a little," but readily admits today that POWDR made a lot of mistakes in its implementation. "My father always said 'Do what you need to do, and then tell everyone.' That doesn't always work. I've learned how important it is to explain your intent up front. Killington was an important learning experience for me ... We were not respectful. That was a mistake." It certainly did not help that these changes occurred during the 2007–09 financial crisis, followed by the devastating impacts of Hurricane Irene in 2013.

POWDR has finally found equilibrium at Killington, honing its mastery of operations, winning back the clientele in droves and ensuring a bright future for the franchise. "It could not be going better now. It's a badass mountain, and it will be more so," he says.

POWDR built the Skye Peak Express in 2010, repaired the snowmaking infrastructure while adding energy efficiency, and made upgrades to its Grand Hotel. For 2018–19 and 2019–20 seasons, it built a new K-1 lodge, installed the new North Ridge triple and Snowdon Six Express bubble, and made K-1 Express gondola upgrades and restored lift service in the South Ridge area. Work included trail widening and new tunnels and bridges at busy intersections; those latter two particularly impressed the diehard skier base. The Killington Peak Lodge was a complete make-over. POWDR was also investing in Pico, long Killington's stepsister but an attractive mountain in its own right, with water line and snowmaking expansions.

The company has emphasized experiences beyond lift tickets, with tubing, yurt dining, and snowcat-drawn sleigh rides, and has refurbished slopeside bars. Given John Cumming's continued support of ski racing and the U.S. Ski Team and building a bridge to the community, the resort now hosts women's World Cup races over Thanksgiving weekend, drawing a two-day crowd of close to 40,000 in the race-crazy East, much larger than the preceding host, Aspen. Worldwide TV coverage to 62 countries promotes its early winter conditions; the resort had a stunning amount of terrain open to the public for the 2018 event. It also awarded more than $250,000 in grants to ski-development programs around the country with proceeds from its VIP packages.

In summer, Killington has concentrated on downhill mountain biking, adding zip lines and rope courses, and hosting a variety of events, including the Fox U.S. Open of Mountain Biking and Under Amour Mountain Running series.

And for the future, SP Land, a Dallas-based developer led by Paul Rowsey, is finally making tangible progress on the base village that was first proposed in the mid-1990s, securing Act 250 approval in January 2017 for the first phase of its Six Peaks Village. SP Land is working on a new lodge, a skier bridge spanning Killington Road, and a pedestrian village and town green. The first stage includes 193 residential units in the village core, 30,000-plus square feet of retail and commercial space, and 32 slopeside single-family homes. Build-out would add another 1,700 units and up to 91,500 square feet of additional commercial development, according to SP's website and published reports. Cumming counts SP Land's Rowsey as one of his mentors, and the two each have a small stake in the other's operation at Killington. In this way they have a stake in their mutual success, but stick to their areas of expertise.

Killington, under POWDR and with Mike Solimano leading efforts on the ground, is back—and still honoring its roots to a die-hard clientele. In its 2018–19 magazine, *4241*, the resort honored the passholders who had skied 100-plus days the previous season. There were almost 300 names on the list.

Following the 2007 Killington/Pico acquisition, Cumming would insert POWDR into arguably the most competitive ski market in the world, Colorado's Front Range, buying Copper Mountain from Intrawest in December 2009. Sandwiched between Breckenridge and Keystone in Summit County, and with Vail and Beaver Creek just up the road in adjacent Eagle County to the west, this four-on-one matchup is as brutal as it gets. But it allowed Copper to position itself as the "authentic" Front Range skier's mountain, a unique brand, and there is an undeniable audience for that product. Cumming cringes at the term "anti-Vail" ("I believe we run to things, not from them"), but that's how a lot of dedicated skiers view Copper.

Copper's transition to POWDR ownership would be much smoother than Killington's. After a decade of Intrawest's real-estate focused operations, chasing the dream of a Whistler-like village experience along I-70, Copper would segue happily from a corporate vibe to a skier's vibe. POWDR focused on the skiing, not real estate. POWDR seemed to be a good fit. Continuing the family tradition of staunch racing support, Copper created the U.S. Ski Team Speed Center in 2011 on the east side of the mountain at the Super Bee lift. This new complex provided the only early-season, top-to-bottom downhill training in the world and drew top racers from around the globe. Priority training space has always been allocated to the U.S. Ski Team. Although these closed trails on the east side of the mountain are a sore point for the local customer base, Copper has built a strong bottom line from renting race lanes to clubs from across the U.S., also requiring them to book lodging in the village at a time when the beds would otherwise be empty. Under Cumming, Copper found a profitable niche in an unusual way.

For the 2018–19 season, POWDR launched a multiyear, $100 million capital improvement project. It dramatically improved its Center Village experience, but with cutting-edge lifts to replace first-generation quad-detachables rather than with new condos. The resort spent $20 million to replace its flagship American Eagle high-speed quad with a chondola (alternating six-pack chairs and eight-person gondola cabins), increasing uphill capacity by more than 40 percent. The chondola would disembark at the new Solitude Station midmountain lodge, now under construction and set for completion by the 2020–21 season. Once open, it will offer evening dining service, rounding out the resort experience. Copper also replaced the American Flyer with six-pack bubble chairs and a 33 percent jump in capacity. The openings of both new lifts, vital to the main base area, saw frustrating delays, but Copper is charging forward for the 2019–20 season with a three-person chairlift to the expert high-alpine terrain on Tucker Mountain and with the Woodward Peace Park.

Copper also got a new president and GM, Dustin Lyman, who replaced 20-year veteran Gary Rodgers as an out-of-the-box hire by POWDR. Lyman, a Colorado native who played tight end for the Chicago Bears for five seasons, had most recently served as CEO of Famous Brands, which includes Mrs. Fields cookies and TCBY yogurt. Lyman had also worked for Vail Resorts, providing lead financial support for its properties, and in a similar role for DISH Network.

All was not rosy for POWDR elsewhere. A couple of years after POWDR acquired Copper, it became embroiled in a lengthy lawsuit against its landlord, the Talisker-owned United Park City Mines, over whether it had, by virtue of an administrative error, lost its lease to some 3,500 acres of terrain, essentially everything but the base area and lifts.

Talisker, a Canadian real-estate company, was, not coincidentally, also the owner of the adjacent Canyons Resort. The PCMR lease was for 80 years and dated back to the 1970s, but it had to be renewed every 20 years by PCMR before a specified date. By 2011, the annual $155,000 lease payments were also well below market, and the two parties had been discussing a rent increase, among other things, but could not reach agreement. At some point, Talisker discovered it had not received the renewal in time (it was two days' late), and assumed the position that the lease had expired. Talisker told PCMR to vacate the premises. PCMR promptly sued Talisker.

PCMR ultimately lost the case, with the court determining that it had failed to timely renew the lease, and ordering its eviction. PCMR appealed.

The situation was dramatically exacerbated when Vail Resorts acquired Canyons from Talisker. That purchase included the Talisker-PCMR litigation, so Vail Resorts was now the party with the right to evict PCMR, subject to the appeal. It appeared that Vail had overpaid for Canyons if it lost the PCMR litigation, but as we all know, it won. The court of appeals also ruled in favor of Talisker/Vail Resorts, leaving Vail Resorts as PCMR's landlord, and leaving PCMR with an expired lease.

The catch was that POWDR still owned the base area, all the lifts, and the amenities, and by threatening to not allow access, it could theoretically thwart any other operator of the resort. Cumming had no choice but to threaten this nuclear option, even if it meant the economic collapse of the vibrant town he loved at the base, in order to get the most leverage and best deal on the sale price. After months of legal wrangling and back and forth, POWDR agreed in September 2014 to sell its facilities for what was reported by Vail Resorts to be a $182.5 million cash deal.

Vail Resorts almost immediately announced $50 million in upgrades, including a gondola connection between the Canyons and Park City, creating a mega-resort of 7,300 acres, the nation's largest. Besides the pain from the loss of their crown jewel and hometown resort, Cumming and POWDR also had to endure endless commentary from various industry experts stating that Vail Resorts would be a much better steward of the resort anyway.

The ordeal was "excruciating" for John Cumming. He lived in Park City, raised his family there, and embraced the town, its residents, and everything about it. His community involvement and dedication were unrivaled. Now he was labeled a "pariah" in news headlines for threatening to close the very mountain that was Park City's lifeblood, and all because of an administrative error, but one that was ultimately his responsibility and his burden. Despite the horrendous circumstances, Cumming did everything he could to preserve POWDR's financial health in the exit from a bad situation. "My commitment was to make the best decisions I could with the perpetuity of POWDR in mind," he said. As for his hometown, he adds, "I want nothing more than to make Park City the best it can be."

Little known to the public, Cumming was diagnosed in 2000 with multiple sclerosis. The first sign was deteriorating vision, and then a two-day bout with the spins. He has courageously fought the debilitating disease, and has undergone various treatments and two stem cell transplants. Cumming no longer climbs mountains ("I do climb in and out of bed," he says), but has chosen to aggressively confront the condition. "Use it or lose it," he says. "It can be emotionally difficult. I can't see out of one eye." When told his executives and colleagues say they can hardly detect the impacts, his quick retort is, "I notice it."

Moving beyond the PCMR sale, POWDR has further defined its purpose and followed the unusual, forward-looking paths that are true to its core. That includes buying the former Resort Sports Network (RSN) and transitioning it to become Outside TV, branded to the magazine of the same name, and also launching POWDR Enterprises, charged with creating events, sponsorships, and media opportunities to leverage the POWDR assets. Cumming turned to Wade Martin, who had launched the Dew Tour, to run the new business. POWDR also purchased Human Movement Management, a Colorado-based company that had launched participatory events such as the Dirty Girl Mud Run and today serves as the experiential arm of POWDR.

In 2017, Cumming found a perfect fit for his POWDR family with the purchase of Eldora, a day-ski area located just above Boulder, where Cumming went to school at CU, climbed in Boulder Canyon, and raced on its slopes. He bought it from managing partner Bill Killebrew, a longtime friend, who also had two partners with long industry ties, the ski-insurance veteran Graham Anderson and the family of the late Chuck Lewis, who had founded Copper Mountain. Although Killebrew had done many good things in his tenure at Eldora, including salvaging it from the brink of bankruptcy and then investing in a first-class snowmaking system and new lifts, he became extremely circumspect later on with capital investments, which caused considerable consternation among locals. He was also often at loggerheads with the local governing authority, Boulder County, which didn't help in securing approvals for any capital projects.

POWDR installed the resort's first high-speed lift, a burnt-orange six-pack called the Alpenglow that goes straight up the gut of the main mountain, and made numerous improvements to the base area. In a lesson to resort managers across the land, perhaps the most lauded makeover came with the bathrooms, which were transformed into state-of-the-art facilities with a "cabiny," Western motif. Cumming's goal at Eldora is to run it with his community-first, craft-beer approach and to become Boulder's go-to ski resort. One of its biggest assets is easy access, which avoids the often mind-numbing traffic on I-70.

In his purchase of Eldora, Cumming certainly had his eye on what might be happening with Intrawest, which, ironically, had been an earlier bidder for the resort. He knew Intrawest was on the blocks and, depending on the new ownership, his deal at Copper (participating with Winter Park and on a limited basis with Steamboat in the Rocky Mountain Super Pass), to which Eldora was also a partner, could be at risk. Buying Eldora was a sound defensive move. No matter what happened, an Eldora/Copper pass would remain appealing to Front Range skiers. Imagine if he had not bought Eldora, and Copper had been cut out of the Ikon Pass.

Thanks to a burst of new business from the Ikon affiliation and new investments, Eldora is now working to catch up with its own success. Having instituted every parking-efficiency measure imaginable to handle more cars (including PR campaigns promoting carpooling and its status as the only resort to have regular RTD bus service, plus a host of satellite parking lots and smarter parking guidelines), it is still hamstrung by a lack of parking. This is a trend we are now seeing across ski country, most notably at A-Basin here in Colorado. The spring 2019 NSAA convention devoted an entire seminar to parking.

Eldora's personable and savvy GM Brent Tregaskis, a 30-year industry veteran who previously spent 18 years leading Bear Mountain in California, has brought a refreshing breath of air and 'round-the-clock expertise to the resort and its relationships. Tregaskis seems to know everyone on the mountain, is a passionate skier, and has gone out of his way to repair and rebuild relationships in nearby Nederland and in Boulder County. For the 2018–19 season, fueled by new Ikon Pass scans and early snow, the resort's attendance exploded. While POWDR does not release skier-visit numbers, the resort appeared on track to break the 350,000-skier-visit mark, roughly a 25 percent increase from the previous season.

Eldora is now working with Boulder County to expand its parking by as many as 980 spaces by 2019–20 or for the following season. In the spring, Eldora earned USFS approval for the new high-speed Jolly Jug lift, opening access to new, much-needed low-angle terrain, even winning support from once-bitter environmental groups, who say they actually enjoy working with the resort now that POWDR owns it. Tregaskis is also optimistic about eventually building a 12,000-square-foot lodge in the beginner area: The "Ignite" adaptive ski program would occupy the ground floor, with a new children's ski school facility on the second floor.

Cumming had participated in the M.A.X. Pass with Intrawest and Boyne and knew many of the Mountain Collective folks. Also, he had years of experience working with Intrawest on its Rocky Mountain Super Pass. So it was no surprise that POWDR became a strong partner on the Ikon Pass. Eldora was actually the first Ikon resort in the West to open for the pass's inaugural 2018–19 winter.

Cumming admits that he was initially a naysayer when the unrestricted Epic Pass launched, not trusting the business model, and he viewed its evolution with patience. "I resisted. I was wary," Cumming says, referring back to his concerns about "paying payroll with skier visits." For the time being, he readily admits he was wrong. "There's no doubt Rob [Katz] was right on that. I give him a ton of credit for that. He did incredibly great work for his shareholders, which is and should be his first priority. He's made it more attainable for more people. I think the customers have been well-served."

Cumming agrees that the resort outlook is as bullish as ever, with its house now in order and the heightened attendance thanks to the mega-passes as the big cherry on top. But still, he worries—about everything from traffic congestion (which is building from Colorado's I-70 to Little Cottonwood Canyon in Utah) to future, unseen ramifications, including the difficult housing climate in mountain towns and the cost of living there. "The mountain communities are expanding. The drive from Copper to the Front Range [on I-70] can be four hours or more. How long are people willing to do that?"

He fears Yogi Berra's famous Yogi-ism actually could come true: "It's so crowded nobody goes there."

"I worry about where this model will lead us in 10 years, with the loss of price integrity," Cumming says. Specifically, he questions whether price alone can create long-term demand, and whether over time the concept will lose its luster; travel activity will likely slow after skiers have marked off all the resorts on their "bucket list." Airlines initially lowered their fares when they consolidated, but then came all the new add-on charges that effectively increased the price. Cumming also notes that Vail Resorts is in the driver's seat with its vertically integrated, mostly high-end resorts and their ability to reap revenue from the pure volume the Epic Pass brings. Others, he says, might be challenged to make money on pure pass volume alone. At the 2019 NSAA spring convention in San Diego, as other resort speakers were citing the incredible success of the mega-pass and just-completed, fourth-best-ever season, POWDR co-president Wade Martin joined the chorus. But he also cautioned everyone about the need to deal with the blowback from the inherent increased crowding, from traffic-snarled access roads to long lines for lifts and other services.

POWDR is looking ahead to ensure that it can deliver fully on its "experiential adventure lifestyle company" motto. So it keeps working to polish its community resort properties and its Woodward action-sports incubators. When Cumming first saw the enthusiastic kids training at Woodward in Pennsylvania, he immediately knew they could be complementary for POWDR resorts, and he saw a huge potential for Woodward to recruit and inspire the next generation of skiers and riders. POWDR acquired Woodward in 2011, and today, to varying degrees, Woodward is a key and growing differentiator for POWDR.

At Copper Mountain and Boreal, action-sports enthusiasts have opportunities to play and train at indoor Woodward facilities; then they can take their skills to the resorts' on-mountain Woodward Mountain Parks. In summer 2018, POWDR introduced the Woodward WreckTangle, and for the 2018–19 season it unveiled the Woodward Peace Park, a partnership between POWDR and U.S. Snowboard Olympian Danny Davis that unveiled unique, ever-evolving terrain parks at Killington and Boreal. In addition to creating environments at its resorts that tap the passion Woodward instills, POWDR has expanded and grown the core Woodward camp business at its namesake town, Woodward, Pennsylvania, and in Tehachapi, California, two hours south of Los Angeles. POWDR is also opening a new Woodward location, Woodward Park City, a short drive from Salt Lake City, at the site of POWDR's former Gorgoza Park tubing hill and unveiled the Woodward Riviera Maya at the Hard Rock Hotel & Casino in Mexico.

In February 2018, Ian Cumming died at age 77 after a difficult struggle with Alzheimer's, surrounded by family and friends at his home in Jackson, Wyoming. With that, John's family-business obligations multiplied, including serving as chair of the family's American Investment Company (AIC), the Crimson Wine Group, and The Cumming Foundation. (His brother David also has executive roles with AIC and POWDR).

In June 2018, Cumming announced that he was relinquishing the

POWDR CEO role, but would keep a strong hand in shaping the strategy and vision as chairman. He named Wade Martin, from the original POWDR Enterprises, and his POWDR CFO, Justin Sibley, as co-presidents of POWDR, while Tim Brennwald would continue as COO. In that complementary trio, he has a marketing guru, a numbers guy, and a ski-operations expert. The five-person POWDR executive team also includes Emily Loeffler, the senior VP on the legal/HR side. The fifth member is Megan Baroska, the senior VP of corporate strategy and communications. As a nine-year veteran of the noted Edelman D.C. public affairs office on Capitol Hill, a former FBI spokesperson, and even a campaign staffer for Mitt Romney's 2014 presidential run, she brings plenty of high-level experience to the team. She worked with the company on the delicate PCMR issue when she was at Edelman, and looking back on that difficult time, the POWDR leadership team believes it was actually a pivotal and positive turning point, when the company decided to buck up and learn rather than fading away.

Like Boyne, the POWDR culture embraces centralization only where logical. It makes sense to base some infrastructure under one roof, and the Park City HQ includes functions for accounting, finance, legal, HR, marketing services, experiential marketing, youth development, and technology. POWDR has roughly 40 employees in Park City and another dozen at an office in Louisville, Colorado (original home of Human Movement, which shed its name and is now just part of POWDR's experiential marketing unit).

Cumming, like his friend Stephen Kircher, is a patient survivor, and the role of POWDR (and Boyne) in Ikon cannot be overstated. The two share many similarities and yet have distinct differences, starting with political leanings that align geographically with their home bases, Cumming to the left and Kircher to the right. While Kircher's resorts tend to be vertically integrated from birth, Cumming has focused on the mountains. Kircher's Boyne promotes a dozen high-end golf courses in summer and a kids' waterpark, youth soccer, and lacrosse; Cumming's counter-seasonal emphasis is all about edgy youth, experiential adventure and Woodward camps. It's healthy to see them and their friendship—and diverse views—at the head of the two biggest Mid-Majors, and the fact that they share this long-term goal in common: They both want to pass the resort business down to their kids, and their kids' kids after that.

Cumming is a resort leader in fighting climate change, with POWDR commissioning the first climate-change industry study in 2006 ("Save our

Snow") and hiring a director of sustainability. He is a staunch backer of other progressive initiatives, including diversity in hiring (his longtime executive vice president was Jody Churich, a 20-year company veteran who worked at Soda Springs and Boreal before guiding Woodward's growth; she departed the company in 2018 and now works as an executive with Vail Resorts). When Churich won a 2012 SAMMY Award for leadership, she told the magazine this about her mentor, Cumming: "I've learned the very valuable and critical pieces of business acumen from him. He's humble, honest, smart, and approachable. His story and true character is one that is grounded in a love for mountains, sports, family, and the environment."

On POWDR's 25th anniversary in 2019, Cumming reflected on his reason for entering the business in the first place, and on finding "balance" in weighing the objective with the subjective. Pointing to the fulcrum mark on the top of the "W" in the POWDR logo, he said it's there as a representation of this balance.

"It is a reminder that we are in this business because we are passionate about what we do, and it is a visual cue for living a balanced life full of adventure.

"If we only looked at things objectively, we would never have gotten into this industry in the first place. It's an industry replete with volatility, competitiveness, climate fluctuation, revenue model shifts, and so on. We balance the objective data points we use to assess risk and measure progress by also accounting for the subjective, which is our belief that these activities make our lives and our customers' lives better. We think we are creating long-term franchise value by being good shepherds of our sport, being good shepherds of our community, and being good shepherds of our environment."

Cumming has developed into a savvy resort operator over the decades. He has more wealth than he can spend. He's not in this for the money. Cumming is always on the lookout for acquisition opportunities in the right circumstances, but in this era of extreme valuations, those opportunities are tiny or nonexistent. He owns an enduringly profitable business, one that has good future prospects and sells goods and services that really mean something to him personally, and one in which he has invested his life's work—and he doesn't need to wear a suit and tie very often. When asked if he would consider selling POWDR, he says: "Who would sell such a thing?"

CHAPTER 8

Peak Resorts:

'Former' Metro-Area Dynasty
Grew on Simple Formula

The latest bombshell in the ever-evolving resort industry came in steamy late July 2019, as Vail Resorts announced its plans to acquire Peak Resorts, the first major foray by one of the giants into this market. It's only appropriate to review how this collection of mostly small- and medium-sized resorts built the track record to attract a robust purchase price from the biggest player of all.

Back in the fall of 2018, Peak Resorts operated 14 ski resorts, primarily located in the Northeast and Midwest, 13 of which it owned. Most are within 100 miles of major metropolitan markets, including New York City, Boston, Philadelphia, Cleveland, and St. Louis. Starting from humble roots at Hidden Valley in Missouri, the company discovered success in the operation of day-ski areas near large cities with a simple formula: lean operations and a relentless focus on snowmaking.

The company's founder, Tim Boyd, was a golfer, not a skier. During college he worked at a St. Louis–area golf course and returned there after graduating from the University of Missouri. He worked his way up through the ranks until he became the greens superintendent and general manager in 1977. A competitive collegiate golfer, he was chasing his passion. Boyd eventually purchased the course with a couple of partners and was looking around for something to do in the winter.

Then, Boyd says, he experienced "divine intervention." He had traveled with his wife to Lake Tahoe with some skiing friends, and the couple had their first skiing experience at Homewood, a small resort on the northwest shore of Tahoe. According to Boyd, they spent several days learning to ski in the pouring rain and never got off the beginner hill. Returning home, he thought, "Well, I know a place in St. Louis where there's the same amount of vertical that we experienced. Why don't we build a ski area there?"

So he purchased the land under what would become Hidden Valley, adjacent to the golf course he owned, and created a ski area with a modest 320 feet of vertical, just about what he had tackled on the lower slopes at Homewood. Much to his surprise, this winter adventure attracted 30,000 visits in its first season. So he did the same thing in nearby Kansas City (Snow Creek) a few years later. From then on, growth came by way of acquisitions, with the next purchase bringing Paoli Peaks in southern Indiana into the fold.

I asked him if, in those early years, he had a vision of what the company might become. His response: "I had no clue." That said, he obviously recognized early on that no one in the ski business was focusing on metro areas. He liked the idea of occupying a space where he didn't have a lot of well-capitalized big players. He has remained a "niche" player ever since, with remarkable success.

Peak's flagship is Vermont's Mount Snow, which was acquired from the ailing American Skiing Company in February 2007 along with Attitash, located in North Conway, New Hampshire. Peak later increased its New Hampshire presence with the purchase of Crotched Mountain and the small (in volume) but legendary Wildcat Mountain, located across Pinkham Notch from Mount Washington. In Pennsylvania, Peak acquired Jack Frost and Big Boulder, two of that region's leading ski areas.

In an investor presentation in May 2018, Peak identified its acquisition criteria as follows:

- Undermanaged and undercapitalized resorts
- Opportunities for targeted capital projects
- Proximity to major metropolitan areas
- On-site water resources for snowmaking

The criteria of "on-site water" is no doubt a lesson learned from the Mount Snow acquisition. For decades, Mount Snow's owners struggled to find a long-term water solution. Located at the headwaters of the North Branch of the Deerfield River, the local streams could not provide adequate water without very large storage ponds. A number of potential solutions were analyzed (such as a pipeline to Somerset Reservoir), but none made it through Vermont's sticky permit process. Finally, for the 2017–18 season, Peak was able to complete a new water project called West Lake, which dramatically boosted its production capabilities. As a result, Mount Snow opened early and had the most terrain open in Vermont for the critical Christmas holiday (as a percentage of total terrain).

Ski areas south of Vermont's Route 4 have historically been more prone to adverse weather events, aka rain. Killington, which sits just south of Route 4, typically enjoys relatively better weather than areas farther south. In this modern era of global warming, all areas benefit from snowmaking, but for areas like Mount Snow the ability to respond to adverse weather events in a dramatic and timely fashion is critical to success. Following completion of the West Lake project, Mount Snow reportedly has the ability to convert some 13,000 gallons of water a minute to snow with temperatures in the low 20s. That is a stunning four- or five-fold increase over the system in place in the 1980s and '90s when I was there. With that kind of firepower, Mount Snow can refresh 240 acres of critical, popular terrain overnight and, with an additional 24 hours, be back in pre-weather-event shape. In those earlier days, we could never put the mountain back together quickly enough to meet guests' expectations.

Other areas in the Northeast have developed similar firepower. Loon, Killington and Sunday River come to mind. The importance cannot be overstated. In booking a ski vacation weeks in advance, a skiing family can be confident that even with some adverse weather, their vacation has a high likelihood of being fun and rewarding. For areas without the major snowmaking capabilities, savvy skiers really need to watch weather patterns carefully before finalizing plans. A segue: In the 1960s and '70s, the Northeast enjoyed a robust ski vacation business. There were significant price incentives to book a mid-week vacation, not to mention the lack of crowds. And weather in those days was not as cruel to ski resort operators—not to say that a miserable cold snap couldn't occur, or a disappointing rain event. But as weather patterns began to change, providing more rain/thaw events, the market for ski vacations longer than a few days shifted west. Rained on one time: bad luck. Rained on twice: "Let's try Colorado."

Certainly, advanced snowmaking will not shift the weather/snow advantage that the West enjoys. Temperatures at night fall dramatically, keeping the snow cold and soft. Low humidity also helps the West. But for areas with major snowmaking in the East, there is a new level of reliability and a material improvement in the quality of the snow surface and the overall ski experience.

Back to Peak Resorts. Tim Boyd's team was one of the first to embrace snowmaking as the very foundation of its business plan. For close-in, metro ski areas, snow quality determines demand. As Boyd says, "we don't normally have a demand problem; if we have snow, people come." In the Northeast and Midwest, snowmaking trumps any other resort attribute. Boyd expects his smaller, urban areas to be able to open 100 percent of their terrain after 48 hours of snowmaking. The same would be true of resurfacing efforts (48 hours). Given the marginal temperatures and frequent rain events that many of the Peak resorts experience, this is a critical capability.

On November 30, 2015, the company announced an agreement to purchase New York's Hunter Mountain from its longtime owners, the Slutzky family, for $36.8 million. "Huntah," as its guests fondly called it, prospered during the boom years of the 1960s and '70s. It was early to embrace snowmaking, but as time passed, the overall experience diminished. End result: a significant loss of market share, which created financial issues, which in turn exacerbated its already-tired facility infrastructure.

When Hunter was being actively marketed in 2013, many potential buyers were no doubt put off by the physical condition of the assets and attendant environmental challenges. Peak was part of that process and communicated to the Hunter management that they needed to make significant improvements to their operation in order to raise EBITDA and justify their asking price. Hunter was taken off the market, but they had established a relationship with the Peaks team and, eventually, Hunter was sold to Peak and never offered to another buyer. Peak knew that Hunter also needed new technology to go along with an expanded snowmaking system, and they were well suited to provide that. For the 2018–19 ski season, Hunter saw a $9 million investment, increasing skiable terrain by 25 percent, adding a new parking lot for 250 cars, and installing a new six-person detachable chair. "We just can't feed that beast enough," Boyd says, referencing both the need for capital and its productivity at Hunter. Obviously, he's bullish on the short- and long-term growth opportunities. Peak expects these most recent investments to return $1.5 million to $2 million in additional EBITDA annually (Hunter has plenty of advanced terrain; it lacked intermediate trails). Given its proximity to the Eastern megalopolis, it has the opportunity to be a veritable factory for creating new skiers and riders. The 2018 expansion creates a new entry portal and, with that, the opportunity for real-estate development. Some new beds, restaurants, and retail would go a long way toward reestablishing Hunter as a major player in the northeast. With NYC being only 2.5 hours away, Hunter should quickly approach 350,000 annual skier visits. In short, Hunter was the poster child for a Peak acquisition. Its primary criteria, "undermanaged and undercapitalized resorts," fit Hunter to a T.

The addition of Hunter also created the opportunity to market a Peak Pass, with the clever marketing tag of "How the East Was One." If you think only the big guys are finding success with season passes in the modern ski industry, consider the following metrics from Peak, released in spring 2018 in the wake of the Ikon–Epic battle and before the 2018–19 season:

"Consolidated season-pass sales through April 30, 2018, increased 14 percent on a unit basis and 16 percent on a dollar basis, compared to the prior year (as of late March, Peak was reporting an 18 percent increase in units and 20 percent in revenue), driven by continued broad interest in the Peak Pass among Northeast skiers and riders, including a 47 percent increase in unit sales of the unlimited, unrestricted Drifter Pass for 18- to 29-year-old … Season-pass sales now provide over 35 percent of total lift income."

So here we have an owner/operator of 14 resorts that seemed to be successfully carving out a niche in a space avoided to date by the two giants, with the exception of Vail's ownership of three Midwestern resorts. In terms of pass products, Peak has pretty well mimicked the multi-resort products of the big guys, but added a new one, the Drifter Pass, aimed at 18- to 29-year-olds. This is a perfect product for the Northeast, given its huge number of college and university students. Their demographic skews younger than most other resorts, as is evident in the proliferation and popularity of their terrain parks (Mount Snow is recognized annually for offering the top terrain park in the East).

Peak Resorts is vertically integrated in terms of product sales. They operate their own retail, rental, F&B, and lodging operations, but they primarily focus on mountain operations. All five of Tim Boyd's children were active in the business and learned it from the bottom up.

Before the sale to Vail Resorts, Boyd's oldest son, Jesse, was expected to take over the reins when his dad retired. They have virtually no corporate-headquarters staff, with the exception of a finance team that focuses mainly on the reporting required of a public company. Like their individual resorts, the corporate team was lean.

In fall 2018, Peak had dropped its own bombshell into the mega-consolidation ski craze. It announced the acquisition of three mid-Atlantic ski areas from privately held Snow Time, Inc. for $76 million. Its Pennsylvania trio of Liberty Mountain, Whitetail, and Roundtop Mountain resorts recorded 600,000 skier visits in 2017–18, and are all within driving distance of the 10 million residents of the Baltimore–Washington, D.C., market. The combined resorts offer 65 trails, more than 325 acres of terrain, and an average vertical drop of 700 feet. Snow Time also operated two 18-hole golf courses and a 20,000-square-foot conference center at Liberty, plus more than 20 F&B locations across the three resorts. It generated $50 million in revenue and about $11 million in EBITDA for the 12 months ending March 31, 2018, so the multiple was 6.8x. These smaller, non-destination resorts simply don't demand the kind of multiples we're seeing out west (10x or more). That doesn't mean that the math doesn't work. Boyd got a good deal.

"The transformative acquisition offers a rare opportunity for Peak Resorts to dramatically grow by expanding the number of resort destinations for our Peak Pass holders in the Northeast, while growing our presence in the very attractive and densely populated markets of Baltimore and Washington, D.C.," Boyd said. He praised Snow Time's legacy and deemed the resorts "exceptionally well-cared for," adding he expected the bottom-line benefits to accrue "immediately" with the 2018–19 season.

Snow Time, Inc., headquartered in York, Pennsylvania, was founded by Irv Naylor in 1964 to develop Ski Roundtop. In this sense, Snow Time began much like Peak, with one small, urban resort and a lot of passion for the sport. Naylor was an accomplished horseman, an amateur steeplechase rider, the owner of racehorses, and an avid skier who regularly attended heli-ski camps. His business interests included significant real-estate holdings in the York area and ownership of a corrugated-box manufacturing company, Cor-Box Inc. Naylor acquired Liberty Mountain Resort in 1974 and Whitetail Resort in

1999. The three resorts served skier markets in Maryland, northern Virginia, Pennsylvania, and Washington, D.C. All offered a full range of skier services, and Liberty provided four-season amenities, including golf, a hotel, and conference facilities. From 1981 until 2005, Naylor also owned Windham Mountain in New York. Windham is very close to Hunter Mountain, so Naylor would have been very familiar with Hunter's challenges and the changes brought by Peak ownership. Naylor's Snow Time resorts were respected within the industry as well-managed businesses.

I had the pleasure of working with Naylor on both the NSAA and USIA boards in the 1980s. Some of my fondest memories are of traveling to Europe with him as part of an NSAA junket (touring resorts, lift companies, and such). He had a tough, challenging intellect with high expectations from everyone he worked with and little patience for anything "average." Travelling with Irv was never boring.

In 1999 he was seriously injured in a horse-riding accident, which resulted in significant paralysis. Although he regained some use of his arms, there was little further progress, and he has remained in a wheelchair since that date. Cor-Box Inc. was sold in late 1999.

The accident must have been devastating to a man with such business and athletic passions. How he continued to function at such a high level and maintain a positive attitude is credit to his innate toughness. His wife, Diane, has stood by him through all the challenges. Theirs is clearly a very special relationship.

About 40 years ago, Naylor transferred ownership of the company to his three grandchildren in what would have been a very advantageous tax transaction for them. All were probably younger than 10 years old. He probably hoped that they would eventually take over the operations. His grandson, Chet, spent several seasons working at Steamboat in mountain operations, learning the ropes. He then worked at all three of the Snow Time areas but, apparently, never wanted more responsibility.

After Peak's purchase of Hunter, Snow Time and Peak executives began talking. According to Naylor, after several months of mutual tire-kicking, Peak made the $76 million offer. That valuation stunned Naylor. He brought it to his grandchildren, now all in their 30s and 40s, who then made the decision to sell. Conventional wisdom would have it that at 82 and still confined to his wheelchair, Naylor was ready to sell. The reality may be quite different. He remains passionate about the business. He expressed to me his hope that the now-grown grandchildren would be engaged in the resorts and not interested in selling. Had he retained some ownership percentage, he probably would have worked to decline the sale (author's opinion here).

At a high level, the Snow Time resorts bring some $49.4 million in revenue and $11.1 million in EBITDA to Peak. The deal closed prior to the start of the 2018–19 ski season and will bring an additional 600,000 skier visits to Peak. This represents dramatic growth in the company's Northeast operation. It adds three more destinations to the Peak Pass lineup and extends the company's reach deep into the Baltimore and Washington D.C. markets.

This transaction also significantly expands Peak Resort's scale. Here are the updated metrics: 17 resorts, 164 lifts, $181 million in annual revenue and $36.7 million in EBITDA. Unquestionably, the purchase will drive pass sales and visitation to their resorts across the region. Given Peak's focus on operational efficiency, there will probably be cost savings from new management protocols, centralized purchasing, and reduced corporate overhead (as a percentage of sales).

With all these acquisitions, Peak is prospering. On May 10, 2019, the company announced: "Consolidated initial sales for Peak Resorts 2019–20 season pass products increased 20.8 percent on a unit basis and 19.8 percent on a dollar basis over the prior year through the springtime sales window, inclusive of Snow Time (Liberty, Roundtop, and Whitetail in Pennsylvania) pass sales in both periods.

"The sales results include the flagship Peak Pass family of products, which, starting in 2019–20, will provide unlimited access to 14 of the company's ski areas [author's note: the pass does not include Boyd's original Missouri and Indiana resorts]; the additions of the Snow Time resorts as well as the company's four Ohio ski areas double the number of areas available on the pass, from seven areas last year.

"To serve the expanded number of passholders, work has already started on approximately $3.5 million in upgrades to the snowmaking infrastructure at Liberty Mountain, Whitetail, and Roundtop. The investments will increase pump power and water capacity and add new state-of-the-art snowguns to improve energy efficiency and overall snowmaking capabilities."

So, the 14 Peak areas were now 17. It was a collection of resorts with broad appeal that could compete regionally with Epic and Ikon, especially if the buyer had no plans to travel west. Peak's strategy was to motivate mid-Atlantic passholders to head north for long weekends or midweek adventures at resorts like Hunter, Mount Snow, or Attitash. For former passholders at one of the three Snow Time resorts, being able to head north adds a week at each end of the season.

So that was the situation in mid-summer 2019, with Peak an important player, touching hundreds of thousands of guests, introducing many new skiers and riders to the sport, and finding a way to transform resorts that might have been considered marginal into performing assets. This was good for the ski industry.

It also became appealing for Vail Resorts, whose $264-million agreement represented a 116-percent premium on the stock price. It was a big payoff for the Boyd family, for top managers who held options, and for shareholders.

"We are very proud of our track record over the last two decades in building the breadth, quality and accessibility of our resorts," Boyd said of the sale. "We are thrilled that our guests will now have access to some of the world's most renowned resorts.

"Vail Resorts has a proven track record of celebrating the unique identity of its resorts, while continually investing in the guest and employee experience. For this reason, we are confident that our resorts and employees will continue to thrive within the Vail Resorts network."

When the transaction closes this fall, the 2019–20 Epic Pass, Epic Local Pass and Military Epic Pass will include unlimited and unrestricted access to the 17 Peak Resorts ski areas. Guests with an Epic Day Pass will also be able to access the new ski areas as a part of the total number of days purchased. For the 2019–20 season, Vail Resorts will honor and continue to sell all Peak Resorts pass products, and Peak Resorts' pass holders will have the option to upgrade to an Epic Pass or Epic Local Pass, following closing of the transaction.

Vail also said it would add $10 million annually to its CapEx budget for the new resorts, and spend $15 million in one-time capital improvements over the next two years. The company will no doubt face new challenges in aligning these resorts with the high bar it has set for the guest experience. It will also likely rely on its deep bench of managerial talent to fill, as needed, top positions in the former Peak portfolio.

While Vail and Alterra have few new avenues for growth in the domestic destination category, this gives Vail a growth opportunity in a segment where there is a long runway. Importantly, when you look at the long-term prospects for the ski industry, Peak's ski areas provide the feeder ground from which generations of new skiers are created and then disembark, headed eventually to the destination resorts of the Rockies. The success of operators like Peak is intimately connected to the long-term health of Vail, and in hindsight, the acquisition seems like a no brainer. The majority of Peak's customers haven't historically traveled west, but with an Epic Pass in hand that could well change. Vail, and Alterra, for that matter, have reached a size and scope where a large part of their future success depends on bringing new skiers to the sport. This looks like a win-win, and another interesting new chapter in this unprecedented story of resort consolidation.

CHAPTER 9

Mini-Majors Prosper on Best Practices, Shared Overhead

The key to success in today's ski business is "be profitable." There are many reasons for the steady enhancement of operating margins, and the new pass-pricing model is clearly a major component. In addition, acquisitions have been a key strategy for the big guys, reducing fixed costs and leveraging best practices. But the same principle operates on a smaller scale as well. A collection of smaller resorts can distribute and minimize overhead costs, and improve margins. I've already discussed the two Mid-Majors and the former Mid-Major (Boyne, POWDR, and Peak). There are several others, I call them "Mini-Majors," that are evolving in a similar fashion.

Mont Saint-Sauveur (MSS), located about an hour's drive west of Montreal, has been a leader in the Canadian ski industry for decades. It is often referred to as "the home of Quebec skiing." The Laurentian region boasts a large number of ski areas in close proximity to each other and the Montreal metro area. MSS differentiated itself by the scale of its night-skiing operations and its brilliantly lighted trails. When I first experienced their product in the 1980s, it changed my view of night skiing. You could actually see where you were going.

To leverage its location in a major metro area, MSS developed one of the largest summer attractions/water parks in the region. Over time, under the leadership of Jacques Hébert, MSS acquired five neighboring ski areas, plus Vermont's Jay Peak in 1978. Jay was sold in 2008 to a partnership led by Miami investor Ariel Quiros. (The new Jay Peak owners have had a rough go; they were sued for fraud in misuse of EB-5 immigrant-investor funds by individual investors and the SEC. Jay Peak is in receivership, and the receiver, attorney Michael Goldberg, is suing Mont Saint-Sauveur for "knowingly and improperly accepting $15 million in EB-5 funds from Miami businessman Ariel Quiros for Jay Peak in 2008." Whether the suit has merit or not was unresolved at the time of writing.)

Hébert passed away in 2006, and chairmanship passed to industry veteran Louis Dufour, whose family now has a controlling interest in the company. In 2016, it was rebranded as Les Sommets, and it still controls the largest number of ski resorts in Quebec (they are called "stations" up there). Besides Saint-Sauveur, these include Avila, Edelweiss, Olympia, Gabriel and Morin Heights. I couldn't find any information relative to an "all-area" pass, but a search of the website shows exceptional deals for passes at the individual resorts, priced relative to the size of each. Les Sommets is investing approximately $16 million Canadian in 2018 and 2019 at Saint-Sauveur and its adjacent learning hill, versant Avila, financed in part by the province-wide Tourisme Québec funding initiative, according to *SAM*. The investment is paying off: Les Sommets won the NSAA's Conversion Cup in 2019 for its excellence in teaching the sport to newcomers. The MSS story is a reminder that the consolidation trends we have been studying do not respect borders. MSS is a large, successful, independent and regionally significant player. Quebec's 75 ski areas recorded 6.4 million skier visits in 2018–19, a 10-year high.

Resorts of the Canadian Rockies (RCR) is an even stronger performer among private North American ski resort operators, with six diverse resorts across Canada. Of the mini-majors covered in this chapter, it's likely the largest in terms of skier visits.

RCR was founded by Charlie Locke, the acclaimed climber and mountaineer turned businessman, who was involved in the startup of Lake Louise in the 1970s and became its sole owner in 1981. The resort is often ranked just below Whistler in Canada, offering some 4,200 acres of terrain and unparalleled scenery. It was Locke's dream to build a resort conglomerate, and he succeeded in adding seven resorts to his initial Lake Louise holding. Facing financial troubles in 2001, RCR was refinanced by Calgary businessman Murray Edwards, whose other properties include the Calgary Flames.

Lake Louise is, ironically, not a part of the RCR lineup today (while Locke is now back as its owner). The RCR name is a bit of a misnomer in that the far-flung empire includes Mont-Sainte-Anne and Stoneham Mountain Resort in Quebec as well as Fernie Alpine Resort, Kicking Horse Mountain Resort and Kimberley Alpine Resort in B.C., plus Nakiska Ski Area in Calgary.

RCR joined the Epic Pass for the 2018–19 season, with up to seven days at its resorts on the full Epic and no blackouts, dramatically strengthening Vail Resorts' footprint beyond Whistler in Canada. RCR continues to sell a pass good at all its resorts, which was priced at $1,399 CDN for fall purchase for 2019–20.

Kicking Horse and Fernie are the biggest draws: Both are legendary for their light powder and big mountain skiing, with impressive vertical drops of 4,133 and 3,555 feet, respectively. Kicking Horse gets 444 inches of snow annually. Kimberly is located in the Purcells, just north of the border and within driving distance of Washington, Idaho and Montana. Nakiska, 45 miles west of Calgary, hosted the alpine events for the 1988 Calgary Olympics. Both Mont St. Anne and Stoneham are a short drive from Quebec City and, accordingly, boast huge night-skiing operations. RCR was a major addition for Epic, and a smart move for RCR to spread word of its quality resort lineup to the U.S.

One small, multi-area holding company in the U.S. of note is Wisconsin Resorts, Inc. (formerly known as Alpine Valley Holdings). This is privately held and affiliated with JFK Investment Company, a Detroit-based investment company that specializes in real-estate development, asset management, leasing, and consulting. Portfolio resorts include Alpine Valley in Wisconsin and three Michigan resorts: Pine Knob, Mt. Holly, and Bittersweet. In November 2018, the company added Searchmont, Ontario, and committed to a $750,000 snowmaking investment there.

Put together a collection of small, urban-ish resorts and enhance the snowmaking—sound familiar?

WE MENTIONED EARLIER THE ARRIVAL OF JAMES H. COLEMAN as managing partner and CEO of Mountain Capital Partners (MCP). He's operated under the national radar but has been involved in the ski business since 2000, when he became managing partner of Sipapu Ski and Summer Resort near Taos. Sipapu is reported to be the state's fastest-growing ski resort. Coleman has more than 30 years of investment and development experience and is focused on resort opportunities in the Southwest. His portfolio also includes Pajarito Mountain Ski Area in Los Alamos, New Mexico; Purgatory Resort in Durango, Colorado, and the nearby Hesperus Ski Area; Arizona Snowbowl in Flagstaff and Elk Ridge Ski Area in Williams, Arizona; and Nordic Valley in Eden, Utah.

According to published accounts, Coleman and his partners have invested up to $30 million to acquire the resorts and have made material investments recently (a new detachable quad at the Snowbowl). Coleman developed his connections and significant investor base at Texas Capital Partners. A key company tenet is "family affordability." With the new investments and pricing, Southwestern skiers are enjoying great deals and something of a renaissance at their resorts. As reported in the April 11, 2019 edition of *SAM* Headline News: "Last year (2017–18) we did the best we could with what we had," said Coleman. "But this winter? It's like every day is a celebration. Guests are loving it."

The company's website announces, "MCP is committed to growing our community of outdoor enthusiasts by consistently and dramatically improving the offerings and experience at each of our resorts, accelerating winter and summer visits, and driving revenue growth at existing resorts, while acquiring new resorts that add strategic value." Case in point: MCP's Arizona Snow Bowl announced in June a plan to spend $60 million over the next 10–15 years on new lifts, trails, facilities and night skiing.

Although this is clearly a for-profit company, it is also value-driven. Following the acquisition of tiny Hesperus, Coleman said: "One of our top priorities is to make skiing more accessible and affordable to families." So here's a new player with plans to energize skiing in the southwest. Welcome aboard!

BRIAN FAIRBANK, A WESTERN NEW YORK NATIVE, was 23 years old and working as the ski school director at the Wintergreen Resort in Virginia when he got a call that, he says, changed his life. It was regarding a managerial position at Jiminy Peak, located in the Berkshires of western Massachusetts. He leaped at the opportunity. That was 1969. And the rest, as they say, is history. Fairbank rose through the ranks and eventually became owner. He has been at Jiminy's helm for more than 40 years.

In 2008, he joined forces with his son, Tyler, to create a renewable-energy enterprise, EOS Ventures. Facing a spike in energy costs, they installed a 253-foot-high, $4.5 million wind turbine near Jiminy's summit, the first at a U.S.

ski resort. Dubbed the Zephyr, it paid for itself in seven years and became an iconic symbol at the resort.

Meanwhile, the father-son partnership, the Fairbank Group, LLC, expanded in the following years as they acquired Cranmore Mountain in North Conway, New Hampshire, and took over management of Vermont's Bromley Mountain (owned by Brian's longtime friend and business partner Joe O'Donnell, former CEO of Boston Culinary Group).

They also started a snow-gun sales and distribution company called Snowgun Technologies. As a hands-on operator, Brian knows how important efficient snowmaking is to a ski area's success. He has incorporated his new gun technology into the Jiminy operation and is reaping the benefits of lower costs and improved snow quality. He is also a great believer in staff training and motivation, and he practices as well as preaches a training culture. He and Tyler have leveraged this strength into a company called Bullwheel Productions that provides online training courses, primarily directed at the ski industry (such as lift operations).

Jiminy is a little gem. A modest but well-designed real-estate development at the base area provides 1,244 bedrooms for short-term rental. There's a conference center and a number of summer attractions to keep the resort energized much of the year.

This is clearly a value-driven company with environmental sensitivity, a supportive staff/management culture, an emphasis on creativity and industry leadership. Jiminy has enjoyed remarkable success for a ski resort doing an average of 200,000 skier visits in a relatively remote area of the Berkshires, always in the shadow of its larger Vermont neighbors. Jiminy belongs to the Mountains of Distinction (discussed earlier) but does not sell a Jiminy/Cranmore/Bromley pass (except for the Jiminy Peak College Pass). Adapting to the modern Internet era, Jiminy offers variable pricing on lift tickets purchased online.

You might think all would be rosy in terms of the future from Brian's perspective, but he is anxious. He sees the arrival of multiarea passes in New England as a real threat. For a Jiminy passholder who might be thinking about a trip out West, there are now some options to consider versus the Jiminy pass. While the number of skiers heading westbound isn't high, it's just one more challenge in terms of maintaining his skier base. At Cranmore, he's seeing impact from the Peak Pass, which provides access to competitors Attitash and

Wildcat, that also serve the North Conway market. Cranmore has an ideal location, being essentially in "downtown" North Conway, but it lacks size and variety compared to its neighbors. With the Peak acquisition, the Epic Pass poses an existential threat not just to Cranmore, but to Jiminy as well.

BRIAN SOLD JIMINY IN 2009 TO CNL, but then entered into a long-term lease. The underlying assets were later sold to Oz Real Estate, which as of December 2018 had disposed of all the former CNL resort properties except Jiminy and Sierra-at-Tahoe. Brian succeeded in re-acquiring the Jiminy resort in early 2019. So despite his concerns, he moved forward with a significant investment in Jiminy's future.

The Fairbank Group has done all the right things in terms of a successful ski resort business model: enhanced snowmaking; product-line diversification; and multiple resorts to spread overhead. Bromley has always had to duke it out with the larger Vermont resorts, but now faces a new competitive risk: Virtually all are affiliated with one or another of the major pass products (Epic, Ikon, or Peak). Jiminy seems to have a strong enough brand to survive, but the future could be more challenging for Cranmore and Bromley.

Time will tell if Brian can succeed independently. Would Vail or Alterra consider adding mid-sized regional resorts like these to their passes? Are there other potential buyers? One thing's for sure. The next few years will be anything but boring for Brian and Tyler.

MY ORIGINAL INTEREST IN WRITING THIS BOOK was driven by the continuing expansion of Vail Resorts and the arrival of Alterra, but my research kept turning up incredible stories about what was happening on the margins, particularly with small and medium-sized resorts, such as Resorts of the Canadian Rockies; Les Sommets in Quebec; the Fairbank Group; Mountain Capital Partners; and Peak Resorts before the sale. That is the space where these competitors have chosen to play. They have no desire to compete against the big guys.

I had never heard of Pacific Group Resorts Inc. (PGRI) until Andy Daly gave me the news in the fall of 2018 that he had signed a management agreement with them for Powderhorn near Grand Junction in Colorado, which he owned along with Tom and Ken Gart. Daly said he had been negotiating for some 18 months with Vern Greco, a longtime industry executive, who had joined forces with the PGRI principals. Greco had been president/GM of

Steamboat, Park City, and Durango/Purgatory; COO of POWDR, and is now PGRI's president and CEO.

The majority owner of PGRI is Doug Anderson, a Salt Lake City–based real-estate developer, with a résumé that includes a number of resort base-area projects. The story of PGRI, as Greco related, was something of a series of accidental coincidences. Anderson had discovered Ragged Mountain, a small ski area in New Hampshire with lots of developable land. He purchased it as a troubled asset in 2006, mostly as a real-estate play. The recession hit, and he was left with a small, functioning ski area and lots of real estate for which there was no clear future.

To help him figure out the best future for Ragged, he engaged Mark Fischer, a marketing professional headquartered in Park City. As their relationship was developing (Fischer became a partner in the firm), the Wisp ski resort in Maryland became available via an auction in 2012. Fischer went to the auction representing PGRI and found that their competition was the heavyweight EPR Properties, a large REIT that was now collecting ski resorts in the CNL mode and providing financing to the ski industry. EPR got the resort at auction and then asked PGRI to run it for them under a long-term lease.

That's when Greco was brought in to help, first as a consultant and then on the payroll as president and CEO. Their small corporate office is in Park City. They acquired the lease at Wintergreen Resort in Virginia from EPR and brought in Rod Kessler, a Stowe and Revelstoke veteran, to run the operation. In 2016, they acquired the Mount Washington resort located on Vancouver Island, British Columbia. (How many ski areas do you access by water taxi?) Mount Washington receives an extraordinary amount of snow, reportedly the most in B.C. It is medium-sized (approximately 200,000 visits) and in terms of natural beauty, it's tough to beat. Snowmaking is a challenge given the high humidity and marginal temperatures that come with a maritime climate.

In the fall of 2018, the company entered into a long-term lease with Andy Daly and his partners, the Gart brothers, for their Powderhorn resort. Daly described the agreement as "mission affordable." PGRI was expected to bring a discipline to the operation that would produce improved results and reduce their risk. One can only assume that eventually there will be a sale to PGRI. This latest agreement brings the portfolio to five, with more certainly on the way.

Greco wants to avoid knocking heads with the big guys. Pretty much all the "A" resorts have been acquired, and those that remain are generally well-run. He sees little opportunity there to improve margins and enhance value. The same is not true when you look at the next tier, what he calls the "B" resorts. In many cases, these have been in the same family for a long time and are managed according to an archaic business model. The next generation simply doesn't have the same passion for the business as the original founders. Often, there's a lot of deferred maintenance, and the overall ski experience has suffered. So it's time to sell. There are buyers now.

PGRI has the capacity to deal with immediate issues, whether safety-related or experiential, and then take a longer look at what needs to happen to create a sustainable business model. Given that these can be significant investments, the acquisition cost has to be "reasonable." Greco believes it's important to make an immediate change in the experience so guests understand that "there's a path forward." In some cases, this might mean emphasizing summer business. Immediate attention goes to food and beverage, rental operations, and such. For many of these "B" resorts, it has probably been a long time since rental inventory or cooking equipment was updated. When the menu transitions from burgers and chili to fresher, healthier options, the guests notice. The company has also developed metrics in terms of operating costs, and although each ski area has its unique set of circumstances, bringing costs closer to traditional operating metrics can quickly improve EBITDA. Vern Greco has a well-deserved reputation for being able to ferret out unnecessary costs.

PGRI is trying to develop a sort of "hybrid" centralization model for their corporate office. "Size matters," he says, so there are some elements of purchasing that need to be centralized to realize savings, but this will be done thoughtfully, watching costs, and leaving most decisions to the local management team.

I began this book talking about changes in the typical ski resort's business model. The main reason Alterra and Vail Resorts have invested so heavily in this relatively small corner of the recreation/travel business is that it is or can be profitable. The biggest challenge ski areas face is deferred maintenance, given the capital-intensive nature of the business. This remains one of Vail's core strengths and competitive advantages. Now the rest of the industry is reorganizing itself to improve profitability and create a sustainable future. PGRI is one fascinating example of how this is playing out.

CHAPTER 10

Combos:

Joining Forces to Survive, Thrive

For ski areas struggling for market share in a highly competitive market, a sale or combination with a competitor is often the best way forward. Overhead costs can be shared, and the new entity gets the benefits of scale. These smaller combos actually mimic the ownership model of some of the larger resorts, where nearby competitors joined forces: Killington/Pico; Keystone/Breckenridge; Vail/Beaver Creek; Park City/Canyons; Bear Mountain/Snow Summit; Squaw/Alpine and so on.

As the ski industry grew rapidly in the 1960s and '70s, there were many areas of the country that were just overbuilt in terms of the number of ski areas. New York has more "lost ski areas" than any other state. That said, most were very small, community hills, without snowmaking, which made them victims of climate change. In the Cortland/Syracuse area, there were several ski areas that went out of business post-boom, including Intermont, an upside-down ski area (parking/base lodge at the top). Central New York enjoys a robust college ski market, but the region is prone to challenging weather and has seen a material exodus of industry and, therefore, population. For those ski areas still operating, it's a tough, highly competitive market.

Greek Peak in Cortland has been around for some 60 years and is the largest ski resort in this region. While it often handled more than 200,000 skier visits a year and had a robust summer-activities program, Greek Peak was marginally profitable, stumbling from one economic crisis to another. In April 2013, it got new owners, Elmira businessmen Marc Stemerman and John Meier. The partners were able to purchase it out of bankruptcy for $7.5 million. According to reports, they shared a passion for the sport and were committed to enhancing the recreational opportunities for residents and, thereby, the region's overall quality of life. They became known as the "Saviors of Greek Peak." Since their purchase, they have invested more than the acquisition cost in improving the facility, including installing the region's first quad chair and replacing the restaurant/bar. The partners took advantage of a matching grant program offered by New York's energy research and development agency (NYSERDA) and purchased 68 low-energy/high-efficiency snow-guns. Enhanced snowmaking improves the overall experience and lessens economic risk.

On August 26, 2015, the partners entered into an asset purchase agreement to acquire the neighboring Toggenburg Mountain Winter Sports Center, a smaller facility but one that records about 100,000 visits a year. The combination of these two hills improved their competitive position in the Syracuse market. Toggenburg's owner, Jim Hickey, had acquired the resort from his father. It had been in the family since 1954. Hickey, known for his passion for food, was to continue operating the Foggy Goggle at Toggenburg and provide F&B leadership to Greek Peak. Sounds like a commitment to end greasy burgers. According to published statements from the partners: "We're really just excited to continue to make Central New York a better place for our families."

The joint-pass product they brought to market was designed to compete with one offered by Song Mountain Resort and Labrador Mountain. These had combined in September 2014. In that case, two longtime competitors simply merged into a new corporate entity. Peter Harris, president of Song, became president and GM of the new entity. They launched the Inter-Mountain Passport. As Harris put it: "You will literally get two mountains for the price of one." The joint-pass product was an immediate hit in the market, and no doubt incentivized the Greek Peak owners to move quickly with Toggenburg. So where there had been four competing businesses, there were now two. These new entities certainly have a brighter future thanks to enhanced profitability and strengthened balance sheets. What is happening here is reflective of other trends we have been studying. New investment brings an improved experience. The value and flexibility of the joint passes drives visitation. Win-

win—and not just for skiers and ski area operators. Given the values and interests of the Greek Peak partners, this new energy should flow to the larger central New York region in an outsized way.

The last few years have seen quite the flurry of combinations similar to those described above. In spring 2019, CMR Lands, LLC, the owner of Silver Mountain Resort in northwestern Idaho, bought 49° North Mountain Resort, just a two-plus-hour drive away in northeast Washington. They immediately debuted a combo pass, $459 for adults and $329 for children. Spokane skiers can now drive an hour east or north to take advantage of the two options.

In Michigan's Upper Peninsula, Blackjack Mountain Resort acquired Indianhead and in 2014 merged into a new entity: Big Snow Resort. They are separated by only five miles and offer complimentary shuttles between the two. Their goal: to create a single ski and snowboard resort experience, which now offers 15 lifts on 410 skiable acres, three terrain parks, and roughly 200 inches of annual snowfall.

Rick Schmitz once served as the general manager of Blackjack, in the early portion of his growing ski industry résumé. He grew up with his brothers, skiing at Little Switzerland, which opened in 1941, in Slinger, Wisconsin, just outside Milwaukee and a little more than a four-hour drive south from the Big Snow resorts in the Upper Peninsula. Schmitz became so enamored with the ski industry that, after graduating from college, he dreamed of owning a resort. At age 22, he wrote a business plan, with a foundation of improved snowmaking, to secure a loan and purchase Nordic Mountain in Wild Rose, Wisconsin, 90-minutes north of Milwaukee, in 2005.

Meanwhile, Little Switzerland shut down in 2007. Schmitz, with his brothers Mike and Dave, eventually bought and reopened the area for the 2012–13 season. They spent $1 million updating the lifts, snowmaking, and grooming, and another $1 million was spent remodeling the lodge.

"We invest very heavily in snowmaking and grooming because higher-quality snow and better conditions means a more ideal experience for our customers," Rick Schmitz explained in a small business profile published by his lender, First National Bank. Sound familiar?

Mike Schmitz, a builder accustomed to navigating the loan process, was surprised that several banks initially turned the brothers down before linking up with First National; the ski area was viewed as a risky, weather-dependent startup. The operation quickly blew past its growth goals, and the brothers soon learned that the area's goodwill with local customers had remained strong, even during the five years it was shuttered.

Schmitz Brothers LLC has since taken over operations of another Milwaukee-area ski hill, the Rock Snow Park in Franklin, which was long known as Crystal Ridge. It is part of a four-season complex owned by ROC Ventures that is developing a Ballpark Commons (to attract a minor-league baseball team) and related developments, including housing. When ROC saw what the Schmitz brothers accomplished at Little Switzerland, they were recruited to take over management of the ski hill, according to a July 2017 report in the *Milwaukee Journal Sentinel.*

The Schmitz trio moved quickly, replacing an old chairlift that had proved unreliable with a high-speed rope tow, and restoring snowmaking to the entire complex. And, of course, the Rock season pass now provides access to Little Switzerland and vice versa; it also includes Nordic Mountain for a small upcharge.

In 2013, western Pennsylvania giant Seven Springs acquired neighbor Hidden Valley. The two ski areas are only 13 miles apart. Hidden Valley markets itself as a "family destination" with 11 lifts, 29 trails, and a respectable 470 vertical feet of skiing. The area now operates the nation's largest fully automatic Techno-Alpin snowmaking installation. Joint-pass products followed the acquisition.

One of the early western Massachusetts ski areas was the G-Bar-S Ranch, which opened in 1936. It enjoyed a somewhat up-and-down history until Channing and Jane Murdock purchased it in August 1962. Almost immediately, they signed a contract for a new double chairlift and opened as Butternut Basin— basically a new ski area—in December 1963. Channing, a Middlebury graduate, had learned the ropes from ski legend Walt Schoenknecht at his Mohawk Mountain ski area in Connecticut (Walt was also the founder of Mount Snow).

The Murdocks ran an absolutely first-class operation. They were personal friends with the Kennedys, who often visited the ski area and lent it a celebrity vibe. Channing was deeply involved in industry governance, serving on the NSAA board as its chairman. In 1994, he suffered a tragic injury while cycling, which left him with permanent brain damage. His son, Jeff, took over the family business and maintained the historic popularity of Butternut despite some setbacks from natural disasters.

Massachusetts has a rich and lengthy ski history, with several areas that trace their history back to the '30s. (*Skiing in Massachusetts*, a book on the state's rich history by Cal Conniff and E. John B. Allen, is available on Amazon and worth your time.) Many of these were small, rope-tow-type operations that went by the wayside when the ski boom of the 1960s–'70s passed and weather became more erratic. More than a hundred areas closed. One was Berkshire Snow Basin, where I learned to ski in the '50s.

Otis Ridge opened in 1947, with a handful of trails serviced by rope tows. By 2011, it was struggling to survive, and little investment had occurred to maintain or update the facility. Jeff Murdock's Butternut Basin was literally next door. Concerned about the small area's future, he provided a second mortgage in 2011 to keep the facility operating. But by 2016, Otis Ridge faced foreclosure. Murdock stepped in and invested an additional $195,000. Other notes were discharged, and his Otis Ridge Properties LLC took over at the end of 2016. Otis Ridge is back in business with day- and night-skiing, a small but important regional ski area. A season pass goes for about $200. And day tickets are a real deal.

Just a few months later, Murdock acquired Blandford Ski Area. Blandford, just off the Massachusetts Turnpike, west of Springfield, opened in 1936. It was owned by the Springfield Ski Club, which in its heyday had almost 5,000 members. This was a veritable learn-to-ski factory. But by 2016, membership had dwindled to fewer than 1,000, and the Club found itself unable to continue operations. As you can imagine, there was considerable deferred maintenance on the facilities, including the three double chairlifts. Blandford had a limited vertical of 465 feet, but that served very user-friendly terrain. Murdock stepped in and acquired the area from the Club for $269,000 in 2017. He closed it for a year to deal with significant deferred maintenance issues, particularly on the lifts, then re-opened in December 2018 with updated facilities and improved snowmaking. The website says, "We're Back."

Dick McCann, the GM of Ski Butternut, said at the time of purchase: "We want to build the skier base back up. And we care very much about making skiing affordable. We think the ski industry is better for having these small ski areas."

So here are two small areas that certainly would have joined the heap of "lost ski areas" were it not for the vision and financial resources of a new owner. Guest comments on the websites are over the top, and speak to the quality of the experience and the value. Season passes are around $200, and day tickets are incredibly affordable. Skier visits are on the rise, and the future clearly looks bright for all three of Murdock's ski areas. More investment will likely follow—better insurance, via expanded snowmaking, against bad weather. We've seen this model work time and time again, despite the powerhouse conglomerates and their mega-passes. These skiers may eventually get to a Vail or Deer Valley. For now, they're very happy at these Massachusetts ski areas!

Channing Murdock would be proud. This is his, and Jane's and Jeff's, Butternut legacy.

IN MAY 2018, THE SCHAEFER FAMILY, owners of Berkshire East Mountain Resort in Charlemont, Massachusetts, purchased Catamount, which straddles the border between Massachusetts and New York. Catamount, a 385-acre property, had invested recently in summer attractions, and the Schaefers plan to focus on year-round operations at both resorts.

In July 2018, R.L.K. and Company, which operates Oregon's Timberline Lodge and adjacent ski facilities, purchased Summit Ski Area, in Government Camp, Oregon. Summit, which began operation in 1927, is the oldest continuously operating ski area in the Pacific Northwest. Timberline and Summit are only one-mile apart, and they may eventually be connected by ski lift. Jeff Kohnstamm, the president of R.L.K., commented: "We are very pleased with the acquisition and plan to operate Summit as a family-oriented, friendly mountain resort ... and break down the barriers to skiing and snowboarding surrounding accessibility and affordability." Sounds remarkably like the operating philosophy articulated by Mountain Capital Partners principal James Coleman and Jeff Murdock. For Kohnstamm, this appears to be a logical but value-driven acquisition.

The common themes that run through the stories noted above: a passion for the sport, concerns over accessibility and affordability, a family-friendly focus, value-priced tickets, joint-pass products, and a focus on financial sustainability—and always snowmaking.

CHAPTER 11

Last of the Independents
Standing Strong

The best "Indies" share several traits in common, starting with owners who aren't primarily motivated by shareholders, investors, or profit margin. Sun Valley, Jackson Hole, Alta, Telluride, and Taos all have owners who march to a different drummer, bringing another layer of diversity and flavor to the resort fabric. These resorts tend to be remote, and—with their history and authenticity—they are hugely popular within their loyal constituencies, though it should also be noted that most of them don't top the charts in terms of skier visits, falling primarily in the 250,000-to-500,000 range, with one notable exception. But tellingly, they dominate the customer-driven popularity polls. Telluride has been named the No. 1 resort in North America by *Condé Nast Traveler* for six of the past seven years, and was crowned No. 1 by *USA Today* for the 2018–19 season. Jackson Hole was voted No. 1 by *SKI* readers for 2013–14, and was tops in the Z Rankings (in conjunction with *Forbes*) for the 2018–19 season. Sun Valley often appears in the top three, including in *SKI's* new Best of the West ranking for 2018–19, and Taos Ski Valley usually outperforms its weight class in the popularity polls.

Taos, nestled in the Sangre *de Cristo Mountains* in New Mexico, was founded in 1955 by the legendary Ernie Blake. It remained in his family's hands until 2013, when they sold the resort to billionaire hedge-fund manager Louis Bacon. Known for his conservation ethic, as well as his financial skills,

Bacon had owned land at the ski area's base since 1996, and more recently had partnered with the Blakes in master-planning the base area. In 2007, he purchased the 175,000-acre Trinchera Blanca Ranch in Colorado's San Luis Valley from the Malcolm Forbes family for $174 million. Significant portions of that property have since been placed in perpetual conservation easements. In 2013, he announced a deal with Colorado Open Lands to place 21,000 acres of his Tercio Red River Ranch into conservation easements. If those actions weren't enough to establish his environmental credentials, he has been a significant supporter of the Colorado Coalition of Land Trusts, the Rio Grande Headwaters Land Trust and the Taos Land Trust.

A number of potential buyers had approached the Blakes, but they reportedly reached out to Bacon because of his interest in sustainability and his vision for Taos Ski Valley's future. In 2012, the USFS approved the resort's updated master plan, which calls for a 60 percent increase in skiable terrain. It also authorizes a number of on-mountain and skier-service improvements. Having this approval in place was critical to bringing Taos into the modern era. To say that its infrastructure needed updating would be quite the understatement.

The owner's challenge: How to walk that fine line between maintaining its independent character and low-key vibe (helped no doubt by the fact that skier visits had tumbled from a high of 364,000 in 1993–94 to approximately 230,000 in recent years) and enhancing its facilities to meet current guest expectations. Shortly after the sale, the new ownership group announced a $300-million overhaul. The base area has seen the addition of The Blake, an 80-room, luxury hotel with a first-class art collection (it had an impressive 80 percent occupancy rate for the 2018–19 winter), plus enhancements to children's facilities, restrooms and dining areas. On the mountain, two new lifts have been installed, the most recent being a detachable quad for the 2018–19 ski season. Snowmaking facilities continue to be improved to support a sustainable business model. New summer activities, such as downhill mountain biking, are being added to broaden year-round appeal.

"We are independent" is the message that dominates anything to do with the Taos brand. Although in a concession to the reality of modern ski-pass wars, Taos has joined the Mountain Collective and is now a partner resort on the Ikon Pass. Independence can't fly in the face of reason. New Mexico's eight resorts broke the 1 million-skier-visit-mark for 2018–19, the best season in 21 years, and the growth at Taos was certainly a major contributor.

Outside magazine identified Taos as "one of the top 10 eco-friendly ski resorts in the U.S.," and it is the first ski resort in the world designated as a "B Corp," a strict certification process that measures a for-profit company's social and environmental performance, ranging from employee benefits to energy and waste reduction.

Taos is putting a new spin on ski resort "direct flight" programs. The company purchased a plane and began its own charter operation for 2018–19, with service from Austin and Dallas.

The Taos renaissance will be fascinating to watch. One recent article spoke to the growth in visits from Colorado skiers, who like the resort's environmental ethic. The qualitative enhancements will certainly improve the resort's competitive position in New Mexico.

One thing is sure: Having an owner with deep pockets and the long view is a huge advantage when coming out of a disastrous winter, such as the 2017–18 season, when the Southwest experienced unusually dry and warm weather. Given Louis Bacon's resources and commitment, Taos is likely to regain its former prominence as an iconic ski destination. It's on my bucket list.

WHICH IS A GOOD SEGUE to perhaps the most iconic of independents: Sun Valley. In the long and storied history of American skiing, there's the Sun Valley story—and then there's everybody else. Although it wasn't America's first ski area, it was inarguably the birthplace of destination skiing, the first internationally recognized American resort.

It all began in 1935 when Union Pacific Railroad Chairman Averell Harriman hired Count Felix Schaffgotsch, an Austrian skier, to find the perfect location for a grand American ski resort. Harriman was pleased with the Count's choice, and he began acquiring land in the Ketchum, Idaho, area. In December 1936, the Sun Valley Lodge opened, and the first of many lifts were installed. The following year saw the opening of the Sun Valley Inn and several buildings in the new village. The original ski facilities were near the later-developed Dollar Mountain, close to the village. After a hiatus for World War II, Dollar Mountain and Mount Baldy received their first ski lifts. Baldy, a few miles away in Ketchum, would become the primary skiing center, with some 3,400 feet of vertical, best remembered for its consistent, steep fall-line skiing.

Sun Valley was home to many celebrities, including Ernest Hemingway, who wrote *For Whom the Bell Tolls* while in residence. The magic of those early years is well-captured in the 1941 movie "Sun Valley Serenade," starring Sonja Henie, John Payne, Milton Berle, Glenn Miller, and his orchestra. (Today, when you check into your room at the Sun Valley Lodge, the "Serenade" is playing on TV.)

In 1964, the resort was acquired by Southern California real-estate developer Bill Janss, a former U.S. Ski Team member and developer of Snowmass in Colorado. Janss made a number of improvements on the Mount Baldy side, including the Warm Springs expansion. But by 1977, he was running low on cash, ready to sell, and talking to the Walt Disney Company. Those discussions dragged on, and, eventually, Salt Lake City businessman Earl Holding reached out to Janss and bought the resort through his company, Sinclair Oil.

Holding had begun his incredible business career running the Little America lodging properties along Interstate 80, where he and his wife often served guests in the restaurant. He had a simple philosophy: operate, improve, and hold. That approach, based on creating long-term value, was the antithesis of today's private equity owners, with their usual 10-year horizon. Sun Valley sits in the company's Hotel and Resort Division, which includes the spectacular Grand America in Salt Lake City.

I have many skiing friends who view Sun Valley as the finest ski experience in North America. The Holdings' investments, both on-mountain and in the village, have created a resort that offers absolutely first-class facilities, without the attendant crowds. Some of this is a function of location and limited air service (the resort does subsidize, with partners, direct flights into the nearby Haley, Idaho, regional airport). That said, for decades the Sun Valley difference has been under-promoted at best. Earl Holding was suspicious of marketing and focused on service, feeling that nothing markets like word-of-mouth. I'm quite confident that Sun Valley enjoys one of the highest, if not the highest, service ratings among competitors, but that alone hasn't attracted the kinds of crowds that one would expect, given the experience. Marketing is important.

Even though existing facilities are underutilized by industry norms, the company has plans for a significant on-mountain expansion in Cold Springs Canyon. Additionally, work continues on updating and modernizing properties in the original Sun Valley Village. Like Taos and Sierra-at-Tahoe, Sun Valley is a value-driven organization. The highest service levels occur only with an empowered and motivated staff. The Holdings were notorious for changing their travel plans at the last minute in order to attend the birthday party of a tenured employee. That commitment to staff is reflected in two new staff-housing buildings, adjacent to Sun Valley Village. The first, a dorm-style facility, was completed in time for the 2018–19 ski season. The second was scheduled to open in spring 2019 and features apartments. Together, they will provide the resort with 575 staff-housing beds in an ideal Village location, just steps from public transportation.

Historically, Sinclair Oil has been an energy and lodging company. Although they own significant ski facilities (including Snowbasin in Ogden, Utah), their passion has been on the hotel side. The Sun Valley Lodge has been remodeled multiple times under the Holdings' ownership, most recently in 2014–15. It is an absolutely stunning hotel. The dining room and lounge still look out over the original skating rink and the slopes of Dollar Mountain. The building footprint is virtually unchanged, with the exception of a new wing to support a huge spa expansion. From an exterior perspective, nothing has changed. But the public spaces—the rooms, restaurants, spa—well, they're as nice as it gets in ski country. And the Holdings have done a marvelous job of preserving the storied history of both the Lodge and the resort. A guest can spend hours wandering the hallways and enjoying the old celebrity photos and memorabilia. Sun Valley is a place where the "magic still lives."

Earl Holding passed in 2013, but his wife, Carol, and family members remain passionate about Sun Valley. One could assume that potential buyers have beaten a path to the Sinclair Oil executive offices in Salt Lake. For Vail or Alterra, Sun Valley would be a crown jewel. Ditto for Boyne or POWDR. As time passes, who knows? But in the here and now, Sun Valley can be expected to remain "fiercely independent."

That's not true, however, in terms of pass affiliation. In February 2019, Sun Valley announced it was leaving the Mountain Collective and joining the Epic Pass for the 2019–20 season (along with Snowbasin). Its 2018–19 winter was the strongest in 20 years, with 426,500 skier visits. I think of Sun Valley as a gentle giant in the ski industry. It's wakening to its strength.

And that brings us to Alta, another iconic Indie that represents skiing's American roots and embodies the best the sport has to offer for no-frills powder seekers. With operations dating back to the 1939 winter, and an average of 545 annual inches of light, dry snow, it is one of just three resorts that don't allow snowboarding (along with Deer Valley and Vermont's Mad River Glen).

Skiers can thank legendary skier Alf Engen for the discovery of Alta's slopes. Engen first charted its terrain, up above the silver-mining town of Alta, back in 1935 (and later ran its ski school). But it was a Harvard-educated lawyer, Joe Quinney, who brought Alta to fruition, combining a strong understanding of U.S. Forest Service permitting issues with a savvy legal and financial background. The origins of U.S. ski resorts provide a treasure trove of intriguing personalities, and with Alta we also find the enduring presence of poet and publisher James Laughlin, whose stable of authors included another avid skier, Ernest Hemingway, along with Ezra Pound. Laughlin, heir to a Pittsburgh steel fortune, had skied extensively in the Alps; he owned the Alta Lodge in the early years and forged the ski area's strong conservation ethos.

Located at the end of Little Cottonwood Canyon and sharing a ticket with neighbor Snowbird since 2002, Alta is a true skier's mountain. The Alta Ski Lifts Company was under the same family ownership through many decades, with 51 percent owned by the Laughlins, 25 percent by the Quinneys, and 11 percent by the Dick Bass family, developers of Snowbird. Today's exact ownership mix is a bit of a mystery. Mike Maughan, the resort's general manager, says that ownership mix is not correct today, but it appears Alta's board of directors prefers to keep the details private. There is little doubt that interested buyers have knocked on Alta's door over the years, and it is also likely that they gave up the pursuit after hearing the same refrain: Alta is not for sale.

Although comfortably old-school—with its family-owned, mostly room-and-board lodging that draws the same skiers back year-after-year (no ski-in/ski-out condos or fancy restaurants)—it's not stuck in the past. Alta introduced RFID ticket gates back in 2007 and now has four high-speed lifts, including an oddity, a detachable triple. Its master plan emphasizes renewable energy, adding wind turbines to the tops of several lifts, and solar panels on all resort buildings.

Alta, along with Snowbird, was an early member of the Mountain Collective, and they naturally joined the Ikon Pass for the 2018–19 season, allowing seven days between the two (plus seven at Deer Valley).

With a strong 626 inches of snow for the 2018–19 season, Alta had its fifth best season in its 81-year history (while Utah set an all-time record for skier visits). It doesn't do much marketing, and it really doesn't need to.

In his role as GM, Maughan writes a blog with often-insightful musings. In his March 12, 2019, post, which he titled "Reflections on a Snowy Winter and New Passes," he reviewed the season to date and the increased traffic at Alta—and across the Western ski world. Like many of his operator colleagues, he noted that there was a powder-fueled, double-digit increase in local, Alta-only pass usage that outstripped the incoming Ikon skiers. In an email after the season, Maughan revealed that day and multiday ticket sales were down significantly, because many skiers migrated to the Ikon (roughly half of the Ikon passholders were in Alta's data base as previous customers who had purchased other Alta products).

Also in the blog, he sounded this warning: "The widespread uptick in skier visits across our country suggests that demand in a snowy year may be greater than the supply in some regions of the country." If you've navigated Little Cottonwood on a weekend, you know what he's talking about.

In classic Alta style, he closed like this: "[The] decision [to join Ikon] was not made lightly, and we are closely monitoring the impact multiresort passes are having on the ski industry, skier patterns, and the Alta experience. Please know that we are committed to preserving the Alta experience by matching the number of skiers visiting Alta with our infrastructure, services, and terrain.

"We welcome your feedback, and ask for your patience, as adjustments will take time, given agreements that are in place and the approval process required to make changes. In the meantime, we hope to share more magical Alta moments with you during the remainder of the season. *Thanks for skiing Alta this winter."*

Alta returned as an Ikon partner when Alterra announced its 2019–20 pass-partner roster in early March, before Maughan wrote that blog post. Because of the Snowbird interconnect and joint pass product, it would be difficult for Alta to unilaterally leave Ikon. Alta doesn't allow snowboarders while Snowbird does, so theoretically it could also stop Ikon-skier entry. But it would be confusing at best. Alta will be interesting to watch, and no doubt the resort leadership will do what is best for the longtime Alta skier.

Sierra-at-Tahoe is independent—sort of. Booth Creek Ski Holdings owned it until 2006, when principal George Gillett Jr. sold it, along with his Northstar, Loon, and the Summit at Snoqualmie properties to CNL. In the case of Sierra, he leased back the operation, and today it is the only former CNL (now Oz) resort left under that umbrella.

Gillett had achieved financial success with a radio and television company (Gillett Communications), and entered the ski business in 1985, when he purchased Vail and Beaver Creek. He is fondly remembered for massive investments in detachable lifts and for an emphasis on service. In 1992, the victim of high-interest rates and issues outside his resort business, his Gillett companies were forced to file for Chapter 11 protection. In 1996, he returned to the ski business through his new company, Booth Creek Ski Holdings, and acquired Sierra (called Sierra Ski Ranch at the time). Ski Resort Holdings, a successor to CNL, now owns Sierra's underlying assets. Gillett continues to own Grand Targhee in Alta, Wyoming, but the two resorts operate separately. The Booth Creek corporate staff has long since moved on.

John Rice has been president of Sierra-at-Tahoe for 26 years. He knows what it's like to battle the big guys. His resort, just off Highway 50, approximately 95 miles from Sacramento and 75 miles from Reno, is effectively "surrounded," from a ski resort perspective, by Vail Resorts. Rice has spent most of his long ski-industry career in California. He was HR director and risk manager at Bear Mountain back in the days when S-K-I was the owner. Ever since Vail Resorts acquired Heavenly from American Skiing Company in 2002 and then the Northstar lease in 2010, he has been competing with the big guys. But when Vail acquired Kirkwood in 2012, things got even tougher. Kirkwood was the next-door neighbor, a prime competitor with a large regional following, value pricing, and now a new owner. The arrival of the Ikon Pass in the Tahoe area with Squaw/Alpine Meadows simply raised the intensity of competition.

Prior to Vail's leasing of Northstar, Sierra and Northstar promoted a Double Whammy pass, targeting day skiers traveling the I-80 corridor. (Remember, Northstar had once been a Booth Creek resort along with Sierra.) The resorts shared close proximity to the interstate, one in north Tahoe and the other in south Tahoe. It was a very popular pass product, and Rice acknowledges the exposure that this product brought to Sierra. That exposure, he feels, enhanced the credibility of Sierra's snow quality and quantity. Snowfall records do seem to support Sierra's argument that they are "favored" regionally from a snowfall perspective. The Double Whammy also helped drive pass sales and skier visits.

With Vail's lease, that pass went away. Fortunately for Sierra, the Powder Alliance had been created in 2013 by a dozen western resorts, including Sierra, to drive passholder loyalty and compete against Epic. For 2019–20 it offers three days at 18 resorts. The fact that Sugar Bowl is now a member brings back a product that has similar appeal to the Double Whammy. Sierra is probably breathing a sigh of relief.

Competing in the new world requires a thoughtful pass strategy in concert with the partnership noted above. Price *is* important. The Sierra season pass has four pricing tiers, with the first (and best deal) coming with a spring purchase: $349. That price increases in $50 to $100 increments. The last tier remains in place well into the ski season (while Epic has a mid-December cutoff). So Sierra captures regional day skiers who were late to make a decision and are looking for the best deal once the season has started. There are always reasons for delay: job change; just moved into town; friends bought a nearby condo. A cheaper pass is available to those willing to forgo Saturdays and enjoy Sunday–Friday skiing—in effect, a locals' product.

To compete successfully, Sierra has to go where Vail doesn't. Because Vail's marketing is so Epic-driven (more and more, the pass is the brand, not the resort), they don't participate in the traditional ski-show marketplace, so Sierra shows up ready to greet new skiers and sell passes on site. Technology can't just belong to the big guys. Whether selling passes at a ski show or responding to online requests, these transactions must be quick and seamless. If not, the buyer goes elsewhere.

In Rice's David-versus-Goliath world, brand is very important. To that point, Sierra seems to have established a clear identity: good snow/grooming; quality, reasonably priced food; friendly staff; and excellent instruction programs, including race training (Sierra touts its success in nurturing Olympians). Looking at the other regional competitors, Sierra does seem to have an opportunity in this regard. Alpine Meadows is fully merged into the Squaw identity. Sugar Bowl has a strong brand image and loyalty with its longtime passholders, but not so much with the younger crowd. And Kirkwood, as a Vail-owned resort, gets the expected and almost inevitable jabs from locals: More Epic=Less Kirkwood. Sierra touts its friendly, high-touch, almost boutique model as its primary point of difference. Its pass strategy for 2018–19 was called "Keeping It Real."

In talking to Rice in mid-December 2018, with the season off to a good start, he thought Sierra was on pace, assuming normal snowfall, to set records for pass sales. Independent, and more than just surviving.

John Rice is a very capable resort executive. He has tons of experience, a passion for the sport, empathy and affection for staff and guests. By self-admission, he doesn't take himself too seriously. He has perspective and a great sense of humor. His personality and values are reflected in everything Sierra does. This "Rice factor" will continue until he steps down. Choosing a successor who can be nimble as a competitor and deliver on the brand promise will be critical to Sierra's continued success.

SHIFTING GEARS AND LOOKING EAST, in northern New England there are only three ski resorts of size (greater than 250,000 skier visits) that remain independently owned: Jay Peak and Sugarbush in Vermont and Waterville Valley in New Hampshire. (Smugglers' Notch, in northern Vermont, does not quite do comparable volume, nor does New Hampshire's Bretton Woods, though it is the largest in that state in terms of acreage.) In Maine, there are no independents of size; Boyne owns the two largest resorts: Sunday River and Sugarloaf.

As noted earlier, Jay Peak is in the midst of a terrible SEC brouhaha over the misuse of EB-5 funds. This controversial legislation allowed foreign investors to receive preferential immigration status for their investments, fueling resort improvements that probably could not have been financed by normal lending institutions. Because of those investments, Jay Peak has an asset base that would otherwise not be justified given its location (drive distance from markets) and historic skier volumes. It is in receivership and will eventually be sold, at which time the future will be less cloudy. Federal receiver Michael Goldberg retained Los Angeles–based Houlihan Lokey to assist with the sale of Jay, and it was on the market in spring 2019. No sale price has been set, but news reports speculated it could be anywhere from $60 million to a whopping $250 million—a number 25 times the resort's reported $10 million profit in 2017. That high number is frankly ridiculous. As noted earlier, ski resorts are selling for around eight to 10 times profits in this sellers' market. Jay does have many non-ski assets —hotels, water park, hockey rink, golf course, soccer fields— and while these are certainly revenue producers, they do so at a level that is much lower than typical ski assets. Valuation will be challenging. Given all these uncertainties, I've decided not to include Jay in the "independent" category.

Sugarbush enjoys one of New England's more legendary histories. Founded by Damon and Sara Gadd and Jack Murphy and opening on Christmas day of 1958, its commercial success arguably peaked in the early 1980s, when it was recording close to a half-million skier visits annually, despite its relative isolation on Route 100. The Sugarbush history includes periods when Stein

Eriksen was the short-lived ski school director and when it reigned as Manhattan's go-to-resort, aka Mascara Mountain, with the tony trailside Club Ten and the Kennedy clan in attendance

Nearby Glen Ellen was purchased and became Sugarbush North. Les Otten acquired the resort in 1995 through his LBO Resort Enterprises (later American Skiing Company) and connected the two with a lift over Slide Brook Basin. Its 2,600 feet of vertical and 581 acres of terrain are arguably as good as it gets in New England. It can celebrate legendary terrain like Castlerock, Stein's Run, Upper FIS, and Inverness, training ground of the Green Mountain Valley School. Today, Sugarbush is independently owned by Win Smith Jr., the retired former CEO of Merrill Lynch International and a son of the firm's founder, Winthrop H. Smith Sr. Along with his partners, Smith invested in upscale lodging and amenities and also relied heavily on the EB-5 funding to survive the Great Recession and to reinvest (like Jay Peak, but without running afoul of the law).

Sugarbush has been creative in designing its season passes, launching the For20s young-adult pass for $299 back in 2012. It has been a member of the MCP and joined Ikon for 2018–19, allowing seven and five days respectively with the full and base products. Smith and his partners have made some smart moves at the resort (and invested in the community by renovating properties such as the now sublime Pitcher Inn). Sugarbush faces tough competition, going head-to-head against the Vail Resorts-owned Stowe and Okemo and POWDR's Killington. Given all these challenges, you would think that Win Smith was getting anxious. Not so. I spoke to him at the San Diego NSAA convention where he was celebrating a breakthrough year, more than 400,000 skier visits, and did not look like a man ready to sell.

Waterville Valley is independent, but with a more complicated future than others we've looked at. Waterville was founded in 1966 by Dartmouth graduate and Olympian Tom Corcoran. While it's very close to the Boston market, and easily accessed from Interstate 93, it sits at the end of a 10-mile access road with limited services. It is an absolutely spectacular, pristine setting. Much of the land is national forest. What development has occurred over the past 50-plus years has been limited in scale. There are a number of private homes and condos and a modest village center that, unfortunately, is not at the base of the lifts. Rather, it's a short drive away on the Valley floor. There is no commercial lodging as in Marriott- or Hyatt-type properties, so the number of beds is limited.

And the mountain itself, while offering 2,020 feet of vertical, has a significant wind issue at its summit. Recently, a T-bar replaced a seldom-running older double chair serving the summit. In terms of terrain and lift capacity, nearby Loon, owned by Boyne, is considerably larger. Loon is also the only New Hampshire ski resort that participates in the Ikon Pass. If that wasn't enough of a competitive challenge, Waterville has always struggled with adequate water for snowmaking, while Loon is a superstar in that category.

Because there was no established community at the base of Waterville Valley's Mt. Tecumseh, Corcoran was by necessity both ski area operator and real-estate developer. He withstood a number of downturns but eventually filed for bankruptcy in the summer of 1994. At that time, I was doing business development for S-K-I Ltd. and wound up spending many days in bankruptcy court in Manchester. Our company was in the acquisition mode and Waterville seemed to be a good fit, if we could purchase at the right price and fix the snowmaking. We had no interest in the real estate. To make a long story somewhat short, we succeeded in buying the ski area assets out of bankruptcy while the real-estate holdings remained under protection, awaiting a different outcome. The logic the judge used was that the remaining real estate would have a higher value with a credible operator of the ski area in place. The ski area assets went for $9.4 million.

Very shortly thereafter, Les Otten acquired S-K-I, merged it with his LBO Holdings, and created the American Skiing Company. Because of antitrust issues, Waterville was sold to George Gillett's Booth Creek Holdings in the fall of 1996, along with Cranmore (which Otten had acquired earlier), for $17.2 million.

Although Waterville had struggled over the years, it had a dedicated and politically engaged clientele. In 2010, the Sununu family and a group of investors, with long ties to the area, purchased Waterville. This change was well-received as it put Waterville back under local ownership for the first time in 15 years. In addition to the ski area, the purchase included the Nordic Center, Conference Center and Town Square properties.

Chris Sununu led the efforts to buy the resort and was named CEO. "Our vision is to return Waterville to being the premier resort it was, can, and should be, and that starts with our belief that local control and local management is always best," Sununu said at the time. He was elected governor of New Hampshire in November 2016, and he stepped down from his CEO position before inauguration. Tim Smith is the current president. Chris's father, John H. Sununu, was the former governor of New Hampshire, and his brother, John E. Sununu, a former U.S. senator (John was the youngest serving member of the Senate during his six-year term). The family has a long history with the ski area and owns vacation homes there.

A number of major capital improvements have followed since their ownership. More than 33,000 feet of new snowmaking pipe have been installed, along with high-efficiency guns (it's unclear how they have advanced a solution to the water-supply issue). For 2018–19, the resort opened Green Peak, with 10 new trails—the first terrain expansion in 30 years. The base lodge has seen significant improvements. And as noted, a T-bar has been installed to serve the upper mountain and deal with the wind issue.

Waterville participates in the unrestricted White Mountain Superpass, which offers unlimited skiing at Bretton Woods, state–owned Cannon, Cranmore, and Waterville. It went for $979 for the 2019–20 season, if purchased by May 31. Not a great deal. And not much of a competitor to Ikon in that market. That said, it would appeal to vacation homeowners who want to explore some other resorts reasonably nearby.

Waterville has long been an avid supporter of competitive skiing. The resort's race program, the Black & Blue Trail Smashers, churned out Olympians for decades. The ski area hosted the first international freestyle competition in 1974, was on the women's World Cup circuit in the 1980s, and welcomed the 2019 U.S. Freestyle Championships.

What is Waterville's future in the new world of skiing? Clear as mud. I think that Ikon will be the dominant pass product in that regional market, given Loon's participation, and that will further diminish Waterville's competitive position. Waterville is finally making investments that will satisfy its existing customer base, which means limited leakage there, considering these are largely second-home owners. The real question is: What happens as these aging Boomers move on? Will their children have the same allegiance to Waterville? So, the first challenge is to remain relevant to a younger crowd. But to grow skier visits? They would probably have to, yes, join Epic. That would give Vail a stronger presence in New Hampshire, along with Peak's just-added Attitash and Wildcat, and stem further any market-share losses there.

Regardless, Waterville faces the same historic challenges: lack of beds; the presence of a stronger, nearby competitor; and snow-surface issues, stemming from limited water storage for snowmaking. An optimistic view sees the resort stabilizing, and then growing market share and skier visits through some form of multi-area pass program and additional strategic investments. A more negative scenario sees the resort not joining a mega-pass, continuing to bleed market share, and, eventually, causing the Sununus to look for a new owner.

A-Basin, the Indie with the longest experience in a collective pass (20 years as the original outside partner in Vail Resorts' first Colorado Pass product), announced that it was going it alone for the 2019–20 season, but left open the option of some sort of restricted pass participation to possibly be unveiled in fall 2019 (the choice was Ikon). Its value-priced pass competes with Loveland's. (As noted earlier, Vail has responded with new early/late pass options with extended seasons for Keystone and Breckenridge.) Loveland, another mid-sized Indie, has shunned the major mega-pass trend, but joined the Powder Alliance for 2019–20 (three days at 14 U.S. resorts plus areas in Canada, Japan, and Chile).

Meanwhile, Jackson Hole and Telluride are two iconic and still independent resorts, but have determined that a brighter future lies in affiliating with a mega-pass. Both enjoy owners who have the resources to remain independent. In the case of Telluride, CEO Bill Jensen is now a partner/investor along with the principal, Chuck Horning, a real-estate investor from Newport Beach, California. Legend has it that Chuck was looking for a ranch in the Aspen area some 15 years ago, and when the asking price was revealed, the realtor commented, "For that amount, you could own a ski area." Chuck said, "Let's look at it."

He bought Telluride instead of the ranch in 2004. He has been a quirky, unpredictable owner, but a committed investor in his resort. Recent years have seen major resort expansions and the purchase of several key lodging properties (Inn at Lost Creek and The Peaks Resort). How long will Telluride remain independent? Probably until Chuck gets bored, or an over-the-top offer is placed on the table. You can be sure that Bill Jensen will continue to grow their business and increase the resort's value in the meantime. Given Bill's long history with Vail and the strength of Epic in the Colorado marketplace, it was not a big surprise to see him sign on with Vail Resorts.

Jackson Hole also enjoys stable, committed ownership. In 1992, Jay Kemmerer purchased the resort for his family from an investment group that had earlier acquired the property from its charismatic founder, Paul McCollister. (Back in the 1970s, Marty Wilson, Killington's CFO, and I made the trek to

Jackson to test Paul's willingness to sell. Obviously and unfortunately, we weren't successful.)

For most of the Kemmerers' ownership, the resort was led by veteran executive Jerry Blann, who retired in 2018 after 23 years at the helm. Over those years, the mountain was transformed from an experts-only haven to a huge, broadly appealing ski complex with something for everyone. Blann oversaw more than $200 million in capital improvements. During his tenure, Jackson Hole experienced the largest growth rate of the majors, increasing annual skier visits from 200,000 to 700,000 for the 2018–19 season, with a significant boost from huge snowfalls and the Ikon pass. Steady increases in the resort's direct flight program have aided that growth, with Jackson Hole now easily accessed from major ski markets.

The Kemmerer family made its fortune in natural resources. Jay led the sale of Kemmerer Coal Company to Gulf Oil in 1981, and has since then overseen the family's asset management company, Kemmerer Resources Corp. That's where the ski resort sits. Jackson is one of the last of the family-owned major resorts. I expect it to stay that way for a long time.

CHAPTER 12

Small to Midsized Areas Can Also Flourish

Much been written about the imminent demise of smaller areas, given the increasing competitive threats from the Majors and Mid-Majors and their pass products, as well as climate change and the relatively stagnant growth of the skier base.

According to NSAA, there were 735 operating ski areas in 1983–84 and 476 in 2018–19, a loss of 259 resorts over that time period. These were typically small rope-tow areas, without snowmaking and serving small markets. Few, if any, were doing more than 25,000 skier visits. This is not to discount the losses—every ski area closure hurts the industry and sport—but to put it in perspective.

A closer look tells you that many of the now-defunct areas should never have been built. Most never achieved a size that would be sustainable. Or their remoteness became exacerbated when closer-to-market ski areas opened. Here in Routt County in Colorado, two ski areas are now defunct. One, in Hahns Peak, called Steamboat Lake Ski Area, operated for just one year, the winter of 1973. It had two Heron Poma double chairs that were removed in 1987. One was relocated to Howelsen Hill, the city-owned ski area in downtown Steamboat Springs, which is still operating. Steamboat Lake was a real-estate gamble. The developer, Lifetime Communities of Florida, had plans for a community of 10,000 residents.

Another failed real-estate plan was Stagecoach near Oak Creek, just south of Steamboat Springs. Stagecoach operated for two seasons, 1972–74, with three double chairs. The master plan called for some 22 lifts and five base areas. Funding for the project was pulled in 1973, exacerbated by the energy crisis and oil embargo. A number of condominiums were built that stand to this day. More recently, there was news of the area's imminent reopening. A developer, Don McClean, who brought some ski credentials to the table, had a contract with the property owner (the Wittemyer family) and planned to reopen in 2017. Local real-estate professionals were all abuzz with the news, and a flurry of real-estate transactions occurred in the area. But as of spring 2019, all was silent. Apparently, the developer could not secure financing, and the project is in limbo.

Across ski country, there were many similar real-estate-driven projects that failed. But for the most part, the ski areas that ceased to operate were small, local tows. New York, which has the largest number of ski areas, also saw the largest decline. Many offered just a single rope-tow, with limited service facilities and no snowmaking. The erratic weather that settled in during the 1970s, plus competition from larger resorts with snowmaking and modern chairlifts, put many out of business.

It has been estimated that roughly 350 ski areas have gone out of business in New York State alone (the nationwide number lost is roughly 1,000, spurring the creation of several "Lost Ski Areas of [fill-in-the-state]" posters, but again, most of these places were tiny). Many of these introduced skiers to the sport, so their absence is no doubt detrimental in terms of attracting new participants. It was also an inexpensive introduction. That said, most lacked appropriate rental equipment, and the experience could be daunting (learning to ride a rope-tow is almost more difficult than handling the downhill piece).

It would be an interesting exercise to calculate what the loss of these areas represented in terms of total skier visits. The reality, I suspect, is that the total number is simply not material in the big picture. Most had limited capacity (hundreds, not thousands) and the growth of larger, more mature facilities has more than made up for the capacity loss these smaller areas represented. Again, what was lost was the local, inexpensive introduction to the sport.

Bill Jensen, former Intrawest CEO and current president of Telluride, remarked at an industry convocation in 2015 that he expected a third of the remaining ski areas to close. I think that statement was off base. In my view, he should have said: "Unless they can figure out a new ownership structure or a way to improve their profitability/guest experience, they will go out of business." That I would agree with. Instead of more closures, the recent past has seen the opening of formerly defunct areas, such as Tamarack in Idaho. And looking broadly at the industry, many small facilities are now thriving. How could this be?

Vail made headlines in 2012 when it purchased two Midwestern areas: Afton Alps, next to Minneapolis, and Mt. Brighton, near Detroit. The company had been working for several years on a strategy to acquire urban facilities as "breeder/feeder" areas, hoping to stimulate participation in the sport and, eventually, drive business to its larger resorts. Significant investments to update the facilities followed. In 2016, Vail added Wilmot, midway between Milwaukee and Chicago, to its urban collection.

I had a chance to speak with Blaise Carrig, recently retired Vail Resorts executive, about these acquisitions. His view was that the original concept had been more aligned with a Woodward (POWDR's successful adventure-camp system, including facilities at Copper Mountain and Boreal), creating a year-round urban terrain park, skiing being a piece of it. What Vail learned over time was that the facilities (we're talking 300 feet of vertical here) were primarily places for kids to have fun. Parents would come along, at least to watch, *if* the facilities were attractive, so Vail took care to make sure the parents could enjoy a comfortable lounge and have an adult beverage while the kids enjoyed themselves. The Midwest is one of the larger markets for destination visits to Colorado. Vail figured out how to leverage its urban areas and gain an advantage in that large skier market by providing the Afton, Wilmot and Brighton kids 12 and under with an Epic Local Pass. (Adults and seniors can still buy a local-area-only pass from those three Midwest resorts, or step up to the Epic Local or above.)

If it wasn't going to cost anything to take the kids skiing, "let's buy two adult Epic Passes and go to a Vail resort for this year's winter vacation." So Vail achieved success with its urban areas by making strategic and appropriate investments to improve the experience and, thereby, drive attendance and profitability. And secondly, it allowed deeper penetration into what had been identified as a strong market for their destination resorts. Will Vail expand its urban strategy? The company answered that question with a resounding "yes" in July 2019 with its acquisition of the 17 areas of Peak Resorts, allowing entrance to several metro markets where they can sell more Epic Passes.

CABERFAE OPENED AS A NON-PROFIT IN 1937, the same year as Sun Valley, near the city of Cadillac in the northwestern Lower Peninsula of Michigan. The opening required a combined effort from the Civilian Conservation Corps, the U.S. Forest Service, and the local chamber of commerce. Once hailed as the "Midwest Ski Capital," its devoted customer base has long regarded it as their "Alta of the Midwest."

The resort grew rapidly in the late 1940s through '70s, with a sprawling series of hills served by 20-plus rope tows, five T-Bars and a chairlift, spanning some two miles from end-to-end. It also offered a 30-meter ski jump, cross-country trails, and even two toboggan runs.

Caberfae was and is all about families and affordability within a national park, sitting amidst the 550,000-acre Manistee National Forest. My editor, Andy Bigford, spent his formative ski years there, from age 10 to 15, and in retrospect he can't believe how fortunate he was. This might be a case study in the ascent of Baby Boomer kids to skiing's most vocal advocates.

The Bigfords bought the "family ski pass" and learned to ski at Caberfae. Their "vacation home" was two aging hunting trailers overlooking a pond 10 miles from the resort. They sat around a campfire for après, played broomball, and enjoyed the "outdoor pool" when the pond melted during spring break. Every few days the family would visit the local Y for showers, the indoor pool, and a dinner out.

The outhouse became attractive when the boys found a cubbyhole with a hidden stack of *Playboys*, left by the deer hunters who used the camp in the fall. In another coming-of-age moment, and led on by a couple of their friends who were along for the weekend, they raided the liquor cabinet in the hunters' trailer for an introduction to adult beverages. (According to Andy, all went smoothly until the next morning, when they had to wake up early to catch first rope.)

At the sprawling ski area, there were endless games, with packs of local kids egging each other on. When it snowed, as it seemed to do often back then, the area would open whole new swaths of terrain, rope tows leading to more rope tows and an occasional T-Bar. Glove protectors were a must, as was entering the rope tow at high velocity to match the speed of the conveyance.

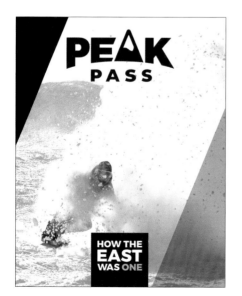

The new face of skiing: Since Vail Resorts launched the Epic Pass in spring 2008 and then Epic for Everyone for 2019–20, the mega-pass has evolved to become the brand for resorts nationwide. The Ikon Pass upped the ante with its arrival for the 2018–19 season, while the Peak Pass, covering primarily Eastern resorts, debuted for the 2016–17 season. With its planned acquisition by Vail Resorts, Peak's 17 resorts get rolled into the Epic for the 2019–20 season.

PHOTOS COURTESY VAIL RESORTS, ALTERRA, PEAK RESORTS

Chairman and CEO Rob Katz is the architect of Vail Resorts' success.
CMO Kirsten Lynch, left, and Pat Campbell, who leads the Mountain Division,
are among the members of his executive team. Blaise Carrig, now retired,
served as the Mountain Division president, and then in a consulting role as
Vail Resorts brought new resorts into its portfolio.

Epic is everywhere: on the rebranded Epic Mountain Express vans (formerly Colorado Mountain Express), Epic Mountain Gear (formerly Boulder Ski Deals), the Epic Burger, and, of course, on the new Epic for Everyone one- to seven-day lift passes.

PHOTOS COURTESY VAIL RESORTS

Rusty Gregory, who spent 40 years at Mammoth, now serves as Alterra's CEO.

KSL CEO Eric Resnick with his daughter Emma at the 2019 World Alpine Championships in Åre, Sweden, where they watched Ikon spokesperson Mikaela Shiffrin win gold; and with KSL founder Mike Shannon.

David Perry moved from the Aspen Skiing Co. to become Alterra's president. Now based in Denver's RiNo neighborhood, Alterra shows its hometown support for the Denver Broncos. PHOTO BY RYAN DEARTH

Stephen Kircher was analyzing resort acquisitions as a child; he's now Boyne's CEO and majority shareholder.

Stephen's father, Ski Hall of Famer Everett Kircher (left), was one of the original U.S. resort pioneers, constantly evolving the industry in every way, including snowmaking.

Everett's all-inclusive village at Boyne Mountain in the 1960s, painted by Cecile Johnson.

The new eight-pack Ramcharger at booming Big Sky; each chair costs more than a Porsche.

John Cumming founded POWDR in 1994; in 2018, he stepped down as CEO but remains as chairman.

POWDR's goals are embodied by the success of the hugely popular Killington World Cup races, bringing the community together, drawing 40,000 fans, and reaching 62 countries with early season TV coverage.   PHOTO COURTESY CHANDLER BURGESS/POWDR

POWDR is spending some $100 million in CapEx improvements at Copper, including the American Eagle chondola out of the Center Village.

PHOTO COURTESY POWDR/CURTIS DEVORE

Inside Woodward at Copper: Cumming views the action-sports incubator as a perfect fit for his portfolio of adventure resorts.   PHOTO COURTESY POWDR/TRIPP FAY

Peak Resorts founder Tim Boyd never wanted to compete with the "big boys" while he assembled 17 small- to medium-sized resorts in the Midwest and East, with his son Jesse serving as president.

Where it all began for Peak: Hidden Valley opened in 1986 as the "only McDonald's" for skiers and riders in the St. Louis metro area.

Acquisition of Mount Snow in 2007 put Peak Resorts on the map, while snowmaking firepower (shown here at Mad River Mountain in Ohio) fueled the rise. With Vail Resorts' planned acquisition, all the Peak areas will be part of the Epic Pass for 2019–20.

James Coleman is the managing partner and CEO of Mountain Capital Partners, owner of six Southwestern resorts, including Purgatory.

Tyler and Brian Fairbank have versatile interests, with ownership of Jiminy Peak, Cranmore, and Bromley, plus a renewable-energy company and a ski-industry-training platform.

The Fairbanks' renewable-energy company drove installation of a 386-foot wind turbine at Jiminy, called the Zephyr.

The author with Bill Jensen in 2007; the two worked together when Jensen was CEO of Intrawest and Chris was president of Steamboat. Jensen is now a partner and CEO of Telluride.

John Rice excels in his "David vs. Goliath" role at Sierra-at-Tahoe, but who will replace him?

To survive in a conglomerate-dominated world, the Indies get creative: Taos has gone beyond offering resort flight subsidies to operate its own airline, while Telluride touts its uncrowded slopes in being named the No. 1 resort in North America for six of the last seven years by *Condé Nast Traveler*.

ROAD WARRIOR

High peaks, lofty prices as skiing prices out middle class

PUBLISHED SUN, DEC 8 2013 · 1:00 PM EST | UPDATED MON, DEC 9 2013 · 3:20 PM EST

CULTURE

Are the ski slopes only for the 1 percent?

by John Nelson / February 27, 2018
Photos by John Nelson

5 Reasons Why We Love the Ikon Pass

One pass, 26 mountains.

February 28, 2018 | By Mattie Schuler

Ikon Pass Seen As 'A Big Benefit' For Steamboat Springs Community

February 26, 2018 at 6:35 pm   Filed Under: Epic Pass, Ikon Pass, Skiing, Steamboat Springs, Vail Resort

The Salt Lake Tribune

How Ikon and Epic passes are changing the game for ski resorts in Utah and elsewhere

Bloomberg Businessweek

ILLUSTRATION: YANN KEBBI FOR BLOOMBERG BUSINESSWEEK

The Battle for the Best Ski Pass

Alterra and Vail Resorts are going head to head
snapping up resorts. Can they save skiing and make
selling lift tickets a viable business?

It's Time to Buy Your 2020 Ski Pass Now

April 16, 2019 | By Sean McCoy

For arguably the first time in its history, skiing's media message has flipped 180 degrees, from a sport viewed as too expensive to one of value, with widespread advice to buy early.

Just about everybody could launch off the notorious ruts that built up on the towpath, complete an aerial 360, and resume the ride up. Ski skills were acquired not just by racing down the vertically challenged terrain, but by skating the endless flats, surviving snowball fights, dodging trees, and navigating the traverses to far-flung hillocks. The whole Caberfae complex was a crazy, informal terrain park.

The main gathering point was the black-diamond run called Shelter, perhaps 250 feet of semi-steep vertical served by a high-speed rope tow. Skier's right usually held a slalom course (Cadillac High was a perennial state champion in skiing), the middle was a mogul field, and the left side featured a series of kickers. Front and back flips were performed virtually all day on weekends. When they were just starting, Andy and his brother Pete, who is now the CEO of Shanty Creek Resort to the north, were known to have broken several pairs of skis through their high jinks. The family would eventually travel all over the West to ski, and the parents would buy a vacation condo in the Colorado mountains, but this is how it all began for two hard-skiing Baby Boomers and their parents.

Caberfae had its ups and downs through the decades, and faced closure in the early 1980s when it was publicly owned. That's when Jack and Tim Meyer, Sr., locals who had previously held a 50 percent stake in nearby Crystal Mountain (which has its own incredible success story), rescued it from bankruptcy. Caberfae is now led by their sons, cousins Pete and Tim Meyer. Pete handles sales and marketing, rentals, and ticketing, while Tim oversees mountain operations.

Jack and Tim Sr. embarked on an endless journey of peak building, what counter-intuitively might be the most successful "ski-resort contraction" in history. The vertical enhancement was launched after they had completed a land trade with the Manistee National Forest to secure ownership of the 500 acres where the ski area sat (they already owned 60). With the land in their name, the Meyers began to move dirt. And move dirt. And move more dirt. Their vertical expansion of two central peaks was accompanied by a horizontal contraction from the far-flung borders and the closing of a dozen-plus lifts, which they could never adequately cover with snowmaking,

Over the years, they increased the vertical drop by some 150 feet, and it now reaches an admirable 485 feet. They installed chairs on the consolidated South and North peaks (rebranding the area as Caberfae Peaks), and also built the attractive 16,000-square-foot Blackmer day lodge, billed as the largest in the state, with the entire first floor dedicated to brown-baggers. The upstairs cafeteria cranks out standard but quality lodge food.

It still wasn't enough, and they faced a weather reckoning in 2005, after which they dedicated themselves to turning their snowmaking infrastructure from weakness to strength. "We were behind the curve for the Midwest," recalls Pete. "We had a very tough winter in 2005–06. We survived the holiday week on pretty much just one run with 40 degrees and drizzle every day, which was a little too close for comfort. From that day forward, we have made significant investments in snowmaking every year. Everything starts with snowmaking. We have gone from 20 fan guns to over 150, while constantly upgrading and expanding the piping, electrical grid, pumping capacity, well capacity. Upgrading grooming equipment is also a necessity to adequately process the larger volume of the snow that is made," he says. To that end, Caberfae recently bought a Prinroth BR 350.

These changes were important, but still not enough given the intense competition from Boyne, Crystal Mountain, Shanty Creek, and Nub's Nob. Pete began ruminating about a potential pricing/value statement that would forever alter that landscape. First, he tested the idea in summer 2004 on the 9-hole golf course at the resort, which had a paltry half-dozen members at the time. He dropped the golf season-pass price to $99, and sold more than 400. Continuing the experiment, he raised it to $119 in 2006, and sales dropped by a stunning 75 percent. He took the price back down and sales responded.

Now, he was ready to apply his theory to the more important product. In fall 2007, a year before Epic was launched, he slashed the price on the roughly $250 season pass, but with a unique twist: Caberfae offered a $99 "season pass" good for either weekends or weekdays, and an unrestricted Peak Pass for $198. (This was a decade before Tim Boyd created his multi-resort Peak Pass.)

"The beauty was the straightforwardness and simplicity of the pricing model, as the passes did not have the usual restrictions (holidays, etc.). Obviously, the Weekend Pass was the most popular, as everyone wants to ski on the weekend. This was counterintuitive, and to this day, I don't think anyone has offered a weekend-only pass." The seemingly illogical move was a huge attention getter. The pass has another wrinkle to help track usage in lieu of sophisticated scanning equipment: Caberfae requires passholders to show their pass to get a lift ticket each day, which also significantly reduces pass fraud.

Pass sales quadrupled, and Caberfae became dominant in the critical Grand

Rapids market, a 95-minute drive from the south, and a place from which customers can day trip or spend a few nights. About 40 to 50 percent of Caberfae's skiers hail from Grand Rapids, where the metro population tops 1 million. The city's local hill, Cannonsburg, has a lock on the race, terrain park, and tubing markets, but can't compete with Caberfae's ski product. Conversely, Caberfae has a small park presence by choice, opting not to channel its resources into this expensive endeavor, but it does offer what it bills as the Lower Peninsula's only backcountry terrain.

Intimately familiar with a family driven clientele that wants value first and foremost, Meyer has held fast to those initial season pass price points for a dozen years. His day tickets are also simple: $39 weekdays, $49 weekends.

After its second earliest opening ever on Nov. 17, 2018, Caberfae recorded its third-best skier visit total in 82 years for the season. Pete and Tim have plenty of skiers for their area's capacity, and are now focused on increasing uphill capacity and expanding their terrain. To that end, they also reinvented the beginner area, adding a magic carpet. For the first time in its history, Caberfae has no rope tows.

When Andy dropped by Caberfae to see Pete Meyer in June 2019, the loaders and CAT 250 dump trucks were making endless loops, moving dirt to build more terrain. The owner was out on a tractor, top-dressing the golf-course greens. One of his longtime staffers was handling the hotel check-ins, the golf course cash register, and also taking reservations for the coming season while selling ski and golf season passes. "I can't complain, nobody works more than Pete and Tim, they're here at 7 every morning and are the last to leave," she said.

When Pete returned, we reminisced about all the state's ski resorts that had closed; more than 150 are listed by the Michigan Lost Ski Areas Project, including 15 in the Cadillac area alone. Andy has his own list of childhood haunts that went under: in Southwest Michigan, the upside-down Royal Valley near Buchanan and Carousel Mountain in Holland; and in the north, Big M in Manistee, Timberlee and Sugar Loaf in the Traverse City area, and Walloon Hills and Thunder Mountain near Boyne (Everett Kircher bought the latter two in the 1970s, and they offered a combo $75 White Season Pass, but he would eventually shut them down. Walloon was converted into Challenge Mountain, an adaptive sports facility.)

Pete Meyer agrees that many of the closures were small, relatively insignificant operations, but every loss hurts. He monitors all the resorts to Caberfae's south, hoping they will continue as breeder/feeders. He's also one of Midwest skiing's greatest advocates, noting that year after year, the Midwest is among the country's most stable skier visit providers, avoiding the relative volatility of the Pacific regions or even the Northeast. For 2018–19, the Midwest reported 6.4 million skier visits, according to Kottke, right in the middle of its 10-year high of 7.8 and its low of 5.4 million, but 5 percent down from the 10-year average of 6.7 million.

Pete Meyer is well aware that because of the Midwest's success in skier development, many of their best customers eventually move west to live near the bigger mountains. "But they come back when they have kids," he says.

Over its eight decades, Caberfae was at times a candidate to join the ranks of the Michigan Lost Ski Areas Project. It is not as flashy or successful in size and scope as Crystal or Boyne, but it's thriving.

How? Know your niche market (Grand Rapids) and stay focused on it. Expertise in snowmaking. Creative value pass/simplified day ticketing. Effective messaging via email blasts and social media. On-site presence seven-days-a-week from inspirational owners. Hard work. More hard work.

Caberfae checks all the boxes.

One downstate urban area that didn't survive is Apple Mountain (formerly called Bintz Apple Mountain), which is adjacent to the Tri-Cities of Saginaw-Midland-Bay City, weighing in with a combined population of 400,000 in Michigan's Thumb. It was actually a counter-seasonal play for founder John Bintz, who wanted to offer his apple orchard/cider mill/bakery/general store workers year-round jobs. With a bulldozer, Bintz created a hill from the flat-as-a-pancake landscape, and Apple Mountain debuted for the 1961–62 season with 30 feet of vertical drop.

By the 1980–81 season, resort brochures claimed the hill had grown to 200 feet in vertical, and John and his wife Joan had also started a successful ski shop. From its founding until 1994, they introduced 800,000 Tri-City students to the sport, an average of 25,000 per season, according to the bio of the Bintzes on the Michigan Ski Hall of Fame website (they were both inducted in 2012). The Bintzes sold the area in 1994, and it's now home to a golf course, restaurant and conference center, but the lifts, including a quad, have not spun since the weather-shortened 2016–17 winter. "Apple's closing was unfortunate for the Michigan ski industry; the downstate resorts play an important role in introducing families and kids. The better they do, the better it is for the northern resorts—and the ski industry overall," Caberfae's Pete Meyer noted.

The owners cited underground snowmaking pipe problems (deferred maintenance?) that could not be accessed for repairs because the golf course shares the same land. With a successful golf course and conference business, the owners likely considered it too much of a hassle or expense to make the repairs. It's not known how many new skiers were introduced from 1994 until its 2017 closing, but if it followed the earlier trend, the loss was material. (Case in point: One of the skiers created at Apple Mountain was Heidi Bintz Friedman, the daughter of the original owners. She went on to lead the award-winning Double Diamond Ski Shop in Vail's Lionshead with her then husband, the late Kenny Friedman.)

There's been talk of a local effort to reopen Apple Mountain, perhaps as a non-profit, but nothing has happened to date, and overtures to Apple from other ski area operators to help out went unanswered.

There are plenty of opportunities for small, urban-ish ski areas to succeed. But three things are needed: Stick to your niche, develop efficient snowmaking, and provide a quality experience. If you look back at Vern Greco's strategy with PGRI, Tim Boyd with Peak, or Vail with its Midwestern properties, they tell their guests that "things are different"—and back that up by delivering. If so, success seems to follow.

PLATTEKILL MOUNTAIN IN ROXBURY, NEW YORK, has been around since the 1950s. It offers 1,100 feet of vertical skiing over 38 trails, plus some steep tree-skiing when conditions allow. Although tested by its location (you have to drive past state-owned Belleayre to get there), it still retained a strong local following given the challenging terrain. In 1992, "Platty," as it's known to locals, went into foreclosure when the previous owners defaulted on a loan taken out to pursue (here we go again) an unsuccessful real-estate project. The Hinkley family had owned Plattekill for 33 years.

The resort was purchased by two former ski instructors, Laszlo and Danielle Vajtay. They met in 1988 while teaching skiing and making the weekend trek from New York City. They understood Platty's uniqueness among the state's 50 operating ski areas and branded it as an intimate, old-fashioned resort for expert skiers and families alike. They know that midweek business is a challenge, so they operate only Friday through Sunday. That said, the mountain is available "for rent" for private groups Monday to Thursday, unless it's the day after a fresh snow ("Powder Daize"), when Platty opens for all. What money they made went into snowmaking. Twenty-five years after their purchase, Plattekill is a thriving Indie, with a dedicated local clientele and growing summer business. They figured it out.

Moving on to larger but historically struggling ski areas, there have been some recent ownership changes and revitalization efforts worth noting. One of the most successful is a local hill, West Mountain, in Glens Falls N.Y., just south of Lake George.

West Mountain had been owned for years by Michael Brandt. During his tenure, the ski area was capital-starved and struggled between boom and bust years, depending on natural snowfall. It is located just beyond the residential areas of the city, only a couple of miles from the Adirondack Northway. In February 2014, West was purchased by Spencer Montgomery and a partner, with Montgomery acting as managing member. Montgomery describes his connection this way: "We grew up in an old farmhouse about a mile down the road from the mountain. Our first goal is to fix up the ski area and make it profitable." Approximately $5 million has been spent to date. Old, abandoned terrain has been resurrected and a new quad chair installed. Summer activities are part of the plan to take advantage of the huge crowds that frequent the Lake George region during the nonwinter seasons. Some $600,000 was spent in food and beverage upgrades to create a "fresh-food cafeteria." Snowmaking capacity has been doubled, with greater pumping capacity and new, efficient tower guns. Sound familiar?

Montgomery, who had a successful career in financial services, has his eye on real-estate opportunities and has acquired significant acreage to support just that. West Mountain, it is hoped, will not only become a successful day area, but eventually will move into the resort realm, with supporting real-estate development. The Glens Falls region, known to ski racers nationwide as the home of venerable vendor Reliable Racing Supply, Inc., has struggled economically (with the exit of textile industries and General Electric) and could benefit from West Mountain's success. If West can grow to 200,000 skier visits, which is Montgomery's goal, the regional impact could be significant.

Another interesting New York success story is that of Windham Mountain, once a private ski area. Irv Naylor's Snow Time Resorts once owned it, but they eventually sold it to a group of local investors. On December 27, 2018, Connecticut-based North Castle Partners bought out the majority shareholder, with four others remaining in the new company, Windham Mountain Partners.

The prior owners had invested in a new six-pack for the 2018–19 season. Windham competes in the Catskill Region with state-owned Belleayre and Vail Resorts' (formerly Peak's) Hunter. This is formidable competition, given the scale of recent capital spending by both. (Belleayre installed a new gondola and, as noted earlier, Hunter has seen a major investment.)

So what is a private equity firm doing investing in a midsized ski mountain in this highly competitive ski market? Well, they're doing it for the money, so they must see an opportunity to increase value in the near term. This speaks to the new reality that many resort operators have figured out how to improve profitability, even those that remain independent, like Windham. North Castle might be a good fit for the ski business, to wit:

"Our mission is to partner with entrepreneurs to build companies that advance Healthy, Active and Sustainable Living, while living our core values and striving to create extraordinary value for these companies, their employees, investors, communities and the North Castle Team."

Its portfolio companies are highly skewed toward those that support an active lifestyle. According to Chip Seamans, Windham president since 2011 and a former senior executive with Kirkwood and Sunday River, this new ownership group embraces the ski culture, with partners often skinning up the mountain before the lifts open.

North Castle has recruited former NSAA President Michael Berry and former SIA President David Ingemie (both now retired) onto its Windham board—a clear signal that the new owners don't intend to skimp on industry expertise.

Windham has a loyal New York metro following, with a large number of vacation homes lining its slopes. According to Seamans, Windham will remain family-friendly, focus on its high-end clientele, raise the service bar, and price its services accordingly. Although the arrival of Peak/Vail Resorts at Hunter creates competitive pricing pressure, he feels that the credibility of Catskill skiing has improved dramatically with their presence and with the facility enhancements at both Hunter and Belleayre. Next season will bring the installation of a detachable four-pack that was removed the prior year to make room for the new six-pack. This relocated lift will provide critical out-of-base capacity for the ski area.

Windham plans to focus on increasing the number of "hot" beds, enhancing snowmaking, growing winter skier visits, and increasing off-season visitation with appropriate summer amenities.

Targeted investment to improve operating results, and then an eventual sale; that's probably Windham's future. Where the cultures are a good fit (owner and ski area), there's an improved likelihood of success. Being just two-and-a-half hours from New York metro's 20 million people doesn't hurt either.

Magic Mountain in Vermont has disappointed many skiers over its almost 60-year history. The Magic may have been there during the early years (it opened in 1960), but it faded through a series of financial crises and ownership changes. I remember skiing there shortly after it opened. At that time, it had only a couple lifts (one T-bar and one double chairlift). Magic was sandwiched between Bromley and Stratton, which explains most of the resort's on-going challenges. "Little Bromley" opened in 1938, and the first J-Bar, more than 2,000-feet long, was installed in 1943. This head start meant that Bromley had an established customer base and loyal following in the Manchester region when Magic opened. Stratton, a much larger mountain, began operations in 1961, and did so with a bang: three double chairs and a three-story base lodge. Stratton's access road was a nightmare during those early years, but it was eventually paved, allowing Stratton to capitalize on its location, closer to major markets than Bromley or Magic. So Magic was geographically challenged and, frankly, did not offer a competitive product during those early years.

In 1985, the resort was sold to the owners of Bromley Mountain (Joe O'-Donnell's Boston Concessions Group [BCG]). O'Donnell had considerable experience in the ski business, because he operated food and beverage concessions at resorts throughout the northeast. But O'Donnell's touch didn't provide the needed magic, and in 1991, BCG closed the area and sold off most of the equipment. Only two lifts remained. Private investors reopened Magic in 1997, and they eventually leased it to an operator from 2006–14, at which time the lease was transferred to one of the original investors, Tom Barker. Barker operated Magic for two years, when it was sold to Ski Magic LLC, led by Geoff Hatheway and a group of 16 investors.

Not a lot of continuity of ownership. Throughout its history, Magic struggled to provide a competitive skiing product, mostly because it lacked sufficient water for an impactful snowmaking system. The end result, as we've seen so often in the business, was a cycle of good and bad years, leaving the coffers dry.

The new ownership group is moving forward with a five-year plan to address its two most critical needs: reliable lifts serving a broad range of skier abilities, and enhanced snowmaking. An Act 250 permit (Vermont's land-use regulation) was issued on August 17, 2018. The permit allows for installation of a new (or refurbished) base-to-midmountain chairlift, a magic carpet for learn-to-ski, enhanced lighting for the tubing area, and a few other relatively minor projects. Also big: the resort announced in June 2019 it had secured approval from the state to double the size of its snowmaking pond (to 9 million gallons) while taking it "offstream" to create a healthier aquatic environment for downstream fish. The permit also allows the in-take of water from Thompsonburg Brook along Rte. 11 for pond replenishment. Magic will now be able to cover 60 percent of the mountain.

Meanwhile, the owners seem to be taking the long view, covering operating losses until the new investments are in place and Magic has a path toward profitability. The website notes the owners' commitment to spend $1.5 million in improvements over the next two years.

It also touts the tagline: "Magic is a place where skiing still has its soul." Sounds remarkably like how most of the remaining independents are positioning themselves. The web site proclaims: "Not Epic, not Ikonic, just Magic." Magic has added some pass options that provide chuckles, if not a lot of sales. For example, the resort offers a "White Out" pass, teasing skiers to escape from the crowds at the larger resorts over the holiday blackout periods. The pass ($199 for 2019–20) is good only on these peak days: the Christmas holidays, MLK Jr. weekend, and President's weekend. I bet the Magic team had a fun time putting this together, but I don't expect a lot of sales.

Somewhat surprisingly, Magic's passes aren't that cheap. Adult unlimited is $599 for 2019–20 with an early purchase, and Shredder (ages 17–29) and Youth (6–17) are $299. Magic has joined the Freedom Pass group to add value and provide some different skiing options for its passholders. And it seems to have found its niche in the Throwback Card. Buy it for $149, and get 1980s pricing ($29) every time you ski, with no blackouts. That would appear to be a good value and provide some flexibility in a poor snow year.

Will the new group succeed? History says no. But with creative marketing, increasing crowds at competitors, and a better on-snow product, there's finally a chance.

ALSO IN VERMONT, but closer to an urban area, is Bolton Valley, located about 20 miles south of Burlington, home to one-third of all Vermonters and one of the few areas to avoid a declining census. Ralph DesLauriers and his father founded Bolton in 1966. Ralph managed to hold on to the resort for some 30 years, but was forced to file for bankruptcy in 1995, and the resort eventually sold two years later. Although Bolton always presented itself as a local ski area, DesLauriers was a real-estate developer by nature, and several marginal Bolton projects probably hastened its demise. In the spring of 2017, Ralph and his three adult children, helped by a number of local investors, re-acquired the resort. So Bolton has come full circle, returning to the DesLauriers after five intervening owners. Ralph's family grew up skiing Bolton. His two sons, Rob and Evan, achieved considerable notoriety as early "extreme skiers" and were featured in more than a dozen ski films. They know the business.

They also have a passion for the ski sport. "My mission is to give every Vermont child the opportunity to ski," Ralph said following the sale. "Our guests can expect to see steady progress toward a major revitalization." The resort's tag line is: "Vermont. Naturally." It offers night skiing Tuesday through Saturday. They're bringing back a corporate race league. Passholders have access to the Freedom Pass, with discounts at 18 resorts. From what I read, they're doing all the right stuff to ensure local support. *Powder* magazine said of Bolton: "Skiing's indie spirit remains."

New investments in snowmaking are helping to take the risk out of the business. I would be surprised to see the risk put back in with an overly aggressive real-estate project. Time will tell. If Bolton is to be successful, it needs to stay true to what it is: a fun, affordable skiing option and community asset for the greater Burlington area.

Shifting gears and moving back out west, just about two hours north of Steamboat, in southern Wyoming, is the not very famous Snowy Range Ski Area. This small area is located in the Medicine Bow–Routt National Forest, about 35 miles from Laramie, home to the University of Wyoming. With a 1,000-foot vertical, four old double chairs and one magic carpet, Snowy Range is as much a "throwback" resort as you could find. About 10 years ago, the owners defaulted on a large note issued by the First National Bank of Wyoming. The bank tried operating the area for a couple of years, until regulators informed them they were in the banking business, not the ski business.

Aaron Maddox, son of longtime Steamboat local Bob Maddox, was working at the time for the Mountain Valley Bank at their Walden, Colorado, branch (about one hour from Snowy Range) when he learned of the bank's decision to sell. Bob and Aaron took a look at the area and decided, "Why not?" A deal was quickly struck for $1.8 million, about $1.25 million of which came in cash from the Maddoxes. I don't have the details, but knowing that the defaulted note covered a new, rather extravagant base lodge, I assume it was a haircut for the bank. According to Bob, the original base lodge had burned down under somewhat suspicious circumstances. Its replacement was over-the-top for the area's skier volume.

Snowy Range was doing about 25,000 skier visits when Bob and Aaron took over nine years ago. Bob had an appraisal business in Steamboat and had previously operated a "flight for life" service in northwest Colorado. Appraisals were his business, but flying was his passion (he currently operates the FBO at Walden and Saratoga, Wyoming, both reasonably close to Snowy Range).

Their first season was a labor of love. Bob reminisces on how he would start early on weekend days, first plowing the parking lot, then piloting a snow-cat for final touch-up grooming, next parking cars, then off to fit boots in the rental shop, and so on—a long day of multitasking. They had a simple formula: Be friendly to everyone, but make it profitable. During the early years, Aaron maintained his position in the bank while helping out at the ski area, but soon the business had grown to the point where it needed full-time management. Aaron took the lead. Bob focused more on the FBO operations (also owned by the two of them). He shrank his appraisal business as the ski area and FBO ops grew.

For the 2017–18 ski season, they recorded about 75,000 skier visits; 2018–19 was another record breaker, just short of 100,000. That represented a fourfold increase in 10 years. Incredible. Although clearly still a "small" ski area, Snowy Range is one of Wyoming's top four ski areas, along with Jackson Hole, Grand Targhee, and Snow King.

Their cash flow on an annual basis is more than their original investment. They've done this while keeping prices so low that a family of four can ski all day and have lunch for about $100. Rentals start at $19. The season pass, if purchased by Labor Day, costs $249. There's a tempting add-on for buyers, which for the 2019–20 season included five days at Steamboat for an additional $169, with, amazingly, no blackouts. This is particularly appealing for college students in nearby Laramie or Cheyenne. The Maddoxes have negotiated a number of lift ticket discounts at regional ski resorts (Jackson Hole, Snow King, Grand Targhee, and James Coleman's Mountain Capital Partners' resorts) as an added value for their passholders. And, passholders get unlimited Buddy Passes (half-off), good Tuesday through Thursday.

When I say Snowy Range is remote, it's all relative. For a skier in fast-growing Fort Collins, Colorado (home to Colorado State University), it's less than a two-hour drive—with no traffic. A trip to the I70 resorts from that same market can run hours longer, depending on the level of congestion. Granted, this is a much smaller ski area (250 acres) but it normally offers good snow, short lift lines, uncrowded terrain, and a fun, family atmosphere. With no nearby lodging, skiers coming for the weekend stay in value-priced motels in the Laramie area. So while the ski area is, honestly, in the middle of nowhere, it is still within a three-hour drive of 3 million people (between southern Wyoming and northern Colorado). The market is anyone who loves skiing and wants a fun day on the slopes, within a limited budget. Bob Maddox describes the skiing outfits as "outerwear:" jeans and Carhartts versus insulated ski pants.

The Maddoxes recognized early on that one thing was missing: some kind of differentiating après-ski. The remedy: They decided to have their own brewery in the large base lodge. The story of the hoops they had to jump through is worth a book in itself. Suffice it to say that the Forest Service eventually approved the brewery plan, reputed to be the only brewery located on *any* National Forest land. The Medicine Bow–Routt leadership understood that keeping small areas successful was a priority, and a brewery would certainly improve the odds for Snowy Range. There was resistance at the Regional USFS level, but with local support and help from Geraldine Link at NSAA, the issue got visibility within the higher ranks of the Forest Service, where it found support and eventual approval. Snowy Range can sell its beer only in the lodge. You won't find it in grocery stores.

The story of Snowy Range is important on multiple levels. It speaks to the opportunities for growth and financial success at smaller areas with the right management and motivation. Also, it highlights how many people aspire to enjoy the ski sport but need an affordable option. That might be for just a few years, until the day when they step up to an Epic, Ikon, or whatever is available and affordable. Or it could be for a lifetime.

The word is out: Snowy Range skiing is good, the people are nice, and the beer is great. What more could you ask for? To Bob and Aaron Maddox, we in the ski industry should say: "Thank you, and well done."

TWO SKI AREAS COME TO MIND that don't neatly fit in the rural or urban categories but deserve recognition as success stories: Wachusett Mountain outside Boston and Holiday Valley in New York.

Wachusett is a little more than an hour's drive from Boston and its suburbs—close enough that train service is available on weekends, yet far enough away to offer that uniquely rural New England ambiance. Eight million people live within a one-hour drive. Wachusett has outsized influence in its market for three reasons: exceptional facilities, a finely tuned operation, and lots of personality.

The ski area, located on State Forest land, has been operated by the Crowley family since 1969, when it was doing a modest 10,000 to 20,000 visits a year on its two T-bars. Prior to that date, it had been state-operated— and as has so often been the case, the state operation floundered. The Crowleys signed a five-year lease, and then annual extensions, while negotiating for a longer agreement (similar to what the State of New Hampshire executed with Sunapee). Finally, in 1981, the Crowleys entered into a long-term lease agreement with the state. That allowed major reinvestment on the leased land.

From 1982 to the present day, Wachusett has grown to become Massachusetts's largest ski area, recording an average of 350,000 annual skier visits on its 120 acres. It offers day and night skiing on a respectable 1,000 feet of vertical. Three modern detachables and a triple chairlift provide the uphill capacity. The entire resort is covered with snowmaking, and its pumping capacity now stands at 9,000 gpm, a staggering amount for an area of its size. Wachusett enjoys the advantage of daily train service from the Boston metro area. Wachusett Station is the last stop on the line. Regarding the train's impact, Jeff sent me an email he had received recently from one of his guests, a Harvard business school professor:

"It's fantastic that the mountain is 'accessible' by commuter rail and Uber/taxi. Reminds me of skiing in Bad Gastein, Austria, where you have dozens of skiers walk off the 8 a.m. train every morning and right onto the slopes."

Although warm-weather events and rain are just a reality of life in this part of New England, Wachusett sits just far enough west and high enough to receive significant natural snow in most nor'easter events. The Crowleys are forever innovating and are currently enjoying the benefits of a new snow-grooming technology called Snowright, which allows snowcat operators to know exactly how deep the snow is that they are traveling over. This ensures that snow is distributed evenly over the varied terrain underneath.

Smaller, urban-ish ski areas tend to focus on the youth market. Wachusett is just big enough to have it both ways. There are plenty of yellow buses, but there's also a dedicated adult clientele enjoying the slopes. A 50,000-square-foot base lodge provides plenty of "après" activities. At an NSAA trade show a few years back, I remember asking David Crowley about how the prior season had gone. His response: "We don't have bad years. We have good years or great years. Last year was a great year."

The Crowley family owns a regional soft-drink company, Polar Beverages, well-known in their market, less so outside New England. Of the five siblings currently involved in the family business, two are focused on the beverage side and three (David, Jeff, and sister Carolyn Stimpson) on the ski area. Polar is in a major growth mode, currently operating in 30 states. I'm told that their secret sauce is less the actual beverage and more their extensive distribution system. When boutique beverage companies want to expand into a region, the Crowleys enter into an agreement that provides a modest equity stake in exchange for distribution. Jeff jokes that Pepsi and Coke watch who the hot "new" beverage players are by checking the back of Polar delivery trucks, and they then become acquisition targets. An example: One of the first small beverage companies to use Polar for distribution was Vitaminwater.

When the Crowley kids were growing up, their dad wanted them to be skaters and hockey players—after all, we're talking Boston here. According to Jeff, they all hated hockey and wanted to try skiing. Their first trip was to Mount Snow. He recounts: "After renting some skis, buying some gloves, and buying the tickets, he [dad] spent more than he expected, so he was thinking that anyone who can get $100 out of Ralph Crowley on a Sunday had to be doing something right. Shortly thereafter, Wachusett came up for lease, and he was all in."

In another Mount Snow connection, Jeff, who had to decide on whether his future would be on the beverage or ski side, went to Mount Snow in 1978 looking for some experience and applied for work. Nothing was available, but Lift Engineering was looking for laborers to help build a new lift. Jeff hired on and spent the next three years learning the ropes and initiating a lifelong ski-industry career.

The Crowley kids have been closely involved with NSAA over the years. They have shared their learnings in terms of rental shop operations and other guest-focused services. They have a well-earned reputation for competence in terms of ski area operations, and have shared their best practices to the benefit of the larger industry. They are also creative marketers. I can still remember their musical version of the 1960s tune, *The Wah-Watusi,* playing on airwaves throughout the Boston area: "Wahhh-O-Wahhh-Chusett!" It used to drive me nuts listening to the kids in the Mount Snow race programs singing that jingle—not fair when a competitor intrudes so effectively in your territory! Small mountain; big influence.

And they have a lot of fun. I loved to refer to the Crowleys as our "improper Bostonians." They still have a passion for the ski sport and everything surrounding it. But the last thing they ever do is to take themselves too seriously. That personality imbues Wachusett Mountain and, in my view, is one of its keys to success.

Find your niche, take good care of your guests, and make great snow. The formula is working in these Worcester hills.

What's the largest ski area in New York State in terms of annual skier visits? It's not in the venerable Adirondacks. It doesn't have 2,000-plus vertical feet of skiing. It's Holiday Valley, in Ellicottville in western New York. And it's a snow factory, lying in what's regionally known as the Buffalo Snowbelt. Especially in the early season, cold northwest winds flow across Lake Ontario, pick up enhanced moisture from the still-warm lake water, and then "dump" snow just east of the lake, right on top of Holiday Valley.

Holiday Valley operates day and night and offers 56 trails and 13 lifts, serving a modest 750-foot vertical. It executes on the formula for success identified so many times on earlier pages:

- Make great snow.
- Take care of your guests.
- Know your markets: western New York (Buffalo, Jamestown), southern Ontario (Toronto), Cleveland, Pittsburgh, and even Detroit (five hours).
- Maximize summer opportunities: adventure park, mountain coaster, and more.

Dennis Eshbaugh has been president of Holiday Valley for more than 30 years. When I called to chat with him about the state of the New York ski industry, he carved out an hour between board and HOA meetings. This was a Sunday. Eshbaugh has been all-in with Holiday Valley, guiding its steady growth over his long career. In '99, the ski area began the transition from ski area to resort with various real-estate development projects. No longer a day area, Holiday Valley is a popular, year-round destination, with the attractive village of Ellicottville as a bonus.

Community Assets/Non-profits

The economics are challenging for smaller facilities, particularly if there's no snowmaking. But many have survived. At the heart of skiing's current renaissance is the growing awareness that a local ski hill provides a deep sense of community. A local ski hill is a visible demonstration of the power of family, kids interacting with their friends but also spending quality time with other family members. There are few activities that can be as rewarding to residents. A thriving local ski hill says, "This is our town, and we like it."

Dynamite Hill in Chestertown, New York, just off Route 8 and the Adirodack Northway, is a classic example of survival. I'm very familiar with the area, having spent many summers at Lake George and nearby Brant Lake. Owned by the town, it offers a modest 65 vertical feet, but opens weekends and holidays and has operated since 1960. Best of all, it's *free*, thanks to volunteer workers, many from the local Rotary Club. I stopped by Dynamite Hill a few years ago and was simply stunned by the energy. The hill was packed with skiers, boarders, tubers and even sledders. I stood by and smiled at the passion. Any passerby would have a similar reaction: "This is a cool place—I could live here." The Schroon Lake Ski Center has reopened with similar community support.

Here in Steamboat Springs, our city owns the local ski area, Howelsen Hill. Howelsen is part of a larger park that includes ball fields, tennis courts, rodeo grounds, extensive mountain-bike trails, even an enclosed ice rink. Howelsen Hill, North America's oldest, continuously operating ski area, opened in 1915. It offers a relatively modest 440-vertical feet, but that vertical serves a steep and challenging slalom run. In addition, the complex includes five ski jumps (two are year-round, with plastic surfaces), an extensive Nordic trail network, a magic carpet for beginners, a halfpipe, and more. The ability of Steamboat kids to access these facilities has produced more winter Olympians than any other community in North America. That Olympic tradition is now part of the community's DNA.

While this is certainly a great success story, until very recently the city showed little interest in the actual ski area, beyond its role as a competition and training site. City staff was responsible for operations, and the budget included a significant annual subsidy, but the Steamboat Springs Winter Sports Club (SSWSC)—which serves almost 1,000 athletes, mostly locals—was de facto manager of the hill. Howelsen has hosted Nordic Combined World Cup events and, for the past few years, Continental Cup events (just below World Cup). Howelsen is a regular stop for regional and national alpine racing competitions. But until recently, it was not considered a recreational option for non-competitive skiers.

Through extended negotiations with the SSWSC over a new operating agreement, city staff and city council became more aware of Howelsen's potential. While the driving force was an interest in reducing the annual subsidy, there was also a desire to expand non-competitive uses. For the 2017–18 winter, the city decided to offer free skiing on selected Sundays. The response was overwhelming. There clearly was a local demographic for which "free" was the right price. And they showed up.

For 2018–19, most Sundays were free. So instead of Howelsen being used almost exclusively by the athletes, it is now serving a larger audience and becoming a more vibrant community asset.

Another change to the fortune of smaller areas comes in the form of new investors (like West Mountain's Spencer Montgomery), who are making a commitment based on an emotional connection and who are prepared to accept less than market returns. A good example here is Blue Knob in Pennsylvania, about two hours east of Pittsburgh. It offers the highest elevation of any Pennsylvania resort at 3,146 feet, and the second-largest vertical drop at 1,072 feet. Despite these advantages, it was relatively small and struggled against larger competitors. Originally, Blue Knob had been an Air Force radar site. It opened for skiing in 1962, and had been owned by the Gauthier family for the past 34 years.

Six Pittsburgh investors, all skiers, purchased the property in July 2017 for $1.3 million. They are applying for a $2.5 million grant from the Pennsylvania

Redevelopment Assistance Capital Program, which they plan to use for enhanced snowmaking (sound familiar?) and other improvements. The partnership is called Sustainable Hospitality & Development LLC. In a statement, the partners described themselves as "skiers who hope to keep the character of Blue Knob intact while making necessary improvements to keep growing the skier/snowboarder base." Let's hope they're successful.

Antelope Butte is a small ski area located 54 miles west of Sheridan, Wyoming, on the east side of the Big Horn Mountains. It's on a well-traveled summer route between South Dakota's Black Hills (Mount Rushmore) and Yellowstone. This is rural, sparsely settled northern Wyoming.

The ski area closed in 2004 after 44 years of operation. Modest by Western standards, it offered three lifts serving 1,000 vertical feet and encompassing 225 acres. The base lodge, which had seen little change over the years, totaled 11,400-square-feet. For several years, there were rumors of new buyers, but by 2010 none had moved forward to close a deal. Since there were no interested operators, the U.S. Forest Service began the process of reclaiming the land. Concerned about the loss of such an important community asset, a group of local residents began negotiations with the Forest Service in an attempt to buy some time and preserve an opportunity to reopen the area. In 2011, The Antelope Butte Foundation was formed, and three years later, they have managed to reopen the area (ironically, the larger double chairlift remained closed during the late 2018–early 2019 government shutdown, because there was no one available to inspect it).

The foundation board reached out to a number of industry experts, including Michael Berry (NSAA) and Blaise Carrig (former president of Vail Resorts Mountain Division) for advice on reopening. Carrig has continued his involvement and directed me to an article describing one mother's recent experience skiing there with her daughter: It was, in her words, "heart-exploding magical!" Wow.

It has been a long road for the foundation, but that parent's expression tells the whole story. It's about local skiers recognizing just how much skiing changed their lives and making a commitment to preserve that opportunity for others in the community. Antelope Butte is regaining its place at the center of northern Wyoming life.

According to John Kirlin, the foundation's executive director, "We are seeing a lot of families and beginners, which is what we are here to serve. Our mission for the foundation is to provide affordable and accessible, year-round mountain training and education, with a focus on youth and beginners."

In February 2019, the foundation hosted about 50 fifth-graders from nearby Woodland Park Elementary School for a weeklong introduction to skiing that fulfilled state physical-education standards. The first few days were spent in the classroom, introducing students to the equipment and different skiing styles. Then came two days outside the school, on-snow, learning positional basics, side-stepping, climbing, and such. The students spent Friday at the ski area, putting all they had learned into action. Kirlin taught the class, and based on this year's success, he hopes to extend the program to other schools. This program highlights the foundation's primary mission: focus on youth.

Fundraising continues, with an ambitious goal of more than $4 million to upgrade the mountain facilities and the base lodge (scheduled for fall 2019), and to expand year-round recreation opportunities. A big advantage: more than 330,00 people drive by each summer on the Chief Joseph Scenic highway.

I should note that the Ski Area Recreational Activities Enhancement Act, passed in 2013, made it possible for small ski areas like Antelope Butte, operating on federal land, to enhance their income stream through summer activities. That, in turn, significantly raises their opportunity for long-term success. Antelope Butte is a case in point. Thanks to all involved for making that happen.

AMERICA'S BEST-KNOWN SKI CO-OP would be Mad River Glen in Vermont, which bills itself as the only such stewardship of a "major mountain." The area, located just up Rte. 17 from Sugarbush, at the foot of Appalachian Gap, offers a rock-solid 2,000 feet of vertical ("Ski It If You Can"—but no snowboarding allowed). It was founded in 1948 by Roland Palmedo, the guiding hand in the creation of Stowe as well as the National Ski Patrol. From the beginning, Palmedo envisioned Mad River as a commercial-free zone for real skiers, and the mountain has stayed true to that mission for 70-plus years.

In 1995, then-owner Betsy Pratt (she had bought it with her late husband Truxton and others in 1972), sold it to the newly created Mad River Glen Co-Op. One share costs $2,000 (payment plans are available), and shareholders are also asked to support Mad River year-in and year-out. They must meet an annual Advance Purchase Requirement (APR) of $200 by Oct. 1, which can be spent on a season pass or converted to Mad Money for anything from meals in General Stark's Pub to ski school. For most shareholders, this is not an additional burden.

About 2,130 shares (generating roughly $4.26 million) have been sold to some 1,800 individuals; the goal is 2,500 shares, but the Cooperative is allowed to sell up to 3,000 shares. The co-op says it has paid off the debt to the former owner and invested nearly $5 million in capital improvements to the mountain's infrastructure, including replacing the famous single chair with a new … single chair. A conservative fiscal structure is designed to provide a cushion for lean years, the co-op says. Audited financial statements are available for potential shareholders.

As expected, Mad River has not embraced mega-pass mania or seen a need to make a bold statement in the value-pass market. Full adult is $769 per season for 2019–20, though it does offer the Twixter Pass, ages 19–29, for an enticing $249, and the 70-and-over Legend Pass for the even better $199.

"Over the next 20 years, we expect to spend another $6.5 million on capital projects such as renovations to the Basebox (Lodge), a rebuild of the Patrol and Ski School building, replacement of the drive on the Birdland double chair, and other projects," the co-op says. Due to a limited water supply, Mad River doesn't make much snow, and it also limits grooming to preserve what has fallen naturally. Many Mad River diehards say the mountain has never skied better. It enjoyed its longest season ever in 2018–19, operating for 136 days.

Two other notable nonprofits are Mt. Ashland in southern Oregon and the National Winter Activity Center (NWAC) at the former Hidden Valley resort in New Jersey, just outside the New York metro area.

Mt. Ashland opened in 1964 as a "mountain for the people by the people," and survived three decades of up-and-down operations and multiple ownerships before the operator in 1991 couldn't find a buyer for the next go-round. A nonprofit group stepped into the breech, successfully using a pyramid fundraising scheme to raise funds and keep the lifts spinning. Each of its original 35 members vowed to find two people who would donate $1,000, and then each of them would recruit another two, and so on, according to a September 2015 account in the *High Country News*. The plan worked.

Located near Medford and Ashland, with a combined population of 100,000, Mt. Ashland's summit tops out at 7,533 feet, with a solid 1,150-foot vertical. For the 2018–19 season, Mt. Ashland recorded its best season in more than a decade, according to the local newspaper, the *Mail Tribune*. General

Manager Hiram Towle reported the nonprofit welcomed 98,677 visitors in a 91-day season that started the first week of December. That was just shy of Mt. Ashland's record of 100,000 visitors, but the highest since the ski area dropped to a five-day-a-week schedule in 2007. And it's 40 percent more than the post-2007 averages of 70,000 visitors per season. "This was a huge year for us," Towle said in a refrain heard 'round the ski world after the past season.

Schone Malliet, a Bronx-born former Marine pilot turned successful businessman, was the driving force behind NWAC, providing a winning second act for the defunct Hidden Valley in New Jersey. Billed as the nation's first such 501(c)(3) winter facility, it draws youth from ages 6 to 17 from all economic backgrounds to the sport, teaching a host of life lessons along the way, including healthy eating and lifestyle. It serves 6,000 participants annually and is designed to be replicable across the country. Kudos to the NWAC. The entire industry would be wise to take note of these sorts of programs and provide appropriate support.

CHAPTER 13

Private Resorts:
Yellowstone Club...
and Then the Rest

There's something about the ski industry that has attracted real-estate developers when otherwise rational businesspeople would stay clear of this niche. Why steer clear? The ski season is short, so the appeal is highly seasonal for buyers and annual occupancies are low for commercial projects. The cost of building in a mountain environment and the relatively brief construction season present additional challenges. Then there's the complexity of permits in resort communities, where the status quo has many votes. And, most importantly, the extended time frame required for a major project often spills into another business cycle. The list of successful resort real-estate developers is a very short one. The arrival of the Great Recession in 2008 virtually ground the resort real-estate industry to a standstill. While all major projects were affected, none were more impacted than those involving private ski clubs.

The investment required to create a private ski area is daunting, when compared with your typical private golf development. The business models are similar: Buy a lot, pay an initiation fee, and then pay annual dues and, usually, some sort of food and beverage minimum. A ski resort is a whole different animal in terms of the magnitude of these costs. We're talking hundreds of millions to create a facility that is large and diverse enough to satisfy members' expectations. This applies to base-area services, as well as the on-mountain lift/trail component. Those who have enough money to join expect the restaurant experience they would find in Aspen or Vail. The ski shop needs to carry popular fashion items, as well as the usual functional gear. And staff has to be friendly and well-trained—and probably housed on-site. And how long will the private ski area be open? Three and a half months. Virtually no one will show up until the Christmas holidays (or cancel if the snow is not satisfactory), and early April is about as far as one can push operations into the spring. Do many spend the whole winter? With the exception of the few who are retired, no. Average use is probably similar to what the club members would do if they had a private home at Beaver Creek. Two or three weeks a winter, typically over the traditional holiday periods. As for summer, unless someone in the family is a hard-core fly-fisherman, summer use will be limited.

The conundrum: Buyers want a high-quality experience, with no crowds, but do not expect to spend a lot of time at the resort. This means it is *very* expensive. So the market is extremely small. In the Vail Valley, there's a lot of noise about how many of the longtime, high-end second-homeowners are packing up and heading to the Yellowstone Club (reportedly, because of frustration with Epic crowding). This makes for great gossip, but we're not talking thousands of people making this move. This is a very small segment of the skiing market.

In my view, unless the club experience was truly extraordinary, members would eventually realize that it simply wasn't worth it, given the amount of time they used the facility, and eventually they would sell and move on. At least that's what I thought until looking at the Yellowstone Club story.

Entrepreneur Tim Blixseth purchased approximately 100,000 acres of Western timberland and then successfully arranged land swaps with the U.S. Forest Service and the federal government. Because of these extraordinary transactions (I don't believe there has ever been a larger ski-related one), Blixseth ultimately ended up with a large amount of developable land and became developer of the Yellowstone Club, a private ski and golf community in Big Sky, Montana. Early members were a "Who's Who" list of American wealth and celebrity: Phil Mickelson, Bill Gates, Dan Quayle. Members had to buy a building lot, and then pay the $300,000 initiation fee. One lot sold for a stunning $16 million. Most homes were in the $5 million to $25 million range.

Blixseth used the Club as collateral for a $375 million loan with Credit

Suisse, where the proceeds were used for other purposes, including an effort to build an exclusive luxury vacation club, with resort properties around the world. This venture failed. Blixseth and his wife divorced, and the Yellowstone Club entered bankruptcy in November 2008, caught in the real-estate shakedown of the Great Recession and Blixseth's machinations. Blixseth's wife ended up with the resort, and she eventually filed personal bankruptcy. In 2009, coming out of bankruptcy, the resort was sold to private equity firm CrossHarbor Capital Partners, led by Yellowstone Club member Sam Byrne, for $115 million. The new owners reestablished credibility for the resort and steadily began to grow membership.

According to Wikipedia, "as of late 2014 the Yellowstone Club has no remaining debt from the bankruptcy, has positive cash flow, and has doubled its membership to more than 500 households. In late 2013, CrossHarbor partnered with Boyne Resorts, the owners of neighboring Big Sky Resort, and paid $26 million to acquire a nearby real-estate project, Spanish Peaks, a 5,700-acre development in bankruptcy. Shortly thereafter, CrossHarbor and Big Sky Resort jointly acquired the bankrupt Moonlight Basin ski club and began consolidation of the newly acquired ski terrain with that of Big Sky Resort." Big Sky now covers some 5,750 acres, making it the nation's second largest resort, and, importantly, thanks to the land swap referenced above, these lands are all in private ownership. In terms of the cost and feasibility of development, this is a dramatic competitive advantage over other destination resorts that have to navigate through a complex and layered Forest Service permit process. This is one reason why Big Sky is in the middle of the largest resort-mountain and real-estate expansion in North America. This place is booming.

Although it took a bankruptcy to make it happen, Yellowstone Club seems to be thriving. It did initiate its own belt-tightening measures, which included nixing the caviar bar and the valets who helped guests put on and take off their ski boots. It also converted a cavernous ballroom on the bottom floor into a youth and teen center, more directly catering to its family clientele.

What separates Yellowstone from other private-club projects is its scale and relative completeness: 2,700 feet of vertical, 18 lifts (including a two-stage Doppelmayr gondola), five on-mountain dining venues, a separate pool and fitness center, base area shops and restaurants, and the spectacular $100 million Warren Miller Lodge! Add to that a Tom Weiskopf–designed golf course, and you have the real deal. Several lifts provide easy connections to the larger, growing Big

Sky Resort. They share a *five-mile border*. This is Montana, so everything operates at a different scale. The Club sits just north of the National Park that shares its name and is surrounded by the 250,000-acre Gallatin National Forest.

It's not cheap. Under the new ownership, members still must buy a lot (or condominium). So let's assume $4 to $5 million to get started. Then there's the $300,000 initiation. Then, annual dues of $41,500 (2018–19). And don't forget the residential association fees that will run $10,000 to $20,000. Membership is capped at 864 families, and reportedly, more than 500 have now joined. The Club notes in a recent promotional piece that average use has grown from 20 to 60 days per year. Impressive and certainly a harbinger of success.

Unlike Moonlight Basin, which opened in December 2003 as a real-estate development within an independent ski area (Moonlight Basin Ranch), the Club at Spanish Peaks tried the private-club strategy. And failed. Covering 5,300 private acres (facilitated by the Blixseth land trade and sold to them by his company), the club had only 200 members when the recession hit. Bankruptcy followed in 2011. On October 1, 2013, the Boyne/CrossHarbor partnership closed on the resort. Members were invited back, without an additional charge, which had been expected and was well received. With the financial strength of CrossHarbor and Boyne, and the positive inertia the Big Sky region is enjoying, one could expect a resurgence of interest in Spanish Peaks real estate.

Both of the private clubs, as well as Moonlight Basin, had to go through bankruptcy before the future got brighter. The Big Sky region is unique in its scale, in the amount of private land for development, and the relatively low cost of doing that. It's one place where the club model may thrive.

For a while, I thought The Hermitage Club at Haystack Mountain in southern Vermont might make it. I am very familiar with Haystack and the Wilmington, Vermont, community, having spent almost 20 years at Mount Snow. Mount Snow owned and operated Haystack from 1991 to 2005, when American Skiing Company (which had acquired Mount Snow in 1996) sold the resort to Robert Foisie, a successful businessman/engineer and 1956 Worcester Polytechnic Institute (WPI) graduate. Foisie was responsible for a $40 million donation, the largest ever made to WPI. His vision was for a private club with heavy emphasis on real-estate development. After a flurry of activity that saw millions invested in infrastructure (but limited buyer interest), Foisie shut it down in 2007, leaving behind unfinished townhomes and construction debris. It looked and felt abandoned.

In November 2011, he sold the ski and golf assets to Jim Barnes for $6.5 million. Foisie's large fortune was smaller thanks to his Haystack experience.

Barnes had made his money in the trash-hauling business (from 1995 to 2009, he was president and CEO of Oakleaf Waste Management). In 2007, he had purchased The Hermitage Inn, adjacent to and just north of Haystack. The Hermitage Inn was an iconic fixture in southern Vermont, owned for many years by my old friend, Jim McGovern. McGovern loved wine and had at one time the largest wine cellar of any New England resort property. One thing McGovern had not done was to put a lot of money back into the inn. Barnes made many upgrades to The Hermitage and, as an active owner, became very engaged in the community. According to Barnes, the offer for Haystack Ski Area was too compelling to turn down.

At the start, he seemed to have a good plan and the money to support his vision: a private club, heavily focused on lot sales to members, and even a hotel. The Hermitage Inn served as a de facto base lodge during the early years. He did eventually complete construction of a huge, 80,000-square-foot base lodge, complete with fitness center, movie theater, and bowling alley. Nothing like this had ever been built at a Vermont ski area. Barnes began buying up properties in the town of Wilmington to provide beds and resort amenities for his club members until they constructed their own homes. The good news: He had refurbished a number of older properties that needed reinvestment (for example, The White House Inn, The Vermont House, The Hermitage Inn). The bad news: He was often working with "other people's money." Sellers were taking back paper. The new Barnstormer detachable chairlift happened only because of a loan ($7.8 million) from some 30 club members. Furniture and fixtures throughout the property were leased. Barnes told reporters from the *Bennington Banner* and *The Berkshire Eagle* that he had invested $70 million personally, but the resort was still highly leveraged.

The mountain is not particularly interesting from a terrain perspective, but it does have decent vertical and, most importantly, location—three and a half hours from New York City and just a little over two hours from Boston. If you look at the amount of wealth that extends along the coast, from Washington D.C. to Portland, Maine, there are enough families passionate about skiing who might have joined a private ski area to ensure a quality experience. Instead of several weeklong vacations (as at a Yellowstone Club), their use would be more flexible: maybe the Christmas/New Year's period, and then a

number of long weekends for foliage visits—maybe even a summer weekend—
all within reasonable driving distance and relatively hassle-free. Barnes thought
this would work, and he put in base-area and on-mountain amenities that were
simply over the top, given Haystack's size and historic market share. For it to
work, he probably needed 2,000 members. Calculating the actual number sold
is difficult, given that so many members had negotiated a different arrangement with Barnes; some may have been comps/trades for service. Somewhere
around 450 was the number that the press kept referencing.

I got the grand tour in the fall of 2016, while visiting friends in the Deerfield Valley. John Santaniello, who once had managed the Steamboat Grand
Hotel for me in Steamboat, had accepted the position of GM for The Hermitage Club. He was excited about the opportunity. Santaniello had a solid
résumé in the lodging business, including a stint with Vail Resorts, but his
passion was on the ski side. Most recently, he'd been working at the Omni-
owned Bretton Woods Resort in New Hampshire. My wife, Eileen, and I met
Santaniello for breakfast at the newly refurbished White House Inn, and he
described his new role and the club's plans. It just struck me as an unrealistic
financial model, and I cautioned him appropriately, which was tough, given
his enthusiasm and optimism. Bottom line, this was still Haystack—and still
Vermont. I was not surprised when, just a few weeks later, he called to say he
had been let go and would have to sue to receive his promised relocation expenses. As of this writing, John is standing in line with a long list of creditors.

It all came tumbling down in the spring of 2018, and the resort remains
shuttered as of summer 2019. Berkshire Bank, which was owed $17.1 million,
initiated foreclosure proceedings on February 23, 2018. Simply put, it's a mess.
Sorting out who owns what, and determining if there is a future for the original
vision, will take time. And as time passes, the resort will probably slip back
once again into disrepair and neglect, and club members will be moving on
and walking away from their original investments, some of which are multi-
million-dollar homes at the base of a now-defunct ski area. How much are
those homes now worth?

The failure has created an economic crisis in Wilmington; tax bills are not
being paid. Many local sub-contractors and vendors, many of the mom-and-
pop vein, have been stiffed and face all sorts of financial challenges. If someone
can acquire Haystack for a *deeply* discounted number, it's still questionable
whether the private-club model can be resurrected. It was just too much, too

fast, with no financial discipline. From the outside, it looked like the classic "too good to be true." And it was. With better management, could it have succeeded? We have no way of knowing, and that's the big problem. Prior members would have to step back and put in more cash, possibly substantially more cash. And so much hinges on successful real-estate sales, while the strength of the New England resort market is still uncertain. Could Haystack have a future as a stand-alone ski area? I'm not sure how it could begin to compete with Mount Snow, given the significant enhancements there in the last decade. There don't appear to be a lot of good options for whoever winds up with the assets.

Like Foisie before him, Jim Barnes has learned, thanks to Haystack, how to make a large fortune much smaller. Barnes is facing all sorts of personal lawsuits. As of January 2019, he did not have legal representation in Vermont and was not showing up at court hearings.

Beyond the high-end, real-estate focused clubs targeting the .1-percenters, there is a colorful and important legacy of family-based, affordable private ski clubs in North America, dating back more than seven decades. Ontario is the epicenter, with nearly a dozen flourishing club hills like Caledon, Craigleith, and Georgian Peaks, typically offering a half-dozen chairlifts and excellent base facilities. The members at HoliMont, located near Ellicottville in New York, share the club with the public during the week. Wisconsin features a handful of club hills, most with origins as ski jumping sites, like Ausblick, Blackhawk, Fox Hill, and Heiliger Huegel, founded in 1935. Another is The Homestead at Glen Arbor in Michigan (though in the northeast part of the state, Otsego Club & Resort recently closed). Sahalie and Meany Lodge operate at Snoqualmie Pass, and the list goes on and on. These clubs all add to the fabric of the sport, creating a meaningful number of new skiers.

CHAPTER 14

Disrupter No. 1:
Climate Change Looms Large

Amid the bullish picture of an overall resort renaissance stand substantial hurdles, and no two are more daunting than climate change and, to a lesser extent, skier participation and demographics.

The headlines are hard to miss: "America's Shrinking Ski Season," "Low Snow Years Cost Ski Towns $1 Billion," "Is Skiing Dead Due to Global Warming?" and, occupying almost a full page on the cover of the Sunday Review section of the February 3, 2019, *New York Times*, this one: "Why Can't Rich People Save Winter?"

From a doom-and-gloom perspective, climate change could decimate the ski business, and skiers are among the first to feel its impacts. Weather does drive the bottom line and is often the single biggest factor in a successful resort season. Early season value-pass deals smartly lock in preseason commitment as insurance against adverse weather, and the big guys have a geographic resort dispersion that spreads the risk, but two or three or four bad seasons in a row can be devastating.

Most in the ski business try to avoid aligning the current "weather" with the overall "climate," not jumping to hasty conclusions because of a poor, or good, week or month or even winter. But the planet is warming; we've seen all the data and causes, and heard the alarming anecdotal evidence.

"Warming is happening faster than we expected; the impacts are going to be greater. The time for climate action is now," says Kelly Pawlak, who came from Mount Snow in Vermont to replace Michael Berry as the head of the NSAA in January 2018.

Everyone might be giddy over the bountiful 2018–19 winter, but that wasn't the case in 2017–18, when a prolonged early-season drought in Colorado depressed visitation. "The whole state is having its worst opening in 20 years. This is the weather and climate we fear. It's already here," said Auden Schendler, the outspoken and beyond-progressive vice president of sustainability for the Aspen Skiing Co., in mid-January 2018.

And yet, at the very same time—and just down the hall from Schendler in Ski Co.'s offices—executives were strategizing their participation in the rollout of Alterra.

What's wrong with this picture? Why are ski resorts large and small, plus investors around the world (all smart people), investing hundreds of millions of dollars in a snow-resort business that scientists say faces such a bleak future? These investments would not be occurring unless the consensus was that increased awareness and political action will slow/temper the worst impacts; comprehensive behavioral changes, legislated or not, will begin to turn things around; and technological advances will help meet the challenge. Warming is out there. It's here now, but the business is steeling itself to survive the increased volatility, and the optimistic view is that somehow it will.

The 1980–81 season was devastating, with skier visits plummeting to 37.7 million nationwide, a 25 percent drop from that era's five-year average. Warm weather coast-to-coast and a dearth of natural snow in the West caused visits to plunge. The response nationally was a major commitment to secure water rights and install or expand snowmaking, investing tens of millions of dollars. It's hard to imagine the resort growth of the last four decades, indeed the very definition of a modern successful ski resort, without this substantial snowmaking infrastructure. Even resorts like A-Basin, with a base elevation at 10,780 feet, owe their current healthy balance sheet to snowmaking efforts that started back then and to a continued effort to improve coverage every season. "Snowmaking put us on the map," recalls Alan Henceroth, A-Basin's chief operating officer. Until those initial snowmaking efforts began, shortly after Ralston Purina purchased the area (and added it to its Keystone and Breckenridge holdings) in 1978, A-Basin was hit or miss, its success depending entirely on snowfall.

Snowmaking still only covers about 12 percent of all Colorado terrain statewide, but that is going up here and nationwide. At least a half-dozen resorts in Colorado have requested or received approval for expanded snowmaking in recent years. Vail Mountain just announced U.S. Forest Service approval to expand coverage to 25 percent, and there will be more of the same across the country (even with energy-efficient systems, environmentalists quickly point out that resorts are expanding their carbon footprint; the Carbondale, Colorado–based Wilderness Workshop in spring 2019 objected to Aspen's planned snowmaking expansion, arguing it was a cause as well as response to the climate problem).

In addition to snowmaking, resorts are investing heavily in summer operations, including off-mountain, non-weather-dependent amenities during ski season. While these are often cast by the media as a response to climate change, the reality is that these just make good business sense.

If people are going to drive or fly to visit a ski resort, they are going to have a negative carbon impact. That's just a fact. Unless we're all willing to give up activities we love in favor of long walks with the dog, we're talking about minimizing the impact, not eliminating it.

Resorts have pursued green initiatives for decades, and in general, with just a few exceptions, have been exemplary stewards. At Steamboat, we were pleased to win an industry Golden Eagle Award in 2014 for making sustainability a cornerstone of our new $5 million Four Points on-mountain restaurant (at 9,716 feet). LEED principles were employed throughout: low-flow fixtures, low-energy insulated windows, composting, and more. We had also installed state-of-the-art, energy-saving Ultra-Tech Lighting in our new night-skiing operation; upgraded our snowmaking system to be more energy efficient; and bought fuel-saving Prinoth groomers. Going through an old stack of press clippings, I dug up these gems from then: "We are thrilled to be recognized with this prestigious honor," I said on the occasion, adding that "these efforts to help sustain our mountain environment playgrounds speak to our staff's dedication, commitment and drive to make a difference." And from this book's editor, Andy Bigford, who was then the publisher of *SKI*: "When *SKI* founded this program in 1993, we wanted to encourage sustainability and recognize resorts for their commitment and proven results to environmental programs. It's gratifying to see how far the industry has come in 20 years, particularly with today's collective focus on addressing climate change."

The point is that ski resorts have long been aware of the severity of the issues, and from the corner office down to the rank-and-file, they work and play in the mountains, so they depend on the climate's health and care deeply about it. Our staff members, particularly the younger ones, are not bashful when it comes to holding management accountable.

NSAA launched its green movement, known as Sustainable Slopes, back in 2000, with 170 resorts signing up to operate by its guidelines, representing 71 percent of the country's skier visits. Its approach from the beginning has been to reduce the industry's footprint, educate the resorts and their customers, and advocate for environmentally sound practices, such as with its early 2000s "Keep Winter Cool" campaign. "We want to walk and chew gum at the same time," says Geraldine Link, NSAA's director of public policy since 1997.

In 2010, it launched the Climate Challenge, and each year resorts sign on to publicly pledge to reduce greenhouse gases, committing to a detailed plan to do so. Importantly, NSAA hired an independent engineering firm to monitor and audit the resorts' progress, saving members money through economies of scale, but the areas still have to pay to be part of the program. Link has worked tirelessly with resorts large and small to assist and encourage their efforts, engaging diplomatically with a broad field of resort types to accomplish their goals. In January 2019, NSAA showed foresight in supporting a House bill (HR 763) that would institute a carbon-fee-and-dividend and put a price on carbon. If passed, it would arguably be the most significant climate legislation ever. All told, given the political diversity of its membership, NSAA has an impressive track record on climate change.

Care for the environment extends to the absolute top in the case of Rob Katz, who significantly ratcheted up sustainability programs when he first joined Vail Resorts, and even had Vail Resorts serve as the sustainability partner for the 2008 Democratic National Convention, when it was held in Denver to nominate Barack Obama. With the longtime Democrat-donor Crown family behind Alterra, the Katz-led Vail Resorts, and John Cumming steering POWDR, the top of the ski industry is actually more blue than ever before. But the vast majority of the small and medium-sized resort operators, who don't feel Democrats are sympathetic to their business needs, remain staunchly Republican.

As the chairman of POWDR, John Cumming is extremely aware of the impacts of climate change on his resort business and the world, and protecting the planet is a core company principle. He first became extremely concerned about climate change back in the mid-1990s, when he started rallying his then-disinterested resort colleagues to get on board. Other resort operators might find some sort of silver lining here: As chairman of his family's American Investment Company and the Crimson Wine Group, Cumming is even more concerned about the climate-change impact on his Arkansas farms and California vineyards than his ski business.

Cumming has backed up the talk: When NSAA unveiled the Climate Challenge, he signed virtually all of POWDR's resorts on to participate. Rather impressively, the company has cut its carbon footprint almost in half in the past decade, through efficiency and clean-energy investments. POWDR touts a long list of green initiatives through its Play Forever campaign, in which it taxes itself 1 percent of revenue to fund sustainability projects.

Cumming today sees positives even in setbacks as harmful as the U.S. pull-out from the Paris Climate Accord. After the announcement, POWDR, Vail Resorts, Boyne Resorts, Alterra, and the majority of other ski resorts all signed the "We Are Still In" letter, pledging to play their own part in adhering to the international pact. Cumming said the Trump Administration's withdrawal is the kind of huge leap backward that will ultimately shock the majority of people into taking personal action themselves, and that's what it's going to take in the long run. "That leaves it up to the individual," he says of the decision. "If you accept that, it's a brilliant move."

Alongside the power of the people to affect change (and the legislation will undoubtedly motivate them), Cumming has confidence in multiple solutions, including technology and science (along with his wife, Kristi, Cumming himself in 2006 funded a community-supported agricultural [CSA] co-op farm, called Copper Moose Farm. The farm's origins and evolution are intriguing; Google it if you are interested).

We could go on and on with resort examples of good stewardship. Taos has turned heads with its unprecedented commitment as a B-Corp, as mentioned earlier. In 2007, Jiminy Peak installed a $4 million wind turbine; within a decade, it was paying for itself, and during windy winters, it provides up to 66 percent of the resort's power. Reality check: All of the above are mitigating responses.

THE ASPEN SKIING CO. IS THE LEADER in the resort fight against climate change; their resorts won so many Golden Eagle Awards in the early years that Aspen stopped entering the industry contest in order to encourage others to do so. It is so out in front of the issue that it makes things awkward for other resorts, and many believe Schendler has hurt the overall cause with pontifications that are seen by some as divorced from reality.

Besides deciding long ago that environmental stewardship would be the company's core value, the Ski Co. took a step that many other resorts still struggle with. Aspen chose to use its unique, powerful soapbox and its close customer relationships to affect change through political activism. For many ski areas, their ability to influence others and create awareness on this issue is almost as important as the actual in-resort initiatives. In that sense, the ski industry has an outsized influence in the climate-change debate. Even by adopting every green initiative possible, resort reformations will not reverse global warming. But maybe the industry's and sport's political activism can make a difference.

Here's an example. Aspen's 2018–19 Give a Flake campaign was its branding/advertising message for the season, including an award-winning print ad with a tear-out, postage-paid card (a million total) that could be mailed to lobby three climate-denying GOP senators in swing states. Directed by CMO Christian Knapp, the online campaign featured an easy-to-use template for Instagram that spreads the #GiveAFlake message. It advocates five steps and guides the way: 1) Spread the Word; 2) Get Social; 3) Make the Call; 4) Mail It In; and 5) Donate. The latter links to Protect Our Winters (POW), which has passionately fought on behalf of skiers and snowboarders, often using high-profile athletes to do so, since its inception in 2007.

POW is a 501(c)(3) nonprofit founded by professional snowboarder Jeremy Jones in 2007. Its mission is to "turn passionate outdoor people into effective climate advocates. POW leads a community of athletes, thought pioneers, and forward-thinking business leaders to affect systemic political solutions to climate change." The staff members are high-profile professionals with deep experience, and avid outdoorspeople to boot. They closely monitor political issues and important races, weighing in for the candidates who support their agenda. In November 2018, POW backed Colorado Gov. Jared Polis, supported a Blue Wave that is enacting across-the-board environmental reforms, and threw its weight behind the approval of Question 6 on the Nevada ballot, which now requires electric utilities to acquire 50 percent of their energy from renewable sources by 2030. With some statewide successes under its belt, POW wants to do the same nationally. Meanwhile, its role in educating, informing, and creating awareness with skiers and snowboarders, especially younger ones, cannot be overstated.

POW has been less successful in engaging with ski resorts to date. Despite this independently funded effort to support the climate health that ski resorts need to survive, POW counted just 20 North American resorts among its resort partners for winter 2018–19, although those 20 included some iconic names: Aspen Snowmass and its four areas (of course), Alta, Taos, Snowbird, Squaw Valley, Arapahoe Basin, Mt. Bachelor, Grand Targhee, Sundance, Sugarbush, Bridger Bowl, Powder Mountain, Mt. Hood Meadows, Homewood, Camelback, and Mountain High. Resort participation in POW is growing: John Cumming recently added his entire POWDR resort lineup to the list, which brings it up to 27 area participants. The Ikon Pass and Mountain Collective Pass are also listed as resort partners, and Ikon Pass purchasers receive a complimentary $50 one-year membership to the group.

But POW still hasn't attracted a broad number of resorts to its fold. Why? POW is the tip of the spear in fighting climate change on the snow front; it is their only issue, and the instrument is extremely sharp. It is a given that POW will aggressively combat any climate-change deniers, and on occasion it is perceived as going overboard. The debate over POW, and over how to fight climate change, is among the most emotional topics I've witnessed in my career.

Ski areas are juggling 50 issues, and although climate change is by far the most important long-term one on the list, its advocacy can sometimes conflict with the other pressing initiatives. What to do when your congressman or senator staunchly supports your resort's need to expand snowmaking, to add summer activities on Forest Service lands, or support a critical highway project … but is a climate-change denier or doubter? It's a nuanced relationship.

Business is business, and politics makes strange bedfellows across virtually every for-profit enterprise in the country. Resorts have always tried to walk a bipartisan line. But the devil is in the details. On the big stuff they are often in accord, for example, the very unified response to the Paris withdrawal.

As the general manager of a POW-member resort, A-Basin's Alan Henceroth understands both sides. He is well aware of the mounting challenges in keeping A-Basin open into June; it used to semi-regularly spin the lifts until the Fourth of July. (It did make it to July 4 in 2019 with top-to-bottom skiing, the first time since 2011; back in 1995, A-Basin stayed open until Aug. 10).

Henceroth sees the ultimate solution coming from changing consumer habits and an increased renewable-energy commitment by power companies. A-Basin's provider, Xcel Energy, which supplies most of the state's ski resorts and covers an eight-state territory, is increasing its use of renewable-energy sources, with the goal of reaching 55 percent of its mix by 2026; it seeks to reduce carbon emissions 80 percent by 2030, and to get to zero emissions of greenhouse gas by 2050. A-Basin is part of POW because of its grassroots skier-education efforts, which Henceroth applauds. The ski area does its part, and Henceroth, who's accustomed to Colorado's relatively advanced experience on green issues, says a lot of out-of-state visitors are unaware of the basics, like single-stream recycling.

At the Outdoor Retailer show in Denver in February 2019, NSAA, SIA, and the Outdoor Industry Association (OIA) announced the Outdoor Business Climate Partnership (OBCP) to "tackle the most pressing environmental issue of our time." The OIA's involvement is big, representing a broad, $500 billion–plus industry, and together the groups front an almost $1 trillion business. The coalition to fight global warming also included seven major state ski associations: Colorado Ski Country USA, Ski Utah, Ski California, Ski Vermont, Ski Areas of New York, Ski New Mexico, and the Pacific Northwest Ski Areas Association.

The combined statement read in part: "As economic drivers in our respective states we urge policy makers to understand that we can't wait for lasting, bipartisan action to reduce carbon emissions, promote energy innovation and support a rapid, responsible transition to a clean energy economy."

NSAA's goal has been to build bridges with lawmakers rather than burn them, and the OBCP has taken the same tack. POW's aggressive stance makes many resort managers uncomfortable. NSAA/OBCP seeks the same end goal as POW, but with very different ideas on how to get there; let's hope they can find common ground as the effort moves forward.

Resorts do "get it," now more than ever. "Climate change is the biggest threat facing our community today," says Pat Campbell, who is the president of the mountain division of Vail Resorts. In 2017, the company committed to reaching zero-net carbon emissions, sending zero waste to landfills, and having a zero-net operating footprint by 2030.

In the big picture, the trend is clear: The ski industry is becoming more unified in its messaging and increasingly visible in D.C. and in the state capitals across ski country.

CHAPTER 15

Disrupter No. 2:
Participation Challenge

A s with climate change, the dire participation headlines are hard to miss as well: "Skiing Is on the Skids;" "Descending Popularity of Skiing in America;" "Bring More Diversity to Skiing;" and "Why Skiing and Snowboarding Need New Recruits."

So, the big question again: Why would so many individuals, investment groups, and sophisticated companies be investing in a business with alarming demographic and participation trends, and a less-than-rosy growth outlook? Would you keep your Apple shares if a shortage of precious metals meant that production was fixed going forward?

Looking at the past, ski resorts have fended off predicted declines for two-plus decades, when that "giant sucking sound" (to borrow the oft-repeated words of then–NSAA president Michael Berry) created by departing Baby Boomers was projected to cut skier visits almost in half—if nothing was done. That didn't happen. Then came the alarm that the huge and enigmatic Millennial generation was rejecting the sport. That didn't happen. Skiing has survived, buoyed by snowboarding and then evolving ski technology. Now, skiing is on the cusp of enjoying a third growth spurt, driven by an improved skiing experience and the new pricing model.

But, as always, demographics matter.

The skier-demographic challenge can be summarized in this way: Baby

165

Boomers (born 1946–1964) were the heroes of the sport—the perfect, loyal customer—and every subsequent generation has been less inclined to ski, or more difficult to recruit and hold on to. Baby Boomers came along just when the resort business was booming, with the founding of some 500 resorts in the U.S. in the 1950s, '60s and early '70s. They put up with terrible commutes on potholed roads, marginal ski equipment and clothing, nonexistent grooming, virtually no snowmaking (or where it existed, poor-quality "ice-making"). It was surprising how many stuck around, and as the industry matured, they reveled in all the new bells and whistles. The advancements made the whole sport/lifestyle easier and more enjoyable—including high-speed lifts that allowed them to rack up more vertical in a couple hours than they used to get in a day. Long live the Baby Boomer: With their continued passion for the sport (still comprising 16 percent of skier visits in 2017–18, according to the NSAA), they also enlisted their children and grandchildren, and they still provide their mountain vacation homes for family get-togethers. These are legacy properties, totaling tens of billions of dollars in value that will, no doubt, be largely handed down to the younger generations.

Gen X (1965–1980) has held stable over the past decade, accounting for roughly a quarter of all skier visits. The Millennials (1981–1996), who declined significantly in the "start-a-family, buy-a-home, pay-off-the-student-loans" phase, have leveled off. They are a huge focus of the industry because of their size, 75 million strong (just surpassing the height of the Baby Boomer generation), and their impact on future success. They don't always respond on the basis of price, though they are deal-seekers. Independent, tech-savvy, and seeking "authentic" experiences that are hard to define, they are a puzzle that begs to be solved, defying stereotypes. The next age group, Gen Z (22 and younger in 2019), have put down their cell phones long enough to comprise 34 percent of skier visits for the 2017–18 season, by far the largest age segment.

There are other worrisome trends. The base is aging, partly because of the alarming cliff drop in snowboarding. Household incomes are going up (though often generated by both spouses working, as opposed to the Baby Boomer one-head-of-household standard), with the $200,000-plus category rising from 18 to 27 percent of the skier population in the past decade. Meanwhile, the $100,000 to $199,999 income category rose from 30 to 35 percent; and skiers earning less than $100,000 and $50,000 dropped from 27 to 16 percent and 25 to 22 percent, respectively, according to NSAA.

There has been only slight growth in ethnic minorities on the slopes over the past decade, compared with the segment's increase in the overall population. (The ethnic percentage in the U.S. is 39 percent, compared with 61 percent non-Hispanic white. Ethnic participation in skiing is 13 percent, up from 11.9 percent a decade ago.) The male/female ratio in participants is 54/46, but more pronounced in skier visits at 59/41 (women tend to ski fewer days). Female participation grew from 39.9 to 42.6 percent from 2008–09 to 2014–15, then dropped back to 41.3 percent for 2017–18.

Participant numbers need to be viewed in the context of the U.S. population growth of 8 percent over the past decade; as the number grows, skiing's share shrinks. As *Powder* magazine stated bluntly in a 2017 clickbait headline: "Skiing is a rich, white person's sport, and that needs to change."

Twenty years ago at the NSAA convention in Charleston, South Carolina, then-president Michael Berry presented research in an effort that would become a cornerstone of his career, showing that aging Baby Boomers exiting the sport would leave a tremendous hole, and that the key to ensuring future health was to get more skiers to try the sport and, critically, do a better job turning them into lifelong skiers. His oft-repeated line (borrowed from management guru Peter Drucker) at the many industry confabs he addressed over the years: "The purpose of any business is to find and retain new customers." So, the effort began.

In 2000, NSAA introduced the Model for Growth, recognizing the participation challenges ahead and targeting a broad new-skier development program that would address the sport's embarrassing retention rate. Most of those who take beginner lessons never return. The trade group in 2002 published a Conversion Cookbook that highlights best practices in beginner lessons. In 2009, Learn to Ski and Snowboard Month (LSSM) was launched. It has introduced nearly a million first-timers to the sport in the past decade. The conversion rate has inched up from 15 to 19 percent, no easy task. NSAA also launched an award program in 2011 to recognize the highest-performing resorts, called the Conversion Cup Challenge.

The explosion of the mega-pass, many industry pundits argue, turns its back on new skiers and even fringe participants: They can't make that upfront commitment, and skiing remains an expensive endeavor. There is some truth in that. Window tickets have passed the $200 mark at top destinations, and the average ticket price in 2018 was $122.30 (this would be much lower if we looked at average yield per skier day, including passes). A first-timer introduction at a major resort can run up to $250. But that's not a big piece of their business model and also not where first-timers typically start out. You don't go to Aspen for a week of skiing if you don't know how to ski. It normally happens at the "local" ski area, where the prices tend to be very attractive. And it's at those local hills that most new skiers have been produced. At Wachusett, not Steamboat.

Mega-passes do have silver linings for participation: The experiential nature of sampling multiple resorts fits perfectly with Millennials, who are also avid Vrbo and Airbnb aficionados, important engines for today's destination resort P&L. And the discounted buddy or friends and family passes that pass purchasers get as a bonus are a huge carrot in themselves for getting ex-skiers off the couch. "Joe," an Epic passholder, books into a cheap Vrbo at Breckenridge and brings lapsed friend "Mary" along. Mary gets to use the buddy pass.

Looking at the big picture: Passholders are opening the door to bring new/lapsed skiers into the sport, and the buddy ticket discount is the means. This is happening naturally. NSAA should assist resorts in providing appropriate "orientation" packages for all these "new" skiers who are just showing up. What's different? They are now showing up at destination resorts so these areas now have the opportunity (and need) to provide an appropriate introduction.

John Fry, former longtime editor-in-chief of *SKI* and founding editor of the defunct but groundbreaking *Snow Country* magazine, has closely followed skier-participation studies and their correlation to the health of the sport for six decades. John is America's pre-eminent ski historian. He sounded the warning that studies (albeit old ones, including the McKinsey & Company research for USIA in the late 1980s) show that the best way to increase skier visits is to get the wide swath of occasional skiers to hit the slopes more frequently, rather than motivating avid skiers to increase their volume. According to the NSAA 2017–18 Demographic Study, 28 percent of 9.4 million skiers and snowboarders accounted for more that 70 percent of the days skied. That percentage will likely increase for 2018–19, with Ikon and Epic passholders taking advantage of good conditions to explore new venues. Is this a problem or not?

Increasing commitment among the hard-core participants helped golf limp through its recent downturn (one-third of golfers currently account for two-thirds of rounds played), but skiing is trending toward an even more pronounced reliance on the core. Fry sees this as a negative. I disagree. Their passion is infectious and draws non-skiing friends into their adventure. One challenge for the industry is measuring how many new skiers are being drawn into the sport due to this new phenomenon versus those attracted in more traditional ways. I disagree with John's premise but, as of now, don't have the hard data to challenge.

Back to existing "grow participation" strategies. Resorts have not been sitting idle; they have been hard at work for over two decades on improving introductory ski school programs, and wooing lapsed skiers back during those life periods when they tend to fade away.

Ski Utah and CSCUSA have had successful elementary-ski-free programs for some 20 years; Ski Utah reports that more than 200,000 fourth graders have learned to ski in its program, and 150,000 have carried it forward into fifth and sixth grade. There are at least six other states offering similar programs: Maine, New Hampshire, Vermont, New York, Pennsylvania, and Michigan. Many destination resorts routinely offer "kids ski free," when paired with lodging as a family incentive.

Learn-to-ski programs have come a long way since beginners struggling on borrowed 210s were pointed in the direction of the rope tow and told to hang on for dear life. Programs like Terrain Based Learning (TBL), developed by Joe Hession and his Snow Operating Company, uses sculpted features to help never-evers grasp the feel for basic skills. TBL embraces both the physical and, perhaps more importantly, the mental side of the sport (one learning drill involves juggling snowballs). Hession and his colleagues at Snow Operating concluded early on that the typical resort approach to teaching wasn't aligned with what the customer wanted or needed. Since its inception in 2012, TBL has spread to some 35 resorts and been adopted by PSIA–AASI.

Hession, perhaps the industry's most persistent advocate for never-evers, will realize a life-long dream late this fall. That's the scheduled opening for what is being billed as North America's first 365-day-a-year indoor ski and snowboard park, "Big SNOW America." It will be part of a mega-mall called American Dream in the Meadowlands in New Jersey, adjacent to the New York metro area. Developed by TripleFive, the group behind Minnesota's Mall of America, the mall will occupy 3-million-square-feet with 450 retail stores.

Snow Operating will run the ski facility, standing 16-stories tall and spanning more than 180,000 square-feet. It will replicate the resort experience, starting with snow rather than a carpet (recycled when it melts) and featuring an 800-foot slope and chairlift. It comes complete with equipment rentals, TBL teaching methods, ski chalet, shopping village and après ski.

With all these new initiatives, learning to ski/ride has never been easier or more accessible. Another big challenge is also being addressed: Because roughly half of first-timers don't go through ski school, resorts are trying other initiatives, such as beginner-terrain-only trail maps that provide self-guided advice for skill development. These are critical, especially given the volume of new/lapsed skiers now tagging along with passholders. Resorts need to be prepared to provide at least some minimal orientation on the spot, especially given the surge in "Buddy Pass" use, as noted above. Michael Berry's always sage advice rings true again: "No one comes without being beckoned by a skier." This is a truism that John Fry first championed in the 1960s and '70s, when the sport was booming. Even better is taking the sport straight to the people: In 2018–19, Tamarack offered free beginner lessons at a tubing hill minutes from downtown Boise for its Idaho Learn to Ski Day.

So what other strategies are in place to broaden participation, attracting the less wealthy and less committed to the sport? Well, price incentives work. In 2012, Sugarbush unveiled its $299 "For20s" pass (yes, that's a sly reference to marijuana's 420 day, April 20), designed to hook them young on the mountain so they would eventually return as a family unit. Having sold just 50 passes to that age group the previous two seasons, Sugarbush set an ambitious goal of 1,000—and doubled it. Young adult passes are now widespread, keeping skiers active in the sport at a time when most have dropped out because of lack of income. Peak Resorts offered its unrestricted Drifter Pass for $99 down and $399 total (it will be interesting to see if Vail continues it). POWDR is all about youth, with its Woodward component and its adventure-lifestyle motif. Vail Resorts does strong grassroots work through the ownership of its three Midwest resorts and has introduced Epic Anyday. Some good things are happening.

Jon Rucker, president of the Head Tyrolia Wintersports U.S. Division, is the first to hold a seat on both the NSAA and SIA boards of directors. He has a less sanguine view.

Under Rucker's leadership, Head has been a key supporter of LSSM and the Conversion Cup (he has also driven impressive market-share gains at Head, while most other brands have declined). He serves on the NSAA's Conversion Committee and its new Growth Committee, and after getting to know his resort colleagues, he views them as innovative, willing to embrace change, and forward-thinking.

Sifting through all the data, Rucker says the macro-trends paint an overall picture that is daunting. Resorts have been smart and are riding high on their recent successes—all well-deserved, he says, but the metrics are not positive in the long run.

As a gear supplier, Rucker presents the other side, a dark one, to the health of the sport. Worldwide, ski companies have essentially lost half their unit sales in the past 20 years (partly because of the rise of snowboarding) and their margins have slipped even more. Citing internal industry numbers, Rucker says global ski factory output has dropped roughly 50 percent since the early- to mid-1990s, while wholesale pricing has remained largely unchanged (and manufacturing costs have steadily risen).

All these challenges might eventually hamper ski-suppliers' ability to innovate, and their technological breakthroughs in gear (first shaped, and then wide skis with rocker, comfortable boots that perform) are a big part of today's resort success story. As a counter trend, each year there seem to be more and more "boutique" ski companies, producing niche products, some at the very high end, though they represent a small part of the market.

Also worrisome to Rucker is the disappearance of the country's retail network, particularly in large cities distant from skiing. Shopping has shifted to the internet or to resort shops, where customers can easily "try before they buy." Most of the successful, independent ski shops were opened by Baby Boomers in the 1960s, '70s, and '80s, in the heyday of ski retail. They are struggling. A beloved ski-retail icon, the exceptionally well-run Danzeisen & Quigley of Cherry Hills, New Jersey, which introduced tens of thousands of skiers to the sport since its opening almost 60 years ago, closed its doors in 2019, and there are dozens if not hundreds of similar stories.

We often forget that some of the largest states in terms of total skiers are often those with no ski areas. Alongside ski-resort saturated states like Colorado (contributing 5.3 percent of skier visits, according to SIA's 2017 participation study) and California (15.5 percent), there are critical skier-visit contributors where there is a limited media message: New York (10.3), Texas (6.2), and Florida (5.5).

"If the ski shop in Miami goes out of business, what happens?" Rucker asks. Those shops used to recruit new skiers, organize ski trips, share information, and create buzz, providing the most "experiential" voice available. "Often times, the only lifeline between the individual and the resorts is the ski shop." Then again, younger generations don't patronize brick and mortar, so how material is the loss in the long run? Social media doesn't respect borders. Facebook posts of a recent ski experience can be as ubiquitous in Austin as they are in Denver.

Exacerbating the situation for local shops is the popularity of demo skis. Some retail pundits argue that this has led to a $500 million shift in business from city shops to the resort demo centers and their ever-growing retail. The business isn't big enough for local shops to survive such a dramatic shift in income. The airlines, with their "extra baggage" charges, were a factor in driving destination skiers to the demo shop. About half of these destination guests do not bring (and in many cases don't own) their own equipment. The arrival of in-room ski delivery companies like Black Tie has brought more revenue to resort communities but also a higher level of guest satisfaction. As local, independent shops have declined, the resorts and resort shops have been the winners. Vail Resorts' retail division, originally called SSV, which Ken Gart launched and directed, is the largest "specialty retailer" in the country, with 180-plus shops. Needless to say, retail/rental income is an important and growing revenue center for the big companies, but their success comes with the demise of local shops. It's a sad passing. Only a handful will survive.

How long can mega-passes and dynamic pricing (along with an improved product) drive the sport forward? The advent of the mega-passes has turned a negative (skiing is expensive) into a positive (no it's not; it's a deal) by pushing the price and value message 24/7 everywhere. In any ski market, especially in the spring, it's all you hear or read about. No lack of awareness here. In reality, skiing remains an expensive endeavor, especially for the family destination vacation. But the new passes and pricing have clearly struck a nerve, and the skier base is responding in a dramatic way. This would not be happening if skiing were not so aspirational. I think the internal debate goes something like this: "I've paid for the pass already. I've used it 10 times. I always wanted to go to Mammoth. Let's do it. At least the skiing won't set us back." So the existing base is skiing more.

John Fry sounded this alarm in the November–December 2018 issue of *Skiing History*, the publication of the International Skiing History Association: "If the experience remains unaltered, and ski areas offer their best pricing to people already committed heavily to the sport, it's difficult to see, with snowboarding participation in decline, and global warming, how measurable downhill skiing activity will grow in the years ahead, or avoid declining.

"The ski industry is not synonymous with the sport, as if we needed reminding. The cross-country ski and freestyle crazes of the 1970s, and later snowboarding, which attracted hundreds of thousands of new participants, were not ski industry marketing programs designed to increase participation. They arose out of the sport's heart, and in some cases the 'industry' didn't initially respond well to them.

"In the long run, the ski industry exists because of the sport, and not the other way around."

I agree that most growth has occurred generically, from the heart and not always with the industry's support. But John doesn't mention the mercurial rise of freeskiing, which has been staunchly supported by resorts and positively influenced by new pricing models. Enormous resources are required to build and maintain terrain parks. This is happening virtually everywhere because resorts recognize how influential this segment has been with new skiers and riders, especially the monstrous Gen Z. Terrain parks are a perfect complement to the GoPro culture. There's arguably more primetime coverage of the X-Games than traditional alpine events. Snowboarding may have declined, but other "generic" activities are growing, including backcountry and side-country skiing.

I also don't agree with John Fry's conclusion that the current pricing model can't support growth. *The best pricing should always go to the heaviest users. That's the way virtually all products are sold.*

As noted throughout this book, there are multiple tranches of pricing offered by virtually all the resorts (not just the conglomerates). These provide significant discounts, especially when there are blackouts. "Frequency" passes were, until this year, the best option for the less committed skiers, usually in the four- to 10-day range—much cheaper than going with a day or multiday product, but not the same value as a full season pass. Vail has expanded the frequency model with its Epic Anyday model for one to seven days, as noted, and you can expect many other areas to follow in a competitive response. The trend is clear: All ticket products will be deeply discounted if purchased early.

Today's modern ski industry has adopted a transformational pricing model. That doesn't mean it can't or won't change or evolve further. But it's apparent coast to coast in North America that this change is driving participation. And isn't it ironic that so many of the people who have been complaining for years about the lack of growth are now complaining about crowds? You can't have it both ways.

While there is considerable momentum for growth, this trend needs to be sustained with thoughtful programs to increase participation. NSAA continues to do its part, and a recent member survey showed that participation growth is the No. 1 priority among its ranks. In April 2019, it assumed management of Learn To Ski and Snowboard Month (LSSM) from the program's longtime champion, Mary-Jo Tarallo. NSAA is expanding LSSM from a month to a season-long focus, formed a Growth Committee, and is steeling itself to address the core and lapsed segments of the skier population. At the spring 2019 Mountain Travel Symposium in Whistler, NSAA president Kelly Pawlak made it clear she is taking the challenge seriously, launching the next chapter in her predecessor's Model for Growth. According to *SAM*, she noted that even with the evolving mega-pass transformation, 55 percent of lift revenue still comes from the ticket window, and the average ticket price grew 60 percent in the past decade. "Attracting new skiers will always be NSAA's primary purpose. But we also want to engage with lapsed skiers who would like to get back to the sport after being away to raise families or pursue careers."

NSAA set a goal of achieving a three-year average of 60 million skier visits per season by 2025–26, an ambitious 12 percent increase over the three-year period ending with the 2017–18 season, but just above the 2018–19 total.

One important factor that influences how the ski sport is viewed and, therefore, its appeal: the success of our athletes in international competition. Lindsey Vonn, who retired after the 2018–19 season, and Mikaela Shiffrin have become two of the most recognized athletes in the world. Both provide a stunningly appealing image for skiing, and even U.S. cross-country skiers are winning Olympic medals. Skiing is hot.

With the 2018–19 season in the rearview mirror, the biggest challenge I see beyond those noted is the increased crowding at our ski areas and resorts. This past year got a boost from exceptional snowfall in most areas, but the trend is obvious. People are skiing more, and there are and will be more skiers. That means pressure on the quality of the ski experience. This will call for better management and more investment. It's a problem the ski industry is fortunate to have.

As an aside, how is the global resort industry faring, and what can we learn from other countries and regions? Laurent Vallant, a Geneva-based ski industry consultant, has produced a global overview for 11 years, compiling statistics that are supplemented by gumshoe detective work to fill in the blanks, where countries only have estimates.

While not based entirely on official numbers, his 2019 International Report on Snow & Mountain Tourism, covering the 2017–18 season, showed an upward tick after three seasons of decline, with overall skier visits increasing by 5 percent. (You can Google and download a PDF of the 222-page report; it's definitely worth a look.)

"Although the worldwide ski industry faces challenges and the numbers of skiers in Western countries tend to be more or less stagnant when not decreasing, the global performance remains at a high level. The 2017–18 winter globally ranks as the fourth best of the new millennium." (It will be interesting to see his report on the 2018–19 season.)

His observations include a spike in China, with rapid growth ahead of the 2022 Beijing Winter Olympics; the country is now third worldwide after the U.S. and Germany in so-called "participants," but lagging well behind in skier visits, with less than 20 million.

Vallant estimates the total number of skiers worldwide as roughly 130 million and says that number seems to be growing, thanks to development in Eastern Europe and Asia (his estimate may be high; his U.S. participant figure is around 25 million, more than double that of the NSAA). Vallant does note that even countries that have no resorts (or only ski domes) include skiers who travel abroad. The Netherlands, for example, accounts for about 1 million outbound skiers.

In terms of annual skier visits, France, Austria and the U.S. have historically been neck-and-neck, in the low- to mid-50s neighborhood (in millions), with the U.S occupying the top spot for 2017–18, despite its relatively weak season. By region, the Alps dominate, with 44 percent of the global market, which Vallant estimates at roughly 350-million skier visits. Canada, facing skier participation challenges similar to the U.S., is just under 20 million skier visits with 4.3 million participants. France and Austria feature the most individual resorts that draw more than 1 million skiers annually, with 13 and 16, respectively. Whistler Blackcomb is sixth in resort skier visits, according to Vallant, below the leader, the French resort of La Plagne, at about 2.35 million annually. (The individual resort list is obviously based on estimates, and perhaps off-the-record embellishments from marketing departments.)

"Nearly everywhere, the industry is facing the challenge of generating long term growth," Vallant concludes in his 2019 report. "In many places, the market is more than mature and the Baby Boomers represent the majority of participants. This generation will progressively exit some of the mature markets without being adequately replaced by future generations with the same enthusiasm for skiing. The need to stimulate the market is extremely important and not always sufficiently addressed. In developing markets this is also an issue. Everywhere, the challenge is to attract a younger generation that has different consumption patterns, that zaps quickly from one interest to the next, and that is in great demand for all kinds of competing activities.

"As already experienced by ski areas that have been actively looking for solutions, gaining new customers by attracting non-skiers and converting them into loyal participants is a far from a done deal. It requires a significant effort and the situation only improves very slowly."

So, even globally, the effort has just begun.

CHAPTER 16

Ski/Mountain Towns Brace for More Change

The ski world has been turned upside down with consolidation and the arrival of widespread mega-passes. What does this mean to the ski towns that are as much a part of the new ski experience as the mountains? Change has played out differently in the East and West. To look forward, we need to spend some time reviewing the history, and because of my Vermont years, I wanted to focus on the Green Mountain State.

The '60s and '70s were a tumultuous time. Many young people, fed up with the deterioration of urban American, poor race relations, and the Vietnam war, were primed for an exit to rural America. The ski towns were logical destinations, given the variety of job opportunities, and Vermont, with its proximity to the urban corridor, was especially attractive. Residents were skeptical of these new arrivals, but overall, Vermont was welcoming and tolerant. It was a place where you could pretty much do what you wanted, as long as you didn't negatively impact your neighbor.

The ski towns where many settled became significant economic engines for the state. Some were virtually brand-new communities, like Killington; others were long-standing resort areas, as in the case of Stowe. Okemo began as a small local area in the manufacturing town of Ludlow and grew to be Vermont's second-largest ski area. In those early years, there was a supportive relationship between the towns and their residents and the ski newcomers, those working at the ski areas and those just attracted to this new scene. These communities were extremely egalitarian. By that I mean you could sit at the local bar and chat with the president of the ski company or the town manager. They were small towns. There wasn't a lot of income disparity, because everyone was broke!

There wasn't a lot happening during the summer (Stowe being one notable exception). People either left or went to work in the construction field. Most of the bars/restaurants couldn't afford to operate in the summer. There wasn't a lot to do once the snow melted. We played a lot of softball at Killington in the '70s. We had our own team of Killington employees (arguably our best player was short-fielder Winnie Allen, Pres Smith's administrative assistant). One of the teams in our loosely constructed "league" was just called The Hippies. Everyone knew everyone else. This was also a time when most Eastern skiers hadn't discovered the West. Winters were cold and the natural snow reliable, at least compared with today's circumstances.

This was an enjoyable lifestyle, and during the ski season there were plenty of opportunities for those willing to work. As with all ski towns then and now, when you were getting started, you needed at least two jobs just to pay the rent. As word got out, more and more young people escaped to these new ski communities in Vermont.

It was a time of rapid growth for the ski industry, and as it grew, a new industry began to evolve: second homes. In the early days, a variety of small to medium-sized lodges and inns provided the housing. But for people who wanted a second home or for those working in the communities, new housing was needed. Some of these developments were done hastily, without a lot of thought to long-term sustainability. Sewer and water issues were not always properly addressed. A backlash eventually arrived as the political landscape changed.

Back in the '60s and '70s, a time when skiing was rapidly growing in popularity, there was also a significant countercultural phenomenon taking place: the retreat to rural America by those frustrated with urbanization and looking for a simpler, more independent and fulfilling lifestyle. For those curious, I would highly recommend Yvonne Daley's *Going Up the Country*. Daley was a career reporter for the *Rutland Herald* and both observed and documented Vermont's historic transformation, from a conservative ("Don't Tread on Me") state to arguably the most liberal in America.

"By 1970, approximately 35,800 hippies were estimated to be living in

Vermont, representing 33 percent of the total population of 107,527 Vermonters between the ages of 18 and 34. The 1980 census showed that Vermont's population grew even more dramatically over the decade, from 444,732 to 511,456, making it the largest increase since the Revolutionary War; 57 percent of that growth were people from out of state." Daley's well-written and meticulously researched book details the transition from commune to statehouse, as these new residents fully embraced the Vermont rural lifestyle and effectively took control of the political process. Where else could Bernie Sanders have been elected again and again, with huge majorities, as Vermont's sole member of the House of Representatives, and then its beloved senator and perennial presidential candidate?

The ski towns had their share of hippies, but the more committed commune crowd generally kept its distance, suspicious of their commercial and capitalistic focus. And so the seeds of conflict were planted. Daley quotes Bruce Taub, a co-founder of the Earthworks Commune:

"We were particularly opposed to our government's military violence, to the competitive behaviors we felt were inherent in capitalism, and to the selfish, male-dominated noncooperative values we then believed were wrongly engendered by the nuclear family. The Vietnam holocaust was to us a course of daily pain. So too was the perceived destruction of our natural environment and the permanent annihilation of other living species. We hoped we could make things better. We intended to be social reformers."

It's not surprising that entrepreneurial ski area founders like Pres Smith represented the enemy to this group. Smith had started his Killington ski area on leased land from the state and with its solid backing. Ditto for Okemo and Stowe, also on state land. In the case of Killington, the state constructed a five-mile access road and the original base lodge to facilitate the ski area's development. The social and political transition Vermont was undergoing was virtually incomprehensible to pioneers like Smith.

In short order, the ski area operators became the bad guys, the most visible incarnation of the capitalist beast, to these newcomers. Over time, this enmity—or, at a minimum, distrust—was formalized in a regulatory structure that made day-to-day business life incredibly difficult. Capitalism brings a certain messiness and unpredictability, something the new political majority would not tolerate. Vermont basically tried to have it both ways: a healthy economy and some of the nation's most restrictive land-use laws. Given a ski area's impact on the natural and social environment, they were disproportionally impacted. Water-quality regulations made it impossible or extraordinarily expensive to expand snowmaking operations. Other criteria under the state's landmark environmental law, Act 250, were aimed at growth issues. The permitting process gave significant influence to those representing the status quo. So it shouldn't be surprising to note that, generally, the status quo was protected. For most rural areas, that meant zero or slow growth. An unintended but inevitable result: As decades passed and people moved on, the population base began to shrink. Faced with a declining population, Vermont is now paying young people $10,000 to move there.

My view is that the current situation would be less dire if the state's ski communities were as economically vigorous as their Western counterparts. Near the end of her book, Daley quotes Lars Nielsen, raised in a single-mother hippie household: "It all seemed like a good idea ... It succeeded but was trumped by other factors, many of them economic. My generation discovered that there's not a huge job base in Vermont and taxes are high, so it's hard to stimulate business and living is more costly now ... Not that I don't dream of going back there some day." Nielsen currently lives in Plano, Texas.

During the '90s, growth in most of Vermont's ski towns ground to a halt. A notable exception was Okemo, where the Mueller family managed a significant terrain expansion, a second base area, and related real-estate development. Although their operating competence and focus on service were largely the catalysts, they also benefited from their location in the former manufacturing-based economy of Ludlow. Here the status quo was arguably more focused on economic survival. The Muellers also proved themselves exceptionally skilled at navigating the permit processes.

The biggest challenge for most Vermont resorts remained water for snowmaking. Most have finally managed to navigate their way to a solution and now offer a competitive product, albeit at great cost and with significant delays. (For Mount Snow that process took over 30 years.) With that, and all the other changes that are occurring within the ski realm, I do believe they face a brighter future. Vermont ski towns will continue to evolve into important economic centers. But in my view, they will not be what they might have been.

Out West, the move to the mountains started a little later, but with largely the same effect: large numbers of young people moving to ski towns, this time specifically for the allure of skiing and good times they offered. The term "ski bum" was coined in the post–World War II late 1940s, and many ski bums were college graduates there to blow off steam for a couple of years before getting a "real job." Some were hippies, just looking for an alternate lifestyle.

Hunter S. Thompson helped define Aspen's early ski-town culture before his ashes were blasted skyward. (Just stop by the Woody Creek Tavern, and you'll get the picture.) In his run for Pitkin County sheriff in 1969 as part of the Freak Power ticket, Thompson's platform included changing the town's name to "Fat City" to keep the greedy out-of-town developers and other capitalists from profiting off its name. He lost the election by less than three-dozen votes, but his anti-growth legacy would remain a defining factor in Aspen politics for decades to come.

Being there early, finding a job, and buying a home: If that happened, the earliest ski bums who stuck around were sitting on pile of dough, with Aspen land prices being some of the most expensive in ski country.

In the Western ski towns, the combination of' transplants and newer, wealthier arrivals (originally second-home owners, and then retirees) often led to no-growth efforts. Vermont's "hippie" factor was present, but not at the same scale. Projects could be fought using local politics, zoning, and land-use rules to stop or delay development. But land rights in the West are more sacrosanct than back East, so the communities grew—and continued to grow through economic downturns and low snow cycles. Some were brand new: Beaver Creek, Copper Mountain, etc. Aspen was a bit of an outlier in terms of the anti-development sentiment.

My editor has told me his tales of survival in Colorado's ski towns in the 1980s, particularly in regard to affordable housing. He ran the newspaper in Breckenridge in the early '80s, and lived in five different houses or condos over four years. Then he did the same for the newspaper in Aspen, where the market was even tighter, eventually winding up in 1987 in a carriage house (horse barn) in the tony West End. It was roughly 600 square feet, the rent was $1,200 a month ($2,473 in today's dollars), the wind blew through its foundation cracks, and you had to keep the taps running with a trickle of water during winter or the pipes would freeze and implode (which they did). But his neighbors included movie stars and corporate tycoons, and his humble abode, located at the rear of a $10 million Victorian property, included the services of the estate's gardener, who tended the flower beds. He and his wife-to-be left after three years for Vermont ski country, where they could afford to buy a house. (He returned to Colorado in spring 1997, when as editor-in-chief of *SKI* he helped move the magazine from Manhattan to Boulder.)

With its incredible housing costs, Aspen became one of the first ski towns to address the employee-housing problem. Aspen required developers to include affordable-housing units as a part of new projects, or had them pay cash into a fund for building housing elsewhere, regulations that are common across ski country today. Lotteries among locals were held for the right to buy or rent a unit. Demand so outstripped supply that when the housing authority offered single-family units for the first time in the late 1980s, locals were getting married and even having children because it gave them more qualifying points, improving their one-in-a-hundred chance of earning the right to buy an employee-housing unit. Virtually every ski resort offers seasonal employee housing while the ski towns are increasingly focused on the larger issues of affordability and accessibility.

Mountain towns monitor the percentage of employees they can house in-town, a critical barometer for sense of community and a life-and-death matter when those workers are firefighters, doctors, or other essential personnel. According to a March 2017 account in *Powder*, Vail and Aspen house 30 percent, Breckenridge 50 percent, Mammoth and Jackson 63 percent. The leader is Whistler, housing 79 percent in 2015, because of an aggressive housing authority and second-home restrictions that date back to its founding.

Now, partly because of the trend of more second-home owners using Airbnb or Vrbo for short-term rentals rather than placing their units in the local housing pool, the acute shortage has reached new heights. Ski resorts across the West are increasing their efforts to build or seed new housing. "Workforce housing is one of the biggest challenges facing the ski industry in Colorado right now, and it's even broader than Colorado," Telluride's Bill Jensen told *Powder*. "Ten, 15 years ago, communities hoped solutions would happen—and now look at Telluride, Vail [Resorts] and Aspen Skiing [Co.]: We are realizing we have to be the leaders in creating the solutions."

Another major ski-town transformation started in the 1980s and continues today: The demise of the ski bum, replaced by an immigrant workforce. These new workers are not in the mountains to ski but to find better-paying jobs, and in many cases to send money home. Some fled life-threatening conditions in Mexico or other violent Central American countries, and now live in more peaceful, accepting communities. Many stuck around, raised families, started their own businesses. Many more rotate in and out, taking the entry-level service jobs that temporary ski bums once performed. They work at an incredibly high level, happily taking on overtime hours, and many ski-town economies would grind to a halt without their contributions.

It is difficult to pinpoint the exact numbers, because many who work in the tourism trade are undocumented. (Yes, ICE does make periodic visits to ski towns.) According to the July 1, 2018, U.S. census, Hispanics comprised 30 percent of the population in Eagle County, home to Vail and Beaver Creek, and 14 and 7 percent, respectively, in the counties of Summit and Routt (home to Steamboat). It has been estimated that almost half of Colorado's tourism workforce in construction, service, and housekeeping is comprised of immigrants. In Mammoth Lakes, California, the Hispanic population is roughly 35 percent per the 2018 census, but the school district is 60 percent Hispanic. Many mountain school districts are bilingual, teaching both languages to all students. Some of the schools in Eagle County's district had a 60 percent Hispanic enrollment way back in 2002. Eagle introduced a dual-language program in the early 2000s. Ski town and resort leaders must constantly weigh the diversity of their communities, and they face ever-escalating challenges in merging these needs into in a common vision.

Another new dynamic has arrived. Instead of moving to town for the skiing, people are coming for the mountain lifestyle. (This trend is contrary to the much larger mass exodus from rural America to the cities.) Skiing for them is an important part of the lifestyle, but not the end-all it had been previously. The biggest change is summer. Ask any new arrival to one of the popular Western mountain towns, and you'll hear the same refrain: "I came for the winter, but stayed for the summer."

Summer at elevation is to die for. In my case, my great fear in relocating from Vermont some 20 years ago was that I'd miss the lakes and ocean waters of the Northeast. Although I missed the sailing and my old friends, it was never really an issue. In Steamboat, each night the temperature drops into the 40s or lower 50s—open the windows; no air conditioning. The daytime high occurs around 4 p.m. and seldom gets much over 80 degrees. We might have one day when the temperature hits 90. Oh, and the humidity is so low that 90 degrees is painless. It's not unusual to get a brief shower in the late afternoon, but no steady rain. No serious rain—sometimes for 40 or 50 days at a time. It's not good in terms of wildfire suppression, but what a blessing in terms of enjoying the outdoors.

The West certainly has distinct advantage in terms of weather. But most of the larger Eastern ski towns are at elevation, and elevation is relative. During my many summers in Vermont, I could never understand why more people didn't visit the mountains rather than wait in line trying to get to the Long Island beaches or to cross the Sagamore Bridge to Cape Cod. Talk about a hassle! Most Vermont nights were cool, with a damp stillness in the morning.

When Vail Resorts made its deal for the Triple Peaks resorts, it wound up with Crested Butte in Colorado. I'm sure they had numerous internal discussions that ran like this: "Why do we need another Colorado ski area?" Especially a relatively small one with access issues, limited air service, and a remote location relative to the Front Range ski market. (Not unlike Kirkwood, the smaller, third member in the company's Tahoe lineup.) My guess is that if they could have kept Crested Butte out of their deal, they would have.

I don't think they will regret holding on to Crested Butte. Why? It is one of the most unique ski communities in the Rocky Mountains. The town of Crested Butte has tons of personality, reflecting that of its residents. Dining options are fantastic. The setting and physical environment are spectacular. And there are all sorts of activities to round out the skiing experience. My view is that the prior owners simply did not appreciate how blessed they were with the broader community offerings and failed to properly brand Crested Butte. In fact, for years, the ski area was in a very public permitting process with the U.S. Forest Service in an attempt to add more skiing terrain, particularly at an intermediate level. It was very controversial, even locally. So here was the ski area telling the world that it really wasn't a good place to ski, because it lacked important terrain. Hogwash. There's plenty of great skiing at Crested Butte for all levels, and the community has a charm and quirkiness that stands out even among some very strong competitors for "personality." The expansion plan was never approved, but I don't see any reason why that should hold back Crested Butte.

One of my favorite questions to ask my skiing friends is: "What ski town do you love to visit?" The leading contenders in my unscientific survey: Jackson Hole, Steamboat, Telluride, and Crested Butte.

In the case of Crested Butte, I'm pretty sure Vail will quickly appreciate its appeal and start marketing the larger resort experience, and over time, build a successful business model. Its inclusion in the Epic Pass will encourage trial, and it's my bet that those skiers will become Crested Butte regulars.

Ski towns are an enviable place to live and do business, or just plain retire. These communities have become centers of entrepreneurial energy and economic engines for their states. And they can do much more in the future. There's absolutely no reason why this model couldn't work in the East.

There are some basics requirements for success. In no particular order, these are:

Quality Recreation

Les Otten had a tagline for his American Skiing Company that I thought was brilliant: "Live in the Outside." An awkward expression, but everyone got the idea. Be outside. Recreate. Get away from your cell phone and web streaming, and be active. Outside. Skiing, hiking, biking. It made all the sense in the world.

Earlier I mentioned the passion I had seen in Steamboat and other mountain communities for what I would call outdoor athletic adventurism. Whether skinning up the mountain at 7 a.m., "gravel grinding" in the summer on largely undiscovered back roads, winter camping on hut trips, or backcountry adventuring, these recreational options were seldom considered by my generation. Boomers were satisfied just to ski. But I'm full of respect for these new adventurers, living "in the outside." They have a clear passion, not only for their activity, but for the natural world that hosts them. It is a deeper, more personal kind of environmentalism, based on setting new athletic goals in a shared value structure (with the other participants). I observe this regularly. And I'm jealous. My generation just didn't have these options. Perhaps, we wouldn't have recognized the opportunity even it was presented. The West doesn't have a patent on the new athleticism, but it is more thoroughly a part of the culture here. It seems to drive every aspect of the community's social life, and for those who haven't made the move to the mountains, it's very aspirational.

Central to the ski-town lifestyle is this culture of adventure, athleticism, and fitness. If you think you're a great athlete, or that you're in great shape, try competing against a ski-town athlete. It's humbling.

Using Steamboat as an example, one of the more visual testimonies to this

culture can be seen on any morning, just as the lifts are opening, on skiers'
right of Heavenly Daze (the popular trail that parallels the gondola line), there
is a steady line of aerobic machines "skinning" up the trail. This is early-morn-
ing exercise for most of these folks. Some may just ski back down; others spend
the next few hours enjoying the mountain via the lift system. And some will
continue up to the summit of Mount Werner and then head off for backcountry skiing. To put this in perspective, the vertical distance to Thunderhead
Lodge (the top of the gondola) is just over 2,000 feet. To the summit of Mt.
Werner, it's an additional 1,600 vertical feet. That's some serious climbing.

On Saturday mornings, there are *hundreds* of skiers making the climb to
Thunderhead. Most are locals who have jobs during the week, so the crowd is
always greater on Saturday.

While ski-town athletes are certainly more conditioned than the average
skier, there is an inevitable impact on other participants rubbing elbows with
them. Ski culture historically emphasized the "après" side. Are you old enough
to remember 1984's "Hot Dog ... The Movie"? It was so bad, it was almost
good—guaranteed to offend just about everyone. It was symptomatic of a time
when much of skiing was just viewed as "silly."

Now the public perception of skiing is much more centered on the active,
healthy lifestyle. And it's not just for young people. In February 2018, *The
Denver Post* reported that Steamboat Springs ranks first in the U.S. in terms
of population growth among people 65 and older. "Routt County experienced
a rise of almost 80 percent in its senior population compared to the national
rate of just over 15 percent during the study period from 2010 to 2016." According to the study, "... based on the share of new arrivals who are moving
into Steamboat (Routt County), Steamboat ranked first among 933 communities known to be popular among retirees. And it follows that Edwards/Vail
ranked third and Breckenridge, fourth."

In Steamboat Springs, many of the recreational opportunities are centered
at the ski area. But there's so much else: An extensive hiking network on the
National Forest. A rapidly expanding mountain-bike-trail network on private
and public lands. Tubing on the Yampa River. The community has invested
heavily over the years so that virtually every recreational activity you can think
of is covered: indoor/outdoor tennis; ice-skating (year-round), multiple recre-
ation centers/gyms; hot springs; multiple cross-country centers, golf—the list

goes on. Many of these more expensive facilities were constructed using a combination of public and private monies. A local option lodging tax was critical in funding some of the more expensive projects (tennis and golf). In general, what the community has invested in has benefited both guest and residents alike. This seems to be the magical formula: If the project appeals to both audiences, it's probably financially rational and enhances the overall appeal of the community.

Pedestrian and Cycling Friendly

I can't think of a popular Western mountain town that doesn't have a "core" walking/biking trail. By that I mean a paved path that avoids intersections, and has elements of seclusion, decent tree-cover for shade, and, often, sections that run along an existing water course. These trails are usually plowed during the winter, and on a sunny day the snow-cover can disappear on exposed sections. Walking becomes a way of life, part of the routine for residents and guests alike. The "core" trail is a place to enjoy the outdoors, get a fresh breath of air, and socialize. During my last visit to Mount Snow, I noticed how popular the new, lengthened bike path was. The town had constructed a classic bandstand near the West Dover Center, where outdoor concerts are scheduled from time to time. Hop on your bike or walk to the concert, and then head home, or stop by a local restaurant. I hope they figure out a way to connect the trail all the way to Wilmington. It would be transformational in terms of the overall appeal of the Deerfield Valley.

Every growing community has issues of parking in downtown areas, and at trailheads, parks, or river-access points. The answer isn't always "more parking." In many cases, there simply isn't the space. By making safe and efficient pedestrian and cycling connections, the car can be left in the garage. Most mountain towns have adopted policies that discourage vehicular use and reward the walker/cyclist. They can be as simple as curb bump-outs to shorten the walking distance across intersections, signs to delineate bike lanes, or bike racks placed strategically throughout the community. Bike-to-work day becomes every day for the diehard. June is "bike to work" month. The new "fat tire" bikes have led to a virtual explosion of winter use in the mountains. This is a younger person's mode of transportation, but it works. In many towns, Nordic operators now rent fat-tire bikes and have groomed paths adjacent to the cross-country trails. In general, mountain towns are universal adopters of this walking/cycling culture. It's taken for granted. It's just part of "who we are."

Music, Festivals

Nothing pulls a community together like a free concert. Growing up in my hometown of Easthampton, Massachusetts, I can remember how much fun our block parties were. Periodically, during the summer, the town would close Park Street between the library and high school, bring out a stage, and we'd have a party. It was a wonderful community and family experience. The ski-town equivalent is the free concert. The price is right. Every few weeks in the summer, the city of Steamboat Springs hosts a free concert. A stage is set up at the base of the Howelsen Hill ski jumps, and thousands of people of all ages show up, sitting or standing on the grassy outrun from the jumps. (Private donations, sponsorship, and an annual contribution from the city budget make this possible). This venue is within walking distance of downtown and just off the "core trail."

Outdoor concerts happen during the winter as well. The ski company holds a number of free concerts in Gondola Square, and these, depending on the group, can be as popular as the summer events. Several weeklong music festivals are held over the winter. Musicfest, which occurs right after the New Year's holiday, attracts 6,000 skiers and music lovers, mostly from Texas. (This festival has been coming to Steamboat for more than 25 years.) Look at the events calendar for any ski town, and you'll see their concert schedule. Many are even more extensive than Steamboat's. Telluride built its shoulder season business on the foundation of its Bluegrass Festivals.

Great entertainment happens throughout the year. It's appreciated. It's just acknowledged to be part of the ski-town culture.

Other private or nonprofit musical venues are also typical of ski-town living. Vail has its extraordinary Ford Amphitheater, which hosts the New York Philharmonic orchestra most summers. Steamboat has its Strings Music Festival, which features classical and other musical styles. Its 550-seat pavilion is regularly sold out. Nothing brings people together like good music.

Beer Is Important

Bud Light just doesn't do it anymore. Younger generations have figured out that the secret to good beer is freshness. And nothing is fresher than a beverage at your local beer pub and brewery. I think there are four breweries in our little town of Steamboat Springs. All seem to be thriving. For many residents and guests, given the choice of imbibing a locally brewed product or a national brand, most go local. We even have a whiskey distillery and bar. Breckenridge is well-known for its many breweries and distilleries. Some of their products, like Breckenridge Vodka, are broadly distributed. Just about every ski town now has its own branded beer.

The local breweries tend to be large venues. The beer is important, and the food, but what really sets them apart is the party scene. It's very social, with picnic tables and garage doors that open to the outside in fair weather. There's not much of what you might call "hunkering down" at the bar. Rather, it's more about interacting, meeting people, and generally enjoying the scene.

High-Quality Medical Services

Shifting from beer to wine: Ski towns aren't just about the younger set. In Steamboat, there are really three major demographics: the longtime locals (many with ranching/mining heritages); the Millennials and Gen X-ers looking for quality employment, starting new businesses, and raising families; and retirees.

The latter group pays many of the bills—no kids in the school system; they just spend. Many have since stopped skiing, but they provide accommodations for their multigenerational skiing families. Many are year-round residents; others drift away to warmer climes during the winter but return for traditional holiday periods. They are a major economic and political force in ski towns. What they do need is quality medical facilities to manage the inevitable health issues that come with aging. Fortunately, where you have a ski town, you tend to have good doctors. They are here because the skiing lifestyle is important them, and, yes, skiers get injured. Surgery, when needed, tends to occur at the local hospital because major facilities are too far away, so the doctors tend to be very good. One of the best is The Steadman Clinic in Vail. It has an international reputation for its ability to repair complex sports injuries.

The fact that skiers tend to be of a high-income demographic means that they pay their bills, and that helps both doctors and the hospitals. One significant trend has been the growth of assisted-living facilities. For many ski-town residents, especially those recently retired, there's often a family member who requires transitional housing. With already-excellent hospital facilities, it's an easy decision to move an aging family member, who now requires assisted living, to a quality facility in your hometown. Here in Steamboat, Casey's Pond, founded in 2011, is providing just that service.

Vibrant Arts, Nonprofits

There is a virtuous cycle that many ski towns enjoy: Retirees with resources adopt a cause that matters to them and then support that cause through direct financial contributions and volunteer efforts. I've served on the board of the Yampa Valley Community Foundation for many years. It is a typical community foundation, with donor-advised funds and an annual granting cycle that supports local nonprofits. Our mission is: "Connecting people who care with causes that matter."

It's great not having to ask for money. Our mission is just to make the connection. There are some 150 nonprofits in Steamboat Springs. What is amazing about them is their diversity, which reflects the mixing bowl that is the larger community. In addition to your traditional human services–type agencies, there are a number of nonprofits supporting the arts. We even have opera. I mentioned earlier the Strings Music Festival, and there are more than 10 galleries—so many that it's difficult to visit all of them during a First Friday Art Walk. This is one of the more interactive social events in town, occurring on the first Friday of each month. (Yes, wine is served.) The newest and largest is the Steamboat Art Museum, now showing nationally acclaimed artists in a stunningly repurposed historic downtown building.

The community's nonprofits are a significant economic engine. They employ staff, rent or own offices, and in terms of local spending, behave just as if they were small businesses.

Came for the Skiing; Stayed for the Library

Who says books don't matter? Steamboat's Bud Werner Memorial Library is arguably the city's social center. The original library was repurposed as a community meeting room and became a wing of a whole, new facility constructed in 2008. Voters overwhelmingly approved a property tax increase to fund the expansion, which offers multiple reading areas; more than 85,000 books, CDs, DVDs, and magazines; and even a coffee shop. Although public perception might be that libraries are old-school in a world where so many people access media via cell phone or iPad, sitting alone in front of a screen gets old. The library is a (quiet) social scene, a chance to be alone with your reading but in the company of other inquisitive minds. I was a skeptic when the library was first built, not thinking that enough people would take advantage of the new space. I was wrong. A library does matter. And don't forget your local, independent bookstore. They seem to thrive in mountain towns: Off the Beaten Path in Steamboat, the Bookworm in Edwards, Explore Booksellers in Aspen, Bartleby's Bookstore in Wilmington, and so on.

High-Quality School System

The good news is that teaching in a place like Steamboat or Jackson Hole is pretty appealing, assuming that an outdoor lifestyle is a good fit. The downside is the cost of living, especially housing. I'll offer some thoughts on housing below, because it's a challenge nearly all ski towns face.

Because of Steamboat's steady growth over the past decade (even with the Great Recession and attendant shrinking of the construction industry), the student census keeps rising. The city's education leaders have vetted several proposals to address the issue, but voters have been skeptical of a grand solution and instead have approved what I would call major-maintenance expenditures that do little to address the growing space problem. The issue isn't performance. Steamboat's schools regularly place in Colorado's top ranks. Voters did approve a dedicated sales tax to support education, particularly the technology side. These extra dollars have kept teacher salaries competitive and helped maintain consistently high scores across the system. There's a tendency to blame the childless, retired segment for the difficulty passing a new funding scheme. Voters are knowledgeable and typically engaged on major ballot issues; to date, they haven't been given a plan that passes scrutiny.

Steamboat Springs is fortunate to be home to one of Colorado Mountain College's 11 campuses, which provides associate degrees across the Colorado mountain west. Steamboat is the largest residential campus, with more than

1,500 students (including full- and part-time). That also includes life-long community learners and concurrent enrollment students from the local high schools. It has a recreational focus that befits its location. Recently, it began offering four-year degrees in a number of disciplines. This is a different institution from the earlier version, fondly remembered by locals as "See Me Ski" College. It is a huge community asset, with a large, public auditorium that is often made available for community functions or confabs. Students are able to minimize educational expenses (which are *very* reasonable) by joining the local work force, which many do at least part-time. The two-year program may take three or more years, but students who work can graduate without crushing debt. Many choose to remain in Steamboat.

With a diverse population base and so many opportunities for continuing education, residents are generally informed and engaged. Seminars at Steamboat, a local nonprofit, brings in four or five internationally known speakers throughout the peak summer season. The Steamboat Institute, another local nonprofit, hosts a popular annual conference that focuses on more conservative issues. An educated citizenry usually demands good government, and everyone benefits from that.

Affordable Housing

Well, here's the elephant in the room: housing. Many ski towns are in remote settings with limited private land. Aspen is a good example. Telluride and Jackson Hole as well. Others, like Breckenridge or Park City, are easily accessed from major interstates and have an almost suburban component. Residents who commute to larger cities are competing with skiers and second-home owners for housing. Either way, the housing demand remains strong even during most downturns. Prices are high and, in most cases, beyond the housing budgets of most middle-income earners. Aspen takes the cake, with starter homes downtown running $5 million. The local workforce commutes from Carbondale, Basalt, or even Glenwood Springs and Paonia.

It's beyond the scope of this book to propose solutions, the issue being so complex and emotional in many places. There are those in ski towns who say, "Well, I worked two jobs to buy my first home and made it work. Why can't they?" Most communities have developed strategies for their seasonal workforce. This is not terribly complicated, because it's not a growth/no-growth issue. These workers come and go. Their housing requirements are pretty basic: clean, TV, on the bus route, inexpensive.

The real rub comes when a young couple decides to have a family. The income stream shrinks when one spouse leaves the workforce. Costs go up, and space needs increase. When two- or three-bedroom homes start at $800,000, that's a problem. Older condos can be found, but many are in nightly rental complexes, not a place for a young family.

If my premise about ski towns is correct—that they are going to become increasingly attractive to those aspiring for the active, outdoor lifestyle—then these communities need to have an honest debate about growth.

In Steamboat Springs, we have the blessing of a wide valley floor, lots of land, and few limits to development, whether power, water, sewer capacity, or infrastructure. There is currently a proposal to add 450 units in a mix of subsidized and free-market housing over the next decade. What is different about this project is its size and the fact that it is providing "attainable" housing, the bridge young families need as they age and move up the economic ladder.

The issue is whether the city will annex the land to make new housing available—not that complicated. But here's where the conflict really comes. Providing new housing means more people. There's no getting around that. More people mean more hassles, especially to the older residents who can remember when you didn't have to wait in line at City Market. Or new residents who came assuming the status quo would somehow be maintained.

So opponents petitioned successfully for a city-wide vote on the annexation. Their argument is that City Council didn't get enough from the developer. But it's really a smokescreen for finding a way to slow growth and hold on to the status quo. Many of those supporting the "anti" effort have signed onto similar efforts in the past. On June 27, the election results were released: The annexation proposal won with 60 percent of the vote.

There are certainly changes, some negative, in the quality of life that attend growth: new people, new ideas, new businesses, and more opportunities for new and older residents. But it's a trade-off. It's a debate that needs to be settled, ski town by ski town, each with unique circumstances—and this needs to happen soon if I'm right about the impending rush to these communities. While there's no secret sauce to create attainable housing, one effective strategy is to construct units of a size that would not appeal to those looking for a second home or retiring. Taking those demographics out of the competition for housing improves the odds for affordability.

Summary

The mega-passes will only exacerbate the current migration trends to ski towns. The passes encourage exploration and trial, meaning that a large number of people will be visiting a place like Steamboat who probably never would have otherwise come here. Will they note all the positives acknowledged above? I think so. And they'll aspire to visit again or perhaps live in a place like this. This will put even more pressure on housing prices.

One final note on the broad appeal of ski towns: They tend to be politically diverse but with a growing trend towards Blue. For example, Colorado is moving from a Purple to a Blue state, with Democrats sweeping all the statewide offices in 2018. In some cases, the ski towns exist as something of a political island. Teton County in Wyoming, which includes Jackson, was the only county in the state to go for Hillary Clinton in the last election. I wrote earlier about the "egalitarian" cast in the early days of ski towns. Certainly, it's a more complex fabric now, but these remain easygoing, tolerant communities. Colorado recently approved the retail sale of marijuana, so our Steamboat community now has a number of pot shops. There were concerns early on about negative public impacts, but they haven't materialized. Locals enjoy the new freedom. Guests seem to take it all in stride. While our politics can surprise, we are more often focused on getting along, and, of course, having a great time.

CHAPTER 17

So Where Are We Going?

1. Mega-Passes

To understand where all this might be headed and how it relates (skiers, ski towns, ski area operators, ski company suppliers, and such), we need to look once more at how the mega-passes have transformed the business.

Beginning with the 2018–19 season, when Ikon joined Epic, the passes themselves became "brands." For a significant portion of the "core" skier market, a brand is chosen and actual vacation/travel plans follow much later. The choice of what specific pass type to purchase is much more nuanced than the brand selection. Here's an example. My old sailing friends Jim and Brenda Crane are classic Killington skiers: hard-core. Weather doesn't faze them. They've had a condo at the base of the mountain for 30-plus years and ski with the same group whenever there. When they're not in residence, their adult children are. It's a multigenerational HQ. For many years their travel plans included an annual trek to Alta, sometimes stopping by Steamboat to visit us on the way out or back. They have always purchased a Killington pass, then multi-day tickets for Alta/Snowbird.

In the new world, they've changed their buying habits. For the 2018–19 ski season, they bought Ikon Base passes, which provided five days at Killington. Because they ski more than those five days and can't use the pass for holidays, they packaged a combination of K Tickets (sold in the fall for about $70 a day) plus owners' passes (about $80 a day), which they get for placing their condo in the company's rental program. That owners' pass also comes with food discounts. This winter, they made a "grand tour" of the West, starting in Aspen, then to Alta/Snowbird, finishing in Steamboat. Ikon Base provided the access they needed outside their home base, but they had to work all the angles regarding Killington. I share their story because it demonstrates how savvy skiers are when it comes to pass selection. It also explains how many folks have migrated away from the individual resort pass to a mega-pass. Where there's a deal, they'll find it. Next year, the Cranes may add a second Western trip. They're talking about visiting Big Sky. Unquestionably, the Ikon privileges are driving them to ski more and explore more.

In my view, anyone who has a "home" ski area that is not owned by or a pass partner with Alterra or Vail and plans to ski largely at that resort will likely continue to buy the home-area's pass, unless they can engineer a cheaper combination of products that work or there are extensive travel plans, like the Cranes above. There are so many reasons why it's home: location, racing or freeskiing programs, second home, and such. The lucky skiers are those whose favored resort is now owned by Alterra or Vail Resorts. They just got a big discount compared to what they had been paying and have opportunities to ski elsewhere that were, frankly, unimaginable just a year ago.

There's another, much larger group of skiers: those who currently do not have a home mountain but who are active participants in the sport. This is the group Vail and Alterra are competing for. They venture out somewhere around 10-plus days per season. Historically, they've headed up to the ticket window, swallowed hard, and bought a day ticket. Those on vacation usually bundled a multiday lift ticket with other products (e.g., rentals, ski school, lodging). This reduced the cost, but it was still expensive, especially at the large destination resorts. They typically aren't repeat visitors at a destination, but cycle through three or four of their favorites, taking one week-long ski vacation most years. The media, including ski press, has always groaned about the cost of skiing—and rightly so. Skiing has always been an expensive way to recreate. But first Epic, and then the other competing passes, managed to reset how the public views the cost of skiing.

Compared with prior years, when the cost of skiing was always a popular headline article, the media has been relatively mum on the subject. This year there was a new record for the cost of a single-day lift ticket: $219 at Vail/Beaver Creek over the holidays. You would think that would generate a lot of negative press. Didn't happen. That's because mega-passes have altered the public view of the cost of skiing. Why would you spend $219 for a day when you can have unlimited skiing at more than 60 Vail Resorts partners around the globe for $899? (To put this in perspective, that's less than the cost of a season pass at Steamboat when I arrived here 20 years ago.) The awareness of these passes in the public mind is simply huge. Vail sold 925,000 of these for the 2018–19 season. Alterra added somewhere around 400,000 in its first season.

Here's the biggest change. If, in the consumer's mind, it's a great deal, then it follows that the product will be used more. And that's what's happening, at many levels. It's also changing how skiers react to adverse weather. For example, if you're spending the weekend at a regional New England resort and the weather is less than great, why invest in an expensive day ticket? A rational person would probably decide to save the money and head home early. But, if you had a pass and it's paid for, why not go out and enjoy a few runs? Pack it in if it's not fun. But at least give it a try. This is a major behavioral change.

I think skiers look at the new products this way: If you want to ski around and are expecting eight or more days per season, the choice is probably a mega-pass. (For those planning to vacation at a pricey destination resort over the holidays, this makes sense for as little as five days.) The really adventurous and financially well-off, they're buying both Epic and Ikon!

Then there's the large pool of "infrequent skiers" (skiing just a few days a year and sometimes taking a few years off). The new passes just don't work for this group. They're the ones staring in disbelief at the day ticket price, especially if it's been several years since the last ski trip. While this group doesn't account for a lot of skier days, it does represent a significant number of skiers and keeping them engaged is critical to long-term success.

As noted earlier, for 2019–20, Vail's Epic for Everyone strategy includes the Epic Day Pass (one to seven days at value pricing if purchased in advance, which is by early December). *Voilà!* It's finally happened. More on this below, but high level, the trend is clear: Value pricing has extended down the food chain to the single-day ticket, if purchased in advance. Expect the rest of the ski industry to follow over time. If broadly adopted, it diminishes the challenge noted above with the "infrequent" demographic. And if resorts continue with "dynamic pricing" (aka ridiculously expensive) at the ticket window, they can at least inform the unhappy guest of all the new options, hand over a business card with the company's website, and express the hope that this never happens again.

On March 5, 2019, we got clarity on where the Epic/Ikon pass wars were headed. Both announced new products, payment plans and benefits for the 2019–20 season. Because pass sales begin immediately, no one wants to be caught flat-footed when a competitor announces the plan. So it wasn't surprising that both were prepared to unveil their detailed line-up on the same day.

Alterra announced an increase in its full unrestricted Ikon pricing: up to $949 from $899, a 6-percent jump. To soften the blow for holders of the 2018–19 pass, these individuals could get a $30 credit if next year's pass was purchased by April 24. As speculated earlier, a new payment plan was rolled out: If purchased by April 24, the pass required a $199 deposit, then four monthly payments from June to September. Another value add: The Ikon passholders could purchase up to two discounted Ikons for kids 5–12 ($199/full; $159/base). Again, the passes had to be purchased by April 24.

So for the 2019–20 season, a full Ikon will provide unlimited access to 14 owned resorts, plus seven days each at 24 pass destinations. Vail, by contrast, will offer its full Epic with unlimited access to 20-owned resorts and limited access to 12 others.

Vail has new pass partners for this upcoming season, Sun Valley and Snowbasin, and continues with Telluride; all have negotiated a "per scan" price that Vail Resorts will pay to each. The simple math: Vail Resorts collects all the pass revenue into a pot, then dispenses to Telluride, Sun Valley and Snowbasin based on the number of uses per the agreed upon "scan" rate. This could be a significant payment; for example, if each resort had negotiated a $100 scan rate (hypothetical), and if each resort had 20,000 scans, each would get $2 million. Not bad, assuming that these were mostly incremental visits. In terms of Vail Resorts total pass revenue, it's a drop in the bucket compared to the value that these three resorts bring to Epic.

Likewise, Epic Pass partners in Canada, Europe and Japan bring breadth and value to the pass, and the compensation to those resorts is likely minimal. The Canadian partner, Resorts of the Canadian Rockies, appears to have a usage rate, while the other international pass partners have "reciprocal relationships," meaning no money likely changes hands. For example, the holder of a Les 3 Vallées season pass for 2018–19 could get up to three two-day passes at 10 Vail Resorts mountains. (Vail Resorts does not disclose terms of its international agreements.)

Alterra, by comparison, is writing *very* large checks to partner resorts. Because the company isn't public, we'll never know the details of this math. One could infer, however, that if it were a really bad deal, Alterra would be renegotiating with its partners and modifying the agreements to make sure they work for both parties. So even if assumptions regarding usage (and therefore payments) were wrong, Alterra would be able to respond and adjust appropriately. Given that the March 5 pass announcement included the original partners and that Alterra would have decent metrics on usage by this date, there probably weren't any big surprises.

Vail is forging ahead with its successful marketing strategy: Use data to identify potential customers; draw these folks into a pass product, then keep moving them up the price/value chain to, eventually, a full Epic. The Epic for Everyone completes this process of segmentation. According to Rob Katz: "We have ... taken the window ticket out of the picture. So at this point there is really no reason—as long as you can plan ahead a little bit—that you can't ski for around $100 a day."

With this new product, skiers get one to seven days at Vail-owned resorts. The one-day is $125 unrestricted, $106 if restricted to an individual resort. The seven-day is $621 restricted, $731 unrestricted. Vail was also allowing guests who purchased a day lift ticket after early March in the 2019 season to apply the value of that toward a 2019–20 pass, including an Epic for Everyone, with four or more days. Good business decision in terms of incentivizing sales. And at least for those who purchased an expensive day ticket in late season, it softens the blow. Good PR as well.

For the reasons noted above, it would be difficult for Alterra to offer a product similar to Vail's Epic Day Pass unless it were restricted to its owned resorts. Otherwise, by way of example, Alterra could have an unrestricted Ikon four-day, and if all uses were recorded at a nonowned partner like Jackson Hole, Alterra would likely be writing a check to Jackson for more than it received from the pass sale.

I do think Alterra will find a way to compete with the Epic Day Pass, even if that means customizing it to individual resorts. But those products won't begin to have the widespread appeal of the new Vail offering. We'll see. What's most fascinating to me is the competitive dynamic at work here.

Looking at the full Epic against Alterra's Ikon for 2019–20, it's priced at $10 less (for the early sales deadline, full Epic was $939; Epic Local was $699). There had been speculation that the Epic Military would be dropped (accounting for 100,000 sales at a hugely discounted $99 for 2018–19). That product remains, with the price adjusted upward to $129. An incredible deal for our military.

Epic and Epic Local buyers get a better deal in terms of early deposit requirements: $49 down, and all buyers receive 10 discounted Buddy Tickets, up from six last year, and six "Ski with a Friend" tickets. Balance is due in September.

Both Epic and Ikon are wildly popular and that popularity, I believe, is driven by the many options each provides. Resorts that have been aspirational to hard-core skiers for many years are now getting extra attention. Here in the U.S., Steamboat, Telluride, Jackson Hole, Sun Valley, Snowbird, Alta, Squaw Valley, Mammoth—those are just a few that I think will be winners. Canada will also be a big winner. One unintended but positive consequence of the new passes: The Canadian border has been effectively eliminated for skiers. Historically, the U.S. Pacific Northwest was a major market for Whistler/ Blackcomb, but with that exception, most U.S skiers didn't cross the border. Not true going forward. I was speaking to friends from back east recently. They had just returned from a visit to Stoneham in Quebec. They had stayed in Quebec City at the renowned Chateau Frontenac and described the trip as "an international experience, unbelievably fun, without the complexity and cost of overseas travel." Tremblant will begin to draw more visits from the Boston/New York markets. Favorable exchange rates will enhance this trend.

I wrote earlier in this book about the appeal of European skiing. Nothing quite matches the majesty of the Alps, the ability to ski from village to village, and the food. Hardcore skiers need to bucket list resorts like Zermatt, St. Anton, and Les 3 Vallees (an Epic partner), the latter being the largest skiing complex in the world, with more lifts than the entire state of Colorado. The mega-passes will encourage international travel.

Back to the future. Vail and/or Alterra will eventually find a way to acquire European resorts and tap into the vast market of the Alps. It is difficult or would have happened already. I mentioned John Garnsey who was on this mission for Vail for years, unsuccessfully. With Vail's marketing might, a Vail-owned European partner could expect a significant boost in attendance from North American as well as other international passholders. Looking at just the European market, Epic would be transformational, assuming it signed up attractive partners (it already has a huge head start with major resorts also offering discounts to Epic holders). Alterra would also find equally fertile ground in Europe. With some 150 million skier visits at stake ... you can be sure they will both find a way to compete. Ikon Europe? Epic Europe? It's coming (I count not just the tradition ski countries, but emerging centers like Slovakia and Poland).

Not surprisingly, Europe has developed a competitive response, offering its first mega-pass in spring 2019, with an initial discount price of $440 for up to 10 days at 100 resorts in nine countries: Austria, Italy, France, Switzerland, Germany, Poland, Spain, Slovenia, and Portugal. Called the Snowpass, its price was set to more than double to $1,000 after the first 50,000 passes were sold, which it was on track to pass by late spring. But, the resort partners are mostly second-tier, with few recognizable to Americans. It is affiliated with FIS, the governing body of the World Cup and all international racing, which in Europe still carries some gravitas.

Back here in North America, the big question was will Vail or Alterra begin to draw medium-sized, regional resorts into their mix? Vail Resorts answered that in July 2019 with news of its planned acquisition of the 17 small, midsized and mostly urban ski areas of Peak Resorts. Will Alterra counter in this market, either through purchases or by bringing on non-owned partners for Ikon? Lots to ponder.

2. Growing Participation; Bring a Friend

Another dynamic that we've discussed: passholders bring friends along who are new to skiing or rediscovering the sport. They can use the "friends and family" discounts that the mega-passes include to make this work for their guests. It's worth emphasizing what an incredible opportunity this is to grow the sport. For the lapsed or infrequent skier, taking advantage of a Buddy Pass ticket (usually a 25 percent discount), thanks to a passholder friend, is a great re-introduction. A deeper discount would be even better! We know that of all the many strategies to grow the skier base, none has worked as well as the old SIA-sponsored "Bring a Friend." That's exactly what the Friends & Family options do.

Ski area operators, pretty much across the board and with support from NSAA, have put into place inexpensive introductions to skiing. Because one day isn't enough, most programs have "add-ons" to encourage continued instruction. Once a new skier has survived three days, you typically have commitment.

The mega-passes are helping this process because passholders often take their friends to the ski area; they stay together, and this camaraderie reinforces the learning process. Some people just aren't cut out for skiing. That's fine, but with proper instruction and with friends as part of the journey, the odds of success increase significantly.

Those who have made it through their "introduction" to skiing are probably not ready to jump into a mega-pass. This is a great market for the four-day-type pass discussed previously. It should be offered to new skiers once they complete their introduction—make it a compelling deal, and get commitment up front, recognizing these new skiers need to be nudged.

Any number of strategies have been floated to increase the new-skier retention rate. It hovers around 19 percent, an improvement from a decade ago but still an unacceptable number. If you share my view that the mega-passes are transforming the ski business, then they will play a huge role in developing new skiers. The dynamic: Skiing friends will drag their nonskiing or lapsed friends along. The new context: The long-term cost of participating is not what it once was. This changes the mindset of anxious new participants and, I believe, will start to improve the retention rate in just a few years. This all assumes that the ski areas execute on high-quality, fun instruction and make sure their best teachers spend time with the new participants. Good instructors matter.

3. What of the Smaller Ski Areas?

For those who find their niche and establish deep ties to their communities, the future is bright. Whether as independents, community-owned, or non-profits, they introduce kids to "living in the outside" at a time when too many are glued to their cell phones. Skiing has always been the one sport that families can do together, and small areas are the playground for that interaction.

I've noted earlier that the decline in the number of U.S. ski areas has been misunderstood in terms of the actual dynamic at work, and the impact of overall participation. The impression given is that skiing is declining. But most "lost ski areas" should never have been found! They were small, generally one or more rope-tows, and were built during the heyday of growth, close to major coastal population centers and operated at a time when the ski world was colder. Some were real-estate focused and never made financial sense as stand-alone ski areas. Overall, the skier visits were not significant. What was lost: an inexpensive, local introduction to skiing.

More recently, abandoned ski areas are being reopened, some as commercial ventures, others as community-owned facilities or nonprofits. I expect this to continue where community support is strong. The P&L for even very small areas has improved with new technologies and a better understanding of the business model. Of all the stories I've covered, Antelope Butte in Wyoming is the most inspiring and deserves to be understood more broadly.

4. What About National and Regional Governance?

Melanie Mills is president of Colorado Ski Country USA (CSCUSA). She already knows about the impact of consolidation. Vail Resorts departed from CSCUSA a decade ago, convinced they could handle their own government relations cost-effectively and that the marketing/PR provided by the trade association was not meaningful to them. Following Vail's acquisition of Crested Butte, CSCUSA has one fewer member.

CSCUSA performs key services for its members, especially the smaller ones, by representing ski area interests in the state's legislative and regulatory processes. Often, new laws have an unintended consequence for ski operators, and CSCUSA has, over time, established a great reputation for staying ahead of the curve in terms of legislation or regulation.

But what if Alterra concluded it could go Vail's direction? CSCUSA would transition to a very small office. It might not even survive. Although Alterra owns only two Colorado ski areas (Steamboat and Winter Park), it has a deeply entwined relationship, via the Ikon passes, with the Aspen resorts, Copper Mountain, Eldora, and now A-Basin. In other words, Alterra's political influence extends beyond its owned resorts. I think Alterra is committed to CSCUSA and don't see any big change coming. In a sense, Ski Country, being non-Vail, has a common focus: Vail as competitor. This is the tie that binds. To my view, Vail would have more to gain by getting back inside that group (author's opinion here).

Regarding national governance, I don't anticipate major changes for the National Ski Areas Association (NSAA). The two Majors are committed to growing the sport, dealing with climate change, and continuing to support a proactive government-relations role. Only NSAA is equipped to do this, plus engage with the various quasi-government agencies that oversee lift-safety issues and the like.

4. Who Are the Losers?

When I began writing, I thought this would be a chapter all by itself. But having taken a look coast to coast, at small, medium, and large resorts, I don't see a lot of losers. That said, there are certainly ski areas that will be challenged, if not to survive, then to grow their market share. These are generally the ones that have not joined a mega-pass, or one of the smaller but still-compelling pass deals (for example, the regional Power Pass). I have yet to hear an executive from one of the still-independent but "aligned" resorts say they expect business to be flat. All are counting on a significant boost from joining Epic or Ikon.

What does that mean for the nonaligned? The pie could get smaller. Unless the number of skiers begins to grow, they had better come up with a plan.

In New Hampshire, Waterville Valley will be challenged. It has always struggled to compete, as noted earlier. The state-run Cannon Mountain will probably struggle, as well. Bretton Woods might be a likely candidate for one of the mega-passes. Going it alone will be tough sledding.

In New York, what will happen to the three state-owned properties, Whiteface, Gore, and Belleayre? They can promote a joint value pass focused on the regional market, but can they grow market share in the New York City market against Epic or Ikon? Not likely. These areas seem to have regained some momentum in recent years. That could be halted. It may go negative.

Other issues pop up in circumstances where there are two or more close competitors and one joins a mega-pass. For example, in western New York, what if popular Holiday Valley joined Ikon? Nearby Kissing Bridge would certainly feel some pain.

5. What About Ski Towns? Real Estate?

Hold on to your hats. Unless the economy tanks and we head into a serious recession, expect ski towns to experience significant growth (and internal strife) from the influx of Millennials and retirees. In 2008, major resort real-estate projects ceased. Until then, much of the development energy was focused on creating new or expanded ski villages, many following the Intrawest model.

As we enter 2019, there are several major resort projects moving forward. The biggest by far is Big Sky. This could well be the "canary in the coal mine" for resort real estate, pronounced dead in 2008. Other major projects include

Snowmass, Killington, Taos, and Squaw Valley. Mount Snow is focusing on the redevelopment of its Carinthia area and has aggressive plans. But much hinges on EB-5 funding, which is very much up in the air. In Steamboat, one of ski-country's largest remaining base-area development parcels (the Ski Time Square property) recently changed hands. Development can be expected to begin in the next few years, albeit not on the scale originally proposed a decade ago. The biggest issue the developer faces: cost of construction is said to be pushing $700 a square-foot. Unless those costs come down, we'll be looking at vacant property for a few more years.

The same situation probably exists for other ski towns. If so, the economic return from new projects might not offset the risk. If that's the case, look for even faster increases in prices for existing housing stock.

6. Ski-Industry Suppliers?

This is a good time to be a lift manufacturer. In 2013, the North American ski industry purchased a total of 16 lifts. In 2018, that number was 37. For the first time in my memory, a number of those lifts were not delivered until after the Christmas holiday, something almost unheard of in the past. Expect 2019–20 to be equally strong. As noted earlier, ski areas find themselves on a much stronger financial footing and in position to deal with the big elephant of deferred capital. Most of that relates to lifts. So expect a large number of re-placements and upgrades in addition to new construction.

There are basically two major lift companies (Leitner-Poma and Doppel-mayr). The lift industry's consolidation occurred years before that on the ski area side. This doesn't mean that the ski conglomerates don't have pricing power, but with lifts ... it's limited. The lift companies will focus on getting multiyear commitments from the big guys and reward those commitments with the best pricing. (There is a third manufacturer, Skytrac, headquartered in Salt Lake City, but they do not produce a detachable lift, which is where the bulk of the lift dollars are spent.)

The lift companies are unique. For other suppliers—whether snowcats, snow-guns, ticket systems, ski hardgoods, whatever—they are now dealing with a handful of buyers, those representing the conglomerates, for the bulk of their business. The pricing power of these buyers is significant, meaning lowered margins and a tough business climate for these suppliers.

7. How Has the Work Changed? Its Future?

With all the recent consolidation, the ski industry is a very different place to work from the one I experienced during my career. A large organization like Vail Resorts is very disciplined in its management protocols. With Vail, the GMs role is to rely on functional experts at corporate. He or she is "coordinator-in-chief." For the GM at a non-affiliated resort, there's much more independence, that is, freedom to make decisions within the broad strategic policies set by the board of directors.

The Vail model is relatively new. One of the intriguing aspects of the ski business to me was its complexity in terms of lines of business. You had to learn and know a little about everything to understand how it all fit together: mountain operations, retail, rental, lodging, food and beverage, transportation, ticketing, and so on. This is still the case at independent resorts. It's more like managing chaos, being a jack-of-all-trades—the way it has historically been. With that juggling act in mind, my old friend and Copper Mountain founder Chuck Lewis used to say: "If you can make it in the ski business, you can succeed anywhere."

In terms of career opportunities, if you're in the Vail organization and have a successful track record, there are many personal-growth options. Vail seldom looks outside its own team when there's a new acquisition and a senior-management position needs to be filled.

When Alterra purchased Crystal Mountain in Washington, they moved longtime Intrawest resort executive Frank DeBerry from Snowshoe to Crystal. Like Vail, Alterra is going to provide opportunities to known talent within the company whenever possible. Frank's position at Snowshoe was filled by an Alterra insider. "We are fortunate at Alterra Mountain Company to have a wealth of talent within our 14 destinations and I am confident Patti (Duncan) will continue her excellent work and lead Snowshoe and its staff into the future," said David Perry, president and COO of Alterra. So Alterra appears to be looking inward, like Vail, when it comes to new leadership opportunities. As its corporate office grows, resort managers will have more functional experts to rely on, and the resort chief's role will shift more to managing relationships, as is the case with Vail.

This isn't your father's ski business. It's still one heck of a lot of fun, especially if you find a good boss and a supportive culture. That, fortunately, can be found just about anywhere in ski country.

And in Conclusion…

In the March 1, 2019, edition of *Mountain Town News,* editor Allen Best's lead article asks: "Have 'Ikoneers' ruined locals' ski experiences?" Quoting the *Aspen Daily News,* he reports a reaction to reportedly long lift lines: "We're on our way to becoming more like Vail," said Ian Long, the owner of a local construction company. Over in Jackson Hole, Best reports the same refrain. "I haven't seen it like this in 30 years of skiing this mountain," a local told the *Jackson Hole News & Guide.*

Our local paper, the *Steamboat Pilot,* ran the following headline and article on April 4, 2019: "Ikon Pass Overcrowds Deer Valley."

"Parking lots overflowed and many skiers complained of longer than normal lift lines as visitation numbers peaked. Resort leaders say multiple factors contributed to the high numbers, but the resort's inclusion in the new Ikon Pass for Deer Valley's owner, Alterra Mountain Co., unmistakably played a role. Next year the resort hopes to better regulate the crowds." Later in the article: "Officials report the resort is up 12 percent." Pretty much the same local push back occurred at Aspen. To be fair, when I say "local," I mean all committed, loyal passholders. They are not getting the "Ikon" deal because it provided only limited access to their "home" resort. They are paying more for their unrestricted passes and seeing the new passholders show up on powder days (using one of their five or seven days). Deer Valley, which still charges $2,400 for a pass, may have to initiate further restrictions or risk alienating its loyal skier/second home owner base

My somewhat cynical view is that many of the same people who have been complaining about lack of growth in the ski sport are now complaining about the crowds. You can't have it both ways. That said, I understand the challenges some of the resort partners are facing. How Sun Valley is impacted next season and how their core skier base responds, having been so spoiled for so many years, will be telling. I've mentioned earlier that these pass deals are not in perpetuity. If and when an arrangement isn't working for both parties, it will be terminated or amended. One thing for sure: things will change.

Across ski country, resorts are exchanging deep discounts for commitment and loyalty, and they're getting it. My opinion is that the first step to growing the total number of participants is to increase participation from the core. This measures loyalty to the sport. And it inspires others (non-core) to increase their participation. If you ask a golfer how many times he/she plays each year and the answer is "once or twice," what does that tell you about the commitment to golfing? Ho hum. Overhearing skiers at the water cooler talking about enjoying their 30th day so far this season—that's a different animal. You make that kind of commitment only when you are deeply engaged. Following the 2018–19 season, we have a core group of deeply engaged skiers from coast to coast. Exploring more and enjoying more. The next step should be increased visitation from the non-core segment and eventually, generic growth in the total skier population.

So there will be more and more crowded days across ski country. That's the good news if you're in the business. If you've enjoyed uncrowded slopes in a more remote destination, change is coming, or it's already arrived.

In terms of trend, is there any reason why the number of Epic and Ikon passholders couldn't double as more and more skiers move up the product chain, ski more often, are drawn back into the sport, or are just brand-new?

Big changes are coming.

IT BEGAN WITH VAIL'S INCREDIBLE BUSINESS SUCCESS via its Epic strategy. Then, in 2018–19, for the first time, Epic had a significant competitor. The excitement and the publicity that accompanied Alterra's arrival, enhanced by generally favorable weather, drove near-record skier visits across the U.S. Vail and Alterra weren't the only winners. The many success stories we've studied are testimony to a new competitive dynamism at work in the ski industry. Pressure remains for all areas to sharpen their pencils in terms of pricing. Winter Park announced that its unrestricted season pass for 2019–20 will cost $449. What a deal.

As the pass wars continue, we're also seeing the first rounds of a spending competition. I noted earlier that many industry competitors, like Brian Fairbank at Jiminy Peak, were concerned that they would not be able to match the capital-investment plans of a Vail Resorts and, thereby, would watch their ski facilities' appeal diminish over time. Alterra has announced, along with its new pass pricing, a plan to spend $181 million at its 14 resorts in the coming year. Multiyear capital expenditures are forecast at $555 million. This is comparable to Vail Resorts' already-announced CapEx strategy. Both are already big; they also plan to keep getting better. Just watch how other areas respond. POWDR's Copper just announced a $100 million expansion, and Boyne plans to invest $1 billion across its portfolio in the next decade or so. Get ready. It's coming. As noted earlier, in terms of investing for generic growth, Vail has a huge head start, in that its deferred-maintenance obligations are significantly less than most of the ski industry.

It's human nature to want to look at the world through a lens that separates winners and losers. That predilection is well at work when people look at the newly competitive ski world. I frequently hear the refrain, "So who's the winner here—Vail or Alterra?"

My own view is that both have shown themselves to be creative, disciplined organizations as they proceed to transform the ski business. The leadership and competency in these two companies dwarfs whatever has come before in terms of ski-area holding companies. Alterra is private, so we aren't able to compare it with Vail Resorts from a financial-metrics perspective. That day may come. If it does, the biggest challenge for Alterra will be that it came into the game late and paid a premium, relative to Vail, for its collection. That will impact all aspects of financial comparison. Additionally, size matters in terms of profitability. Vail owns the largest resorts in North America and Australia. Although Alterra has three high-margin resorts, recording more than a million skier visits (Mammoth, Steamboat, and Winter Park), these simply can't compare in terms of profitability with Whistler Blackcomb, Park City, or Vail's big four in Colorado. In California, the year-over-year earnings of Northstar and Heavenly are less volatile than those of Mammoth and Squaw/Alpine, given the size of their snowmaking systems and nearby bed bases. Alterra's Mammoth is already a monster in terms of skier visits (in some big snow years, its bottom line is comparable to the big guys) and stands to benefit when discovered by non-California Ikon skiers.

In terms of profitability, Vail also has a big head start in terms of vertical integration, the size and scale of its rental/retail operations, lodging operations, real estate brokerage, and other key revenue centers like the Epic Mountain Express shuttle business.

In the earlier pages of this book, I noted the dramatic drop in Vail Resort's stock price following the announcement of some softness in pass sales in key markets. Much speculation followed regarding the impact of new competition from Alterra.

For 2018–19, skier visits across the U.S. were up 11 percent. Vail Resorts reported traffic to its North American resorts increased just 6.8 percent (in-

cluding Whistler, so this is not apples to apples; the Canadian behemoth's slug-
gish early season likely dragged down the total). Given the big difference, it's
reasonable to assume that Vail did see slower growth than the rest of the industry. This is a change because Vail typically outperforms. Alterra's arrival had
to be at least partly responsible. Rob Katz says Alterra/Ikon validates Vail's
blueprint; but that doesn't mean he's insulated from new competition.

How did this translate to financial results? Well, Q3 results were announced on June 6, and Vail reported third-quarter revenues that grew 13.7
percent to $957.9 million, narrowly missing the market projection of $958.75
million. Earnings for the quarter grew to $7.12 per share, from $6.17 per share
a year ago. The Q2 earnings were stronger than the analysts' expectation of
$7.06 per share. EBITDA guidance was raised slightly to $702 to $712 million
from prior guidance of $690 to $710 million to take into account recent acquisitions. Vail shares jumped over 6 percent following the earnings announcement, so the decline had dropped to 16.6 percent in trailing 52 weeks.

"We are pleased with our overall results for the quarter and for the full
2018–2019 North American ski season, with strong growth in visitation and
spending compared to the prior year, including a strong finish to the season
with good conditions across our western U.S. destination resorts," CEO Katz
said. "After the challenging early season period for destination visitation, our
results for the remainder of the season were largely in line with our original
expectations. Our results throughout the 2018–2019 North American ski season highlight the growth and stability resulting from our season pass, the benefit of our geographic diversification, the investments we make in our resorts
and the success of our sophisticated, data-driven marketing efforts."

In the same earnings release Katz noted that pass sales through May 28
were up 9 percent in units and 13 percent in revenues (not including the military passes).

Doesn't sound much like a company on the ropes, especially when you consider the stock jumped more than 4 percent, to $235, on July 22, the day it an-
nounced its plans to acquire Peak Resorts. Yes, the world changed for Vail
Resorts when Alterra arrived in April 2017. But the company's creative responses to this new competition have arguably driven it to discover new opportunities for growth and profitability. If one accepts the fundamental premise
that the new pass strategy, encouraging commitment and loyalty, will eventually
grow skier visits across the board, there's room for more than one winner. My

slightly foggy crystal ball indicates that Epic and Ikon sales will grow at approximately the same pace for 2019–20. The longer view, post-2020, will be impacted by new acquisitions and pass partners, such as Vail's Peak addition.

My view is that the ski industry is being led by two huge, dynamic, and successful companies with the financial resources to realize the potential of their individual resorts. There's room for both. Vail is public. Alterra remains private and, given the jumpstart provided by good weather for the 2018–19 season, I'm sure it's exceeding the goals set by its owners and investors. The general consensus among industry insiders is that Alterra will strengthen its holdings over the next five years, perhaps adding more resorts, improve operating margins, and then do an IPO to reward its investors. Another view has the Crowns, committed buy-and-hold investors, taking control of Alterra and then merging it with their Aspen properties. Lots of interesting scenarios.

For both Vail and Alterra, I see a bright future. Another positive that is perhaps overlooked: having two major players creates an opportunity for collaboration on the big, long-term issues of growing the sport, increasing diversity and addressing climate change. If Rob Katz and Rusty Gregory can agree on how to tackle these issues, it's pretty obvious that the rest of skidom will follow. A coordinated, industry-wide effort in the 1980s had mixed results (some would say it failed miserably), the USIA's "Ski It to Believe It" campaign. Could a concerted, big-dollar campaign be mounted again, led by Vail and Alterra? Certainly, the opportunity to do so is greater now than at any time in the past, and Vail and Alterra will not achieve ultimate success if more skiers don't come into the sport.

While these two companies get a majority of the press, I hope it's clear, if you got this far through the book, that there are a lot of exciting things happening in the rest of the ski world. One of the most amazing to me is that, despite the size and popularity of the Alterra and Vail properties, it's the independents that keep winning popularity polls. For 2018–19, *SKI* magazine gave the nod to Aspen Snowmass for "Best of the West."

Small ski areas are finding their niche and regaining their appeal. Some are finding that through mergers or partnerships, overhead costs can be lowered, improving financial performance. Many private club facilities, including Yellowstone, are on solid financial footing while some (Haystack) flounder. Even long mothballed projects like Fortress Mountain in British Columbia are showing signs of life. And resort real estate, just recently declared "dead," seems to be coming up for a second breath. All this means that ski country, defined broadly, is experiencing a renaissance.

To date, skiers have been the beneficiaries. Yes, there are some clouds on the horizon: climate change, demographics, Washington's political chaos, perhaps an economic recession, but the ski business has proven itself durable under much less optimistic circumstances. As my editor, Andy Bigford, often remarks: "All good."

Skiing continues to have an outsized influence on the quality of life for so many people. I'll always remember Eric Resnick telling me how "skiing has been the connective tissue to all the good things that have happened to me." I've introduced a lot of ski executives in this book; some I know well; some not at all. But I can say that all share a deep love of the sport and a desire to share that passion. I can't think of any other business that enjoys this kind of leadership. Doesn't success always start with leadership?

Skiing is in a good place these days. I like golf. I love to ski. I hope you enjoyed these thoughts. See you on the slopes.

APPENDIX

Conglomerates

(as of July 23, 2019)

The *Ski Area Management (SAM)* ski resort ownership timeline (saminfo.com/ownership-timeline) is an excellent real-time resource for updates on resort activity.

VAIL RESORTS, INC.
Founded: January 1997
Headquarters: Broomfield, Colorado

Vail Resorts owns (or operates) 37 resorts, including those from its planned acquisition of the Peak Resorts portfolio (set to close in fall 2019). The seven listed in *italics* were added since June 2016, when the original *Ski Inc.* was published, and the Peak areas are listed separately.

North America
Afton Alps, Minnesota (2012)
Beaver Creek Resort, Colorado (opened 1980)
Breckenridge Ski Resort, Colorado (1997)
Crested Butte Mountain Resort, Colorado (2018)
Heavenly Mountain Resort, California/Nevada (2002)
Keystone Resort, Colorado (1997)
Kirkwood Mountain Resort, California (2012)
Mount Brighton Ski Area, Michigan (2012)
*Mt. Sunapee Ski Resort, New Hampshire (2018)
**Northstar California Resort California (2010)
Okemo Mountain Resort, Vermont (2018)
Park City Mountain Resort (including Canyons), Utah (2013-14)

Stevens Pass, Washington (2018)
Stowe, Vermont (2017)
Vail Mountain, Colorado (opened 1962)
Whistler Blackcomb, British Columbia (2016)
Wilmot Mountain, Wisconsin (2016)

*Operated by long-term lease, owned by EPR Properties.
**Operated by lease, resort is owned by State of New Hampshire.

The below resorts are set to be acquired from Peak Resorts, which was founded in 1997 and headquartered in Wildwood, Missouri. Years refer to when Peak acquired the resort, italics are the recent additions.

Alpine Valley, Ohio (2012)
Attitash, New Hampshire (2007)
Big Boulder Ski Area, Pennsylvania (2005)
Boston Mills/Brandywine, Ohio (2002)
Crotched Mt. Ski Area, New Hampshire (2003)
Hidden Valley, Missouri (founded 1982)
Hunter Mountain, New York (2015)
Liberty Mountain Resort, Pennsylvania (2018)
Jack Frost, Pennsylvania (2005)
*Mad River Mountain, Ohio (2001)
Mount Snow, Vermont (2007)
Paoli Peaks, Indiana (1997)
Ski Roundtop, Pennsylvania (2018)

Snow Creek Ski Area, Missouri (founded in 1986)
Whitetail, Pennsylvania (2018)
Wildcat Mountain, New Hampshire (2010)

*Resort is is owned by EPR Properties and operated under a long-term agreement by Peak/Vail Resorts.

INTERNATIONAL

Australia
Perisher Ski Resort, Australia (2015)
Falls Creek, Australia (2019)
Hotham, Australia (2019)

ALTERRA MOUNTAIN CO.
Founded: January 2018
Headquarters: Denver

(Acquired from KSL Capital Partners)
Alpine Meadows, California
Squaw Valley, California

(Acquired from Intrawest in April 2017)
Blue Mountain, Ontario
Snowshoe, West Virginia
Steamboat Ski & Resort Corporation, Colorado
Stratton, Vermont
Tremblant, Quebec
*Winter Park Resort, Colorado

(Acquired from Mammoth Mountain Ski Area LLC in April 2017)
Big Bear Mountain Resort, California
June Mountain, California
Mammoth, California
Snow Summit, California

(Acquired from Stern/Penske in October 2017 and June 2017)
Deer Valley, Utah
Solitude, Utah

(Acquired from John Kircher in October 2018)
Crystal Mountain, Washington
Also: Alterra also owns CMH Heli-skiing

*Winter Park is owned by the City of Denver and operated by Alterra.

THE MID-MAJORS

BOYNE USA, INC.
Founded: 1947
Headquarters: Boyne Falls, Michigan

Big Sky Resort, Montana (1976)
*Brighton Ski Resort, Utah (1986)
Boyne Highlands Resort, Michigan (1963)
Boyne Mountain Resort, Michigan (founded 1947)
*Cypress Mountain, British Columbia (2001)
*Loon Mountain, New Hampshire (2007)

*Sugarloaf, Maine (2007)
*Summit at Snoqualmie, Washington (2007)
*Sunday River Ski Resort, Maine (2007)

*Resorts had been owned by Oz/CNL Lifestyle Properties and operated under long-term agreement by Boyne Resorts before Boyne bought them in full in 2018.

Also: Boyne has owned the Gatlinburg Sky Lift since 1954, and founded the Inn at Bay Harbor, including a grand hotel and 27 holes of golf, in Petoskey, Michigan, in 1998.

POWDR

Founded: 1994

Headquarters: Park City, Utah

Boreal Ski Area, California (1995)
Copper, Colorado (2009)
Eldora Mountain Resort, Colorado
(2017)

Killington, Vermont (2007)
Lee Canyon, Nevada (2003)
Mt. Bachelor, Oregon (2001)
Pico Mountain, Vermont (2007)
Soda Springs Ski Area, California (1995)

Also: Snowbird, Utah, is not officially part of
POWDR, but has the same shareholders. POWDR
owns six Woodward action sports camp facilities.

THE MINI-MAJORS

Alpine Valley Holding Co.

Alpine Valley, Michigan
Alpine Valley Resort, Wisconsin
Bittersweet Ski Area, Michigan
Devil's Head Resort, Wisconsin
Mount Holly Ski Area, Michigan
Pine Knob Ski Area, Michigan

State of New York

Belleayre Mountain (Olympic Regional
Development Authority)
Gore Mountain (Olympic Regional
Development Authority)
Whiteface (Olympic Regional
Development Authority)

Mountain Capital Partners

Arizona Snowbowl, Arizona
Hesperus, Colorado
*Nordic Valley, Utah
Parajito Mountain, New Mexico
Purgatory, Colorado
Sipapu, New Mexico

*Resort is owned by Skyline Mountain Base, LLC,
operated under long-term agreement by Mountain
Capital Partners.

Pacific Resort Group International

*Powderhorn, Colorado
**Ragged Mountain, New Hampshire
Mountain Washington, Vancouver Island
***Wintergreen, West Virginia
***Wisp, Maryland

*Resort is owned by Andy Daly and Tom and Ken
Gart and operated under lease by Pacific.

**Resort is owned by RMR-Pacific LLC and
operated under long-term agreement by Pacific.

***Resorts are owned by EPR Properties and
operated under long-term agreement by Pacific.

Fairbank Group

Bromley, Vermont
Cranmore, New Hampshire
Jiminy Peak, Massachusetts

CANADA

Mont Saint-Sauveur International Inc.

Edelweiss Valley, Ottawa
Mont-Avila Ski Area, Quebec
Mont Gabriel, Quebec
Mont Olympia, Quebec
Mont Saint-Sauveur Ski Area, Quebec
Ski Morin Heights, Quebec

Resorts of the Canadian Rockies Inc.
Fernie Alpine Resort, British Columbia
Kicking Horse Mountain Resort, British Columbia

Kimberley Alpine Resort, British Columbia
Mont-Sainte-Anne, Quebec
Nakiska Ski Area, Alberta
Stoneham Mountain Resort, Quebec

GEOGRAPHIC RESORT COMBINATIONS
(Partial list)

Greek Peak in Cortland, New York
Toggenburg Mountain Winter Sports Center, New York

Song Mountain Resort, New York
Labrador Mountain, New York

Silver Mountain Resort, Idaho
49° North Mountain Resort, Washington

Little Switzerland, Wisconsin
Nordic Mountain, Wisconsin
Rock Snow Park, Wisconsin

Seven Springs, Pennsylvania
Hidden Valley, Pennsylvania

Butternut Basin, Massachusetts
Otis Ridge, Massachusetts
Ski Blandford, Massachusetts

Berkshire East Mountain Resort, Massachusetts
Catamount, New York

Big Snow Resorts, Michigan (Upper Peninsula)
Blackjack Mountain Resort
Indianhead

Timberline Lodge, Oregon
Summit, Oregon

THE MEGA-PASSES
For 2019–20 season; visit the pass websites for details and updates.

EPIC PASS
Vail Resorts, Inc.

The Epic Pass provides unlimited, unrestricted access to all of Vail Resorts' owned and operated resorts (in *italics*) and additional access to partner resorts around the world. That includes seven days each at Sun Valley, Telluride, Snowbasin, and a variety of days at its other partner resorts in Canada, Japan, and Europe. There are several Epic Local Pass offerings, and the new Epic Day Pass covers one- to seven-days. See the Epic Pass website for details.

When Vail Resorts announced its plans to acquire Peak Resorts, it also said that its 2019–20 Epic, Epic Local, Military and Epic Day Pass will be good at Peak's 17 resorts. Also for the 2019–20 season, holders of the Peak Pass will be able to use the pass as structured, along with the option to upgrade to an Epic or Epic Local following the closing of the transaction, set for fall 2019. The resorts that are part of the Peak Pass are listed separately.

California
Heavenly Mountain Resort,
California/Nevada
Kirkwood Mountain Resort, California
Northstar California Resort, California

Colorado
Vail Mountain, Colorado
Beaver Creek Resort, Colorado
Breckenridge Ski Resort, Colorado
Crested Butte Mountain Resort, Colorado
Keystone Resort, Colorado
Telluride Ski Resort, Colorado

Idaho
Sun Valley Resort, Utah

Michigan
Mt. Brighton Ski Area, Michigan

Minnesota
Afton Alps, Minnesota

New Hampshire
Mt. Sunapee Ski Resort, New Hampshire

Utah
Park City Mountain Resort, Utah
Snowbasin Resort, Utah

Vermont
Okemo Mountain Resort, Vermont
Stowe Mountain Resort, Vermont

Washington
Stevens Pass Ski Resort, Washington

Wisconsin
Wilmot Mountain Ski Resort, Wisconsin

EPIC PASS/PEAK PASS

Alpine Valley, Ohio
Attitash, New Hampshire
Big Boulder Ski Area, Pennsylvania

Boston Mills/Brandywine, Ohio
Crotched Mt. Ski Area, New Hampshire
Hunter Mountain, New York
Jack Frost, Pennsylvania
Liberty Mountain Resort, Pennsylvania
Mad River Mountain, Ohio
Mount Snow, Vermont
Ski Roundtop, Pennsylvania
Whitetail, Pennsylvania
Wildcat Mountain, New Hampshire

(Note: Peak's Boston Mills/Brandywine in Ohio and Hidden Valley and Snow Creek Ski Area in Missouri are not included in the Peak Pass, but are included in the Epic Pass.)

CANADA

*Resorts of the Canadian Rockies

Alberta
Nakiska Ski Area

British Columbia
Fernie Alpine Resort
Kicking Horse Mountain Resort
Kimberley Alpine Resort
Whistler Blackcomb

Quebec
Mont-Sainte-Anne
Stoneham Mountain Resort

*Resorts of the Canadian Rockies offer up to seven days with no blackouts, then 50 percent off tickets.

INTERNATIONAL
Australia
Falls Creek Alpine Resort
Mount Hotham Alpine Resort
Perisher Ski Resort

Epic Europe
Only the unrestricted Epic Pass provides European access and there are additional lodging requirements for some of the

redemptions. Visit the Epic Pass website for more details.

Austria
*SKI ARLBERG
Lech
Zurs
Stuben
St. Christoph
St. Anton

*Up to a three-day lift pass to Ski Arlberg; Epic Pass holders must book at least three nights of consecutive lodging at a participating property to redeem their passes.

France
*LES 3 VALLÉES
Val Thorens
Méribel
Courchevel
Les Menuires
Saint Martin de Bellevelle
La Tania
Orelle
Brides-Les-Bains

*Up to a seven-day ticket.

*Paradiski and Tignes/Val d'Isere:
Les Arcs
La Plagne
Peisey-Vallandry
Tignes
Val D'Isere

*Up to a four-day ticket.

Italy
*SKIRAMA DOLOMITI
Madonna di Campiglio
Pinzolo
Folgarida-Marilleva
Peio
Ponte di Legno-Tonale

Andalo-Fai della Paganella
Monte Bondone
Folgarida-Lavarone

*Up to a seven-day ticket.

Switzerland
*4 VALLÉES, SWITZERLAND
Verbier
Nendaz
Veysonnaz
Thyon

*Up to a five-day ticket; must book at a participating lodging property to receive ticket.

Japan
*Rusutsu

*Epic Pass, Epic Local Pass and Epic Australia Pass for five consecutive days with no blackouts.

**Hakuba Valley

**Epic Pass and Epic Local Pass and Epic Australia Pass will receive five consecutive days with no blackout dates at Hakuba Valley's 10 ski resorts.

IKON PASS

Alterra Mountain Co.
The Ikon Pass offers unlimited skiing with no blackout dates at 14 resorts (in *italics*; this is all of its owned resorts, minus Deer Valley), plus up to seven days at another 25 destinations. The Ikon Base Pass offers unlimited skiing at 12 resorts (all of its owned resorts minus Deer Valley, Steamboat and Stratton), plus up to five days at 27 destinations.

About that tagline: "39 Destinations. One Pass." That's Ikon, but those "39 Destinations" actually include some 48

resorts. Counting as one destination is
Aspen Snowmass, SkiBig3, Niseko United,
Killington/Pico and Coronet Peak, The
Remarkables, Mt. Hutt. CMH*, which has
a dozen lodges, counts as one destination,
but the Ikon only gets early bird savings
there.

U.S.

California
Alpine Meadows
Big Bear Mountain Resort
June Mountain
Mammoth Mountain
Squaw Valley

Colorado
Arapahoe Basin
Aspen Snowmass (Aspen Highlands,
    Aspen Mountain, Buttermilk,
    Snowmass)
Copper Mountain Resort
Eldora Mountain Resort
Steamboat
Winter Park Resort

Maine
Sugarloaf
Sunday River

Michigan
Boyne Highlands
Boyne Mountain

Montana
Big Sky Mountain Resort

New Hampshire
Loon Mountain

New Mexico
Taos Ski Valley

Utah
Alta Ski Area
Brighton Resort
Deer Valley Resort
Snowbird
Solitude Mountain Resort

Vermont
Killington
Pico
Stratton
Sugarbush Resort

Washington
Crystal Mountain
The Summit at Snoqualmie

West Virginia
Snowshoe

Wyoming
Jackson Hole Mountain Resort

Canada

Alberta
SkiBig3 (Mt. Norquay, Lake Louise,
    Sunshine Village)

British Columbia, Canada
Revelstoke Mountain Resort
Cypress Mountain
*CMH Heli-Skiing & Summer
    Adventures

Ontario, Canada
Blue Mountain

Quebec, Canada
Tremblant

INTERNATIONAL

Australia
Thredbo
Mt. Buller

Chile
Valle Nevado

New Zealand
Coronet Peak
Mt. Hutt
The Remarkables

Japan
Niseko United

POWER PASS

Mountain Capital Partners
Arizona Snowbowl, Arizona
Hesperus, Colorado
*Nordic Valley, Utah
Parajito Mountain, New Mexico
Purgatory, Colorado
Sipapu, New Mexico

MOUNTAIN COLLECTIVE PASS

Accessing two days at 17 resorts, with additional days 50 percent off the lift ticket.

Alta Ski Area, Utah
Aspen Snowmass, Colorado
Banff Sunshine, Canada
Big Sky Resort, Montana
Coronet Peak + The Remarkables, New
    Zealand
Jackson Hole Mountain Resort, Wyoming
Lake Louise, Canada
Mammoth Mountain, California
Mt Buller, Australia
Niseko United, Japan

Revelstoke Mountain Resort, Canada
Snowbird, Utah
Squaw Valley Alpine Meadows, California
Sugarbush Resort, Vermont
Taos Ski Valley, New Mexico
Thredbo Alpine Village, Australia
Valle Nevado, Chile

INDY PASS

The Indy Pass, launched for 2019–20, is $199 for two free days at each participating resort plus other discounts. Check for updates on new participating resorts at the Indy Pass website.

Idaho
Brundage Mountain
Silver Mountain

Washington
White Pass
Mission Ridge
49 Degrees North

Oregon
Hoodoo

California
Mt. Shasta

Montana
Red Lodge Mountain
Lost Trail Powder Mountain

Utah
Beaver Mountain

British Columbia
Apex Mountain Resort

Wisconsin
Little Switzerland
Nordic Mountain
Trollhaugen
Tyrol Basin

Michigan
Big Powderhorn Resort
Pine Mountain Resort

Vermont
Bolton Valley Resort
Magic Mountain

Massachusetts
Catamount Mountain Resort
Berkshire East Mountain Resort

Virginia
Massanutten Resort
Bryce Resort

North Carolina
Cataloochee Ski Area

Minnesota
Giants Ridge

New York
Greek Peak Mountain Resort

Pennsylvania
Blue Knob Resort

New Hampshire
Pats Peak

Value-Added Pass Extensions

POWDER ALLIANCE

Purchase a season pass to any of the 18 Powder Alliance resort and visit the others up to three times, non-holiday. Day tickets are free midweek, half price on weekends.

Angel Fire, New Mexico
Bogus Basin, Idaho
Bridger Bowl, Montana
Castle Mountain Resort, Alberta, Canada

China Peak, California
Kiroro, Japan
La Parva, Chile
Loveland Ski Area, Colorado
Ski Marmot Basin, Alberta, Canada
Monarch Mountain, Colorado
Mountain High, California
Mt Hood Ski Bowl, Oregon
Schweitzer, Idaho
Sierra-At-Tahoe, California
Silver Star, Canada
Sugar Bowl Resort, California
Timberline, Oregon
Whitewater, Canada

FREEDOM PASS

The Freedom Pass is a complimentary pass add-on at 19 ski areas across the U.S. Buy a pass at a participating mountain, take it to any other mountain on the pass, and get three free days of skiing with no restrictions.

Black Mountain, New Hampshire
Bolton Valley, Vermont
Buck Hill, Minnesota
Dartmouth Skiway, New Hampshire
Eaglecrest, Alaska
Hesperus, Colorado
Lost Valley, Maine
Magic Mountain, Vermont
McIntyre, New York
Nordic Valley, Utah
Purgatory, Colorado
Pajarito, New Mexico
Platekill, New York
Sipapu, New Mexico
Ski Cooper, Colorado
Snow Bowl, Arizona
Sunlight, Colorado
Whaleback Mt., New Hampshire
Yawgoo Valley, Rhode Island

A Glimpse Back in Time

INTRAWEST-VAIL RESORTS, CIRCA 2007

In 2007, Intrawest was the North American resort leader, with more resorts and market share than Vail Resorts:

Intrawest

Blackcomb Mountain, British Columbia (1986)
Tremblant, Quebec (1991)
Panorama, British Columbia (1993)
Stratton Mountain, Vermont (1994)
Snowshoe, West Virginia (1995)
Whistler, British Columbia (1996)
Copper Mountain, Colorado (1996)
Mont Ste. Marie, Quebec (1997)

Vail Resorts, Inc.

Vail, Colorado (opened 1962)
Beaver Creek, Colorado (opened 1980)
Breckenridge, Colorado (1997)
Heavenly Mountain Resort, California/Nevada (2002)
Keystone, Colorado (1997)

MID-1990s CONGLOMERATES

By 1997, the resort landscape had undergone a major consolidation. It would not last, and only Vail Resorts remains. Here are the companies, the resorts they acquired (with year), plus their ownership today.

American Skiing Co.

Sunday River, Maine (1980) (Boyne Resorts)
Sugarloaf, Maine (1996) (Boyne Resorts)
Killington/Pico, Vermont (1996) (POWDR)
Sugarbush, Vermont (1995) (Winn Smith and partners)
Mount Snow/Haystack, Vermont (1996) (Mount Snow owned by Peak Resorts; Haystack private)

Attitash/Bear Peak, New Hampshire (1995) (Peak Resorts)
Steamboat, California (1997) (Alterra)
Heavenly, California (1997) (Vail Resorts)
Canyons, Utah (1997) (Vail Resorts, rolled into Park City Mountain Resort)

Vail Resorts, Inc.

(All remain under Vail Resorts)
Vail, Colorado (opened 1962)
Beaver Creek, Colorado (opened 1980)
Breckenridge, Colorado (1997)
Keystone, Colorado (1997)

Booth Creek Ski Holdings, Inc.

Northstar-at-Tahoe, California (1996) (Vail Resorts operated)
Sierra-at-Tahoe, California (1996) (Independent)
Waterville Valley, New Hampshire (1996) (Independent)
Cranmore, New Hampshire (1996) (Fairbank Group)
Loon Mountain, New Hampshire (1997) (Boyne Resorts)
Snoqaulmie Pass, Washington (1997) (Boyne Resorts)
Grand Targhee, Wyoming (1997) (Independent)

Intrawest Corp.

Tremblant, Quebec (1991) (Alterra)
Panorama, British Columbia (1993) (Independent)
Stratton Mountain, Vermont (1994) (Alterra)
Snowshoe, West Virginia (1995) (Alterra)
Whistler Blackcomb, British Columbia (1996) (Vail Resorts)
Copper Mountain, Colorado (1996) (POWDR)
Mont Ste. Marie, Quebec (1997) (Independent)

If You Must Get Injured

Do It in France

France sometimes gets a bad rap over its guest service, particularly when the visitor does not speak the language. I've never found this to be true in ski country, and I'll share the following tale to make my point.

In 2009, I headed to Europe with a group of ski operators from the U.S., Canada, New Zealand, and Australia to visit a number of French resorts and French companies serving the ski industry. I had made four or five similar trips in the past (it was called France Neige International, and was sponsored by the French government and the country's ski-industry suppliers). The group's primary sponsor was Leitner-Poma of America, headquartered in Grand Junction, Colorado.

Rick Spear—the lift company's longtime president, who retired in spring 2019 after some 40 years with the company—was our tour director, as he had been on all previous trips. Poma was one of the early ski-lift manufacturers, starting in France and then expanding worldwide. Their surface-lift design, the "Poma lift," bears the company's name. In 2000, an Italian lift company purchased Poma, and the new entity was named Leitner-Poma. Consolidation was occurring on the supplier side as well as the operating side of the ski business.

Bernie Pomagalski, son of the founder of the original company, was skiing with our group for the day. Bernie's father, Jean, was Polish and his mother French. It's an interesting and not well-known fact of the ski business that many of the early, successful lift engineers such as Jean Pomagalski and Jan Kunczynski emigrated from Poland after graduating from the University of Kraków, and became pioneers in the international lift-manufacturing industry. France, in the 1960s, was creating artists, not engineers.

It had been warm for February, as I recollect, but in search of the best snow, we found ourselves in one of the higher lift sections of Courchevel, one of the many resorts that make up Les 3 Vallées (all interconnected). As we disembarked near the summit, we were surprised to discover about 8 inches of fresh, dry powder in that area of the mountain. It was a bluebird day, and this was the best snow we'd seen so far on our trip. Off we went.

I believe it was Jeff Crowley from Wachusett who spotted a beautiful, untouched slope just off-piste on our right as we descended, so like lemmings, we followed Jeff, all separating to find an untracked line. The snow was fabulous, but underfoot, it was bulletproof. About halfway down, I hit an unseen rock midturn and got dumped instantly. As soon as I hit the hard base surface, I knew that my collarbone was broken, having done this before, unfortunately.

Well, unless you are very, very badly injured, you do not call for ski patrol in France. They charge for the rescue service. So I skied down with the group, uncomfortable but not in great pain. I joined everyone for lunch and then was escorted down by Bernie Pomagalski to Hôtel le Oreé du Bois in Méribel, where we were staying (Méribel is a great location in that it provides easy access to both Courchevel and Val Thorens). Bernie took me to the local clinic, where an X-ray revealed a simple collarbone break but a complete separation. The recommendation was to have it repaired then, rather than traveling home in that condition.

I agreed, and the local clinic doctor set me up at a small hospital (Clinique Générale de Savoie) in Chambéry, about an hour's drive away. Rick Spear was awesome through this whole misadventure. He arranged for a taxi to pick me up the following morning. The next stop for our group was Chamonix, so Rick had one of his employees from the factory pick me up the following day, post-surgery, and bring me back to the group.

I was pretty uncomfortable during the drive and didn't say much. My French is limited at best. We got to the hospital around 9 a.m. I gave my credit card to the driver and was informed that he could only take cash, which I didn't have. I asked him if there was a bank nearby. He said "yes" and drove me there, only a few blocks away. I struggled up the stairs, entered and saw about 20 people standing in line and no evidence of urgency on the part of bank staff. Ugh. This was not going to work. I started feeling nauseous and headed back to the cab. I explained my dilemma to the driver as best I could, and he said, "No problem. You send me check when you get home. I know Bernie." He gave me his card with the amount due on it. What a relief. And thank you, Mr. Pomagalski.

I entered the small reception area. No one was there, but in an office off to the side was a woman, looking very clerical, with her desk piled high with folders. I introduced myself, and we confirmed that I was indeed scheduled for surgery that day. She began to check me in, but when she heard "American" she went into something of a panic. "Oh, monsieur, American insurance?" I said, "No. I'll pay cash." I could see the relief on her face. I think I filled out two short forms. No disclaimers. No waivers. Just the basics: what medications was I taking and allergy information.

There were only about eight rooms in this tiny hospital, and as I was led upstairs to my room, I noted that all appeared to be doubles. I was introduced to my roommate, who was recuperating from surgery the prior day to repair a torn Achilles. I met what seemed to be his entire family, who were crowded into the room. Immediately, they wanted to know about my accident and expressed concern.

I met the surgeon, Dr. Francesco Carotenuto, around noon. We struggled to communicate, but I did figure out what he intended to do in terms of the repair (a titanium plate to reconnect the broken clavicle). I also learned that he was Italian and had married a former French ski racer, whose hometown was nearby. I was prepped and put under. I remember the trip up to the operating area, but then nothing. When I woke up, the doctor was standing nearby, holding an X-ray. He looked at it, turned to me, and said, "*Magnifique!*" He had a big smile as he showed me the film.

I mostly slept quietly through the night and in the morning had a wonderful breakfast—no hospital food. Just scrambled eggs, fresh bread with local jellies, and fresh fruit. I felt great. Bandages were removed, and the last thing remaining for the nurse was to remove a small glass jar and drainage tube, which was there to collect any blood from the surgery area. When she went to do that, the tube didn't come out, and she said, "*Mon Dieu, le staple.*" Well, I could figure that out. The small jar was filled with blood, which meant that it had done its job, but in using staples to close the incision, the drain tube had been "stapled."

Next thing I know, I'm in a wheelchair headed back up to surgery. I was settled into the same room where I had gone the day before, sitting on a bed. I hadn't been there five minutes when the doctor arrived through the operating-room door. Gloved hands covered with blood. He obviously had just walked away from whatever surgery he was doing. He cleaned up, came over to me, tugged on the tube, and said, "*Pas de problem.*"

In the next minute, he removed the staples and thereby the drain tube, shook some antibiotic into the incision area, and restapled me—the first time I had ever consciously been on the receiving end of a staple gun. Bang, bang, bang.

Then he said, "Bye-bye," turned on his heels, and headed back into the operating room. Ten minutes later I was back in my traveling clothes and standing in the reception area reviewing my hospital bill: $500 U.S.

I said in broken French: "This can't be right." And at that exact moment, the nurse who had been attending me came running down the hallway and, very apologetically, explained that she had forgotten to get the doctor's bill to the office staff. I looked at it: another $500 U.S.

To the nurse and receptionist, I said, "Are you sure this is right?" "*Oui, monsieur.*" Incredible. $1,000 for the surgeon and hospital. This would have been $10,000 or more in just about any U.S hospital. I gave them my credit card, met my driver from Poma, and off we went to Chamonix.

Several weeks after returning to Steamboat, I had my follow-up appointment with Andres Sauerbrey, one of our local orthopedic surgeons who specializes in shoulder work. I got an updated X-ray. He looked at it, as well as at the one taken immediately after surgery (which I had taken with me). His response: "Incredible. This is exactly the kind of repair that I try to talk my patients into."

If you must break your collarbone, do it in France and have your surgery in Chambéry!

INDEX

BIG SKY
MONTANA

**BOYNE
HIGHLANDS**

Sunday River

BOYNE RESORTS
EXPERIENCE THE LIFESTYLE

BOYNE MOUNTAIN

THE SUMMIT
AT SNOQUALMIE